Partnership! A Question of Business, Friendship, and Marriage
(Volume I)

Dr. Sarah Von

Tweaking The Question Ministries – Belle Glade, FL
ISBN - 978-1-949-5490-0-3
Library of Congress Control Number: 2020911986
Partnership! A Question of Business, Friendship, and Marriage (Volume I)
Dr. Sarah Von
Available formats: eBook
Paperback distribution

DEDICATION & SPECIAL THANKS

In memory of my devoted mother, Lizzie B. M. Holmes. Silver and gold she had none, but her love and devotion to God through the teachings of Christ, she shared with all who would receive.

Also, in loving memory of my grandmother, Sarah Rogers, who had the fight of a rowdy tiger.

This book is also dedicated to my husband, my friend, and partner in Christ.

Other titles by Dr. Von:

Partnership! A Question of Business, Friendship, and Marriage (Volume II)

Your review of this book is appreciated.

Contents

About the Author

Dr. Sarah Von is a committed Holy Spirit filled Christian. She was called from her mother's womb who was an anointed Prophet of God. She was born with a veil over her face. As a baby, Dr. Von was the beneficiary of a miracle when her life was restored after succumbing to dehydration, as a result of a severe stomach infection. The doctor told her mother that Sarah had died and directed her to deliver Sarah's dead body to the funeral home. He further told her mother that due to the late hour, he would visit the funeral home the next morning to sign the death certificate.

Instead of following the doctor's instructions, Sarah's mother took Sarah home and petitioned the faithful God of Israel in Jesus' name to heal her child. After three days of praying and watching over Sarah, who was black and blue and had become stiff from rigor mortis, her child's life was restored. Sarah was taken back to the doctor who had pronounced her dead. From that point on, Dr. Simmons would affectionately call Sarah his "little dead girl." Dr. Von recalls having fond memories of being called this by her doctor as a little girl. Unbeknownst to her mother and others, this miracle was a depiction of the calling on Sarah's life.

Dr. Sarah Von was a unique and peculiar child who displayed a number of Spiritual gifts that made her stand out in her family and community. Despite this, Sarah longed to be a "normal" kid. Over the years, she continued to feel the calling of God on her life. Sarah's desire to be "normal" would lead her to turn away from the calling of Christ on her life. Even though she was a committed Christian, Dr. Sarah Von's conflicted emotions led her to shun any position that would shine a light on her Godly gifts.

She instead, focused on her education and career, rather than answer her calling in Christ and petitioning God for a better understanding of the calling she felt on her life. She had a vision of her future and did not want to deal with issues of rejection, stress, and resentment that often challenged those who are focused on accomplishing the things of God in a world filled with many who resist the will of God and are determined to follow their own path. Sarah went on to earn a Bachelor's Degree in Experimental Psychology, a Master's degree in Community Clinical Psychology, and a Doctoral Degree in Clinical Psychology. She convinced herself that she would have plenty of time to do the things of God when she got her personal goals out of the way. She was driven to live in Christ as she saw fit. In November of 2011, Dr. Von had an "on her way to Damascus experience". She was involved in a serious car accident. She went through years of recovery. During this time, her commitment to God strengthened. This improved commitment allowed God to order her steps, allowing her God to fulfill His calling for her to embrace her prophetic ministry and share her Godly gifts through the gospel of Christ, in God's Spirit and Truth, with all who are willing to receive.

INTRODUCTION

As we approach the question of partnership and how to choose the appropriate partner for business, friendship, and marriage, it is important to note, this writing is non-denominational and biblically based. Also, the answer to the question of partnership will be approached from a Christian perspective that is willing to move beyond the restrictions of diplomacy to help Christians gain a constructive understanding of God and living an appropriate Christian lifestyle. This perspective is designed for the strength and longevity of the Christian lifestyle. The goal of this book and its approach to partnership is to help all Christians make Godly choices when choosing partners and to allow God to perfect His light that shines within them. This is an approach with an aim to help Christians function and partner themselves with what God is calling for in these days. In an attempt to help Christians gain a more insightful understanding of salvation and its role in Christian partnership, this book will also address a number of biblical concepts, such as salvation, having a sin nature, living sin free, God's grace and mercy and the definition of the Holy Spirit. This book also briefly addresses the concept of deviant sexual behavior and proactive child raising in Christ as these topics relate to partnership.

CHAPTER ONE

Overview of Some Partnership Issues for Christians

Unknown to many, or perhaps, not acknowledged by many, Christians need to be what God would have us to be, according to "His" Word. Therefore, the primary goal of this book is to help Christians understand that a partnership for a Christian, should be a union that is in line with the will and Word of God. Therefore, the people of God are encouraged to consider the following questions when contemplating any partnership:

(1) How does the particular partnership help maintain and strengthen my relationship with God?

(2) Does this partnership allow me to be what God would have me to be, according to "His" word?

For example:

 (1). Will a given partnership support an honest, truthful, and modest lifestyle in Christ?

(2). Will this partnership also allow you to grow in God and live free in the Spirit of God and in the truth of God's word, according to the gift of deliverance offered by Jesus Christ? Clearly stated, are you free to live and do the will of God in your partnerships or are you in partnerships that are defined by expectations that are outside of the will of God? To state it even more simpler, because this point is very important, do your partners allow and encourage you to worship God in Spirit and in truth, or are the expectations of your partnerships rooted in what is more pleasing to men than God?

One should be able to answer these questions either "yes" or "no." There should be no ifs, ands or buts about it, because appropriate Christian partnerships are founded in the principles and liberty of God. Therefore, partnerships should not be stifling or inhibiting. The concept of partnership was established by God to help all parties live and operate within a supportive system that promotes the liberty of God, offered through Christ, and operates within the liberty of His truth. As a result, a well-founded partnership is one that encourages personal growth; enhances each partner's ability to feel comfortable with self, with their God given characteristics; and is one that helps partners improve their personal skill sets and talents. Well-founded partnerships also function in ways that enhance each partner's ability to achieve personal and team goals (goals of the partnership). The natural byproduct of an appropriate partnership in Christ, encourages all members to grow as individuals in Christ and to grow in their efforts to improve the lives of others, as all partners work together to improve the state of the world and the environment they live within.

Prospective Vulnerabilities and Advantages

Partnerships are imposing! So, if you do not like others imposing on your time and space, do not seek out a partnership. Partners inform, disclose, and share with one another, to improve the condition and state of all parties. Due to the intimate nature of the types of communications and interactions that must take place between partners, **partnerships render their members vulnerable to one another in ways that do not occur outside of the partnership.** Once again, one can never be removed from the fact; when you partner with another, you're making yourself vulnerable to that person or entity.

Many of us are removed and/or too selfish to accept the true nature of a partnership and the vulnerable position it will put its members in. Many do not really contemplate the intimate nature of a partnership and the vulnerabilities associated with being in a partnership. This is because many do not accept the reality that partnerships are not just about what another party can do for them. Too many partnerships are a byproduct of one or more partners evaluating how the partnership could work to his or her advantage. For these individuals, partnership is about making a home run for themselves and if another happens to benefit along the way, that is okay, too. They see other partners as pawns to be used for their gain. For these individuals, being in a partnership is a way of addressing the question; what can others do for "me?" The question of how they can empower other partners and enhance the partnership with their gifts and talents comes only as an afterthought, if at all.

Their style of partnering will only serve to exploit (take advantage of) their relationships with their partner(s). These individuals primarily function as takers in their relationships. Partnering with a taker is draining, and the partner of a taker will always get the short end of the stick. The act of sharing is difficult for a taker and the little that the partner gains from their partnership with a taker will never outweigh the cost of extending one's self to a taker. On the other hand, the committed Christian follows the principle of God, which states: "It is more blessed to give than to receive **(Acts 20:35)."** Therefore, the nature of a committed Christian is that of a giver. With this understanding, it is crucial that a committed Christian adheres to the notion that being involved with the wrong partner(s) can be costly and will place them in a very vulnerable position. This is true because a giver will always be giving and a taker will always be taking. A partnership such as this is the definition of a one-sided relationship. Although there may be times when one partner will have to put in more work than the other partner to work through issues, in an appropriate partnership, both partners are fully vested in addressing the needs of one another and the needs of the partnership, to the best of their ability.

There are no one-sided relationships in Christian partnerships. The goal of this type of partnership is for Christians to unite with those who are committed to achieving self-assurance, self-confidence, personal growth, and personal and team goals according to word and nature of God, as written in God's word and as displayed by Christ Jesus. Due to the goals of Christian partnership, the united effort needed to achieve these goals, and the vulnerable position posed upon all parties of a partnership, Christians should be vested in making sure they choose appropriate partners, whether it is for business, friendship or marriage.

Lifestyle with Expectation and Considerations

It is also important that everyone are in tune with the fact that **being a Christian is a lifestyle, not a statement**. One's lifestyle is a way of living that is apparent in one's daily walk and the impact it has on others. A statement can be a thought or feeling and may have no apparent or conscious history of being acted upon. **Matthew 24:12** informs us that God's reward is for those who endure to the end. To endure implies prolonged action or a prolonged way of conducting one's self. The prolonged way of conducting one's self embodies the definition of the concept *lifestyle*. This concept of living should be embraced by leadership and should acknowledge the timing of God.

Therefore, a person who is truly committed to God, has a history of conducting him or herself in a way that is Christ-driven (defined by the principles of Christ and in accordance with the truth of God's word). However, newly committed or young individuals in Christ must be allowed time to grow and develop such a history. With this in mind, one must be careful about developing expectations, ties and/or partnerships with young and newly founded Christians. Expectations for these individuals should be realistic for a babe in Christ and should not be too demanding **(I Timothy 3:1-15)**. To expect a person who is a newly found Christian (milk drinker) to be equipped for a marital partnership or to function well in a lead role in a business partnership, would be a mistake. Such an expectation can be detrimental to the babe in Christ and to the partnership in question **(I Timothy 3:6)**.

Partnering with other Christians is a key element in living the Christian lifestyle, because as discussed, partners are helpers to one another. **I Thessalonians 4: 1-10** informs us that one of the primary roles of a Christian is to urge (not make) others to adapt to the Christian lifestyle as well as help them understand and maintain that lifestyle. Most will agree that in order to effectively help a person accomplish a goal, one should have a sound understanding of the subject at hand. Therefore, to effectively help another be Christ-driven, a person must first understand who Christ is, and be committed to being governed by the principles of God according to the teachings of Christ. This is because a person who properly understands, embraces, and is committed to the subject in question, will most likely be more effective at helping another accept and adapt to the subject in question, in the appropriate manner.

Having a limited understanding and commitment to Christ and the principles of Christ does not mean one cannot follow or help others adhere to the principles of God. However, it does mean that an individual who is not historically committed to being governed by God in the Spirit and truth of God, according to the leadership of Christ, cannot live in Christ or assist another in living an "effective" and prolonged Christ-driven lifestyle that is pleasing to God. This is because a Christian's hope, faith, effectiveness and endurance in God, is rooted in his or her knowledge and understanding of God and His nature through the teachings of Christ. Appropriate knowledge and understanding of God is a byproduct of having a history with God through Christ that bears witness to one who is obedient to the word of God according to the nature of who God is, made evident by what God has manifested. Therefore, a person, without such a history in God, does not have the experience to effectively live in Christ or help another live in Christ, according to God's word, His Spirit, and His truth. It is also very likely, a teacher in Christ such as this, will fail and cause the student to also fail in his or her ability to live an effective and prolonged lifestyle in Christ.

Clearly stated, adhering to the laws and principles of God alone is not a Christ-driven lifestyle **(Romans 3:20)**. Additionally, it is not a lifestyle that commands the attention or favor of God. God acknowledges all godly acts, but when one is living a lifestyle that, not only adheres to the principles of God, but is in line with and submits to the truth of God's word according to His Spirit and His truth, one is living an effective lifestyle in Christ. One can call on God for support at any time and He will respond. Their lifestyle commands the attention of God. He will hear and respond to those governed by Him, because they belong to Him. **John 8:47; John 10:27; & I Peter 3:12** report that God has a special ear and call for those who are governed by Him. These are the individuals that can be most effective when helping others in Christ, because they have a true relationship with God and an in-depth understanding of what it means to be a Christian.

Command the attention of God

One's ability to command the attention of God is very important for everyone and for Christian partnerships. An effective Christian lifestyle is one that is committed to operating within the will of God. This is a commitment that thrives on one's ability to effectively (in a way that is constructive and favorable) address God daily. It is this type of commitment that is acknowledged by God and causes God to act on behalf of mankind. However, it must be noted: God acknowledging or hearing you does not mean He will give you everything you desire, especially when a person's desires are not according to God's plan for him or her. Nor, does it mean He will bail you out of every uncomfortable situation. This is because God's plan for our lives (as it was for Jesus) is scripted for the success of our redemption and soul salvation.

Also, one of the fruits of the Spirit is the gift of long suffering in Christ. This gift is designed for our spiritual growth and to help mankind discipline the flesh and learn how to acknowledge and commune with God and others in spirit and in truth.

As many will confess, experiencing prolonged periods of discomfort and suffering has a way of helping those in distress look beyond fleshly things for comfort. Due to discomfort, pain, and/or suffering, these individuals are forced to move beyond the flesh to experience hope and joy. Their comfort and joy will most likely be found in the simpler and more spiritual things of life, the smile of another, nature, and the spirit of life. This includes finding comfort in the assuring word of God.

The need for Christians to have the ability to look and function beyond one's personal comfort level is very important. This quality is not only important, it is a necessity for Christians and Christian partnerships. The ability to function beyond one's comfort level will help the people of God accept and adhere to the commands of God, even when one is not comfortable. This ability is also needed to help Christians resist the notion that their relationship with God and others is primarily about one's personal comfort. A Christian's ability to move beyond personal comfort will help the Christian operate more profoundly in Christ. It is also a disposition that commands God's attention and favor, because it fulfills the requirement put forth by Jesus in **Matthew 16:24**: "If anyone wants to come after Me, they must first deny themselves (give up their way of viewing things and their comfort level) and take up their cross and follow Me (press to view things from God's perspective and press to be comfortable with what God has commanded)." When one's personal comfort level is the primary focus of engagement and/or partnership, one cannot fulfill the requirement presented in **Matthew 16:24**. Also, such individuals will perceive and function in partnerships in very fragmented ways. Their behavior will not be in the best interest of everyone in the partnership, because their behavior and actions are dictated by "their" comfort level. Leading many to come together for selfish and fleshly reasons (reasons of comfort) and relate to one another in the context of those reasons.

Relationships that are established and maintained according to one's comfort level are most likely the result of selfishness and are fragments of who and what each party is. These partnerships will not be healthy for the unity of the partnership. These relationships/partnerships will have a form of unity, but this type of unity will be dysfunctional and will not take into account the need for a unified mindset that must exist at the core of any partnership. This type of union will force partners to relate to one another within the confines of each partner's comfort level. This type of relationship can be toxic.

Outside of the communication and interaction they share about specific common interest, engagements, and concepts, which each partner may feel comfortable with, these partners function as independent agents. The members of their partnership share a form of togetherness, but they are not truly united. Not being truly united partners, will make the partnership vulnerable to intrusions and breakups. Also, these partners will not be able to command the attention and favor of God, as seen in **Matthew 18:20**. The more vested each partner is in a partnership, the less energy each partner has to invest in similar partnerships or allow other entities to intrude upon the existing partnership. As a wise person once said, "A chain is only as strong as its weakest link." Differences that are not acknowledged and addressed, by all parties in a partnership, create weak links that weaken the strength of the partnership.

For example, many marriages are established upon physical attraction, fame, education, status, money, and other superficial reasons. These couples deal with one another visually and in the bedroom, address each other's fame, education, and status, and if they are not having money problems, they go about functioning mostly independent of each other. There is very little meeting of the minds. Such a union is not in line with the true definition of marital partnership, Christian or not. A marital partnership is a coming together of the minds, bodies, spirits, and everything else. This includes having a conscience about their differences that may cause one another to feel uncomfortable. It is at the couple's points of difference, divide, and ambiguity that the door is open for frustration, anger, and allowing other entities to trample upon and intrude into the partnership.

As the result of the lack of unity in the marital partnership, room is left for the breakdown of the partnership. Therefore, the breakdown in such a partnership is the byproduct of both parties' inability to recognize, acknowledge, and address prior to and during the partnership, that each had differences that would/could hinder their ability to function in unity. These differences were not addressed, most likely, because one or more of the partners were unwilling to address the points of difference that exist between them. Therefore, each partner chooses to address one another within the fragments of what each partner feels comfortable with. This is a form of conduct that each partner submitted to unintentionally or intentionally. Both partners have summited to overlooking or avoiding the difficult aspect of their union.

Therefore, allowing a type of interaction to develop that is grounded in one or more of the partners' comfort level and not within the reality of what each partner is (as a person) and the reality of what type of relationship/partnership that exists between them. Once a prospective member or members of a partnership appropriately address points of differences, resolutions will began to formulate. These resolutions will be based on facts or the true character of the members and the nature of the relationship. This process will also direct and determine the appropriate course of the relationship. This is a course that will define the nature of the partnership; whether it should end or should continue. If differences are not addressed, the husband and the wife must take the blame for the failure of the marriage or partnership. The failure must be viewed as the legal system views criminal acts that are performed by more than one person.

Within the legal system, when a criminal act takes place by two or more people, all parties are arrested and convicted. They are all legally viewed as one body working together to break the law. This is because it is the responsibility of all parties involved to consider the consequences of engaging in the criminal act prior to performing the act. In the same manner, God's view of partnership is that of two or more recognizing, acknowledging, and addressing differences prior to and during the partnership. This also includes the need for them to have the ability to work together to help one another in unity accomplish goals, and accept, submit, and live in God's plan for their lives.

There is no "You" or "I" in a true partnership. True partnerships are about "Us." This is why traditional marriage vows clearly bind the couple together as one, for better or worse. This is also why God punished both Adam and Eve in the Garden of Eden. Couples should spend intimate and soul-searching time together learning of one another and coming into agreement with one another prior to and after partnering with one another. Christian partners should seek to understand and accept each other, God's word and God's truths on a personal level and as a unit, in spite of their comfort level with addressing personal differences. This approach creates a type of single-mindedness that is impenetrable and fearless in the things of God and when addressing life's challenges, especially when faced with dealing with feelings of discomfort and troubles.

Christ-Centeredness versus Fragmented and Segmented

Although many in our society have given up on the concept of true partnership, Christians do not have this option, because partnership is an integral part of God's design for His people. As a result, Christian partnerships cannot be built upon fragments of personal interest. A Christian does not unite with others for common interest only. Christians partner themselves with others first and foremost to honor God and to help maintain the soul salvation of all partners. Yes, you are your brother's keeper and partnerships in Christ are the epitome of this concept. Christian partners are for the soul salvation of all parties involved! Whether the partnership is for business, friendship or marriage, it is for the sake of encouraging, maintaining, and enhancing the stability of one's salvation and Godly lifestyle.

The Holy Spirit mentors Christians and the Holy Spirit focuses on the totality of a man. This is a focus that supports the concept that God's people do not partner with others based upon fragments of an individual or organization. This may be fragments that were gained from isolated encounters or chance meetings of friendly communication. For example, you meet a person at a function or a club and you share a brief period of positive exchange and because of this positive exchange, you have decided that this person is a good candidate for partnership. This is not an appropriate approach for partnerships. Just because a person behaves well around you for a period of time or treats you well for a period of time, does not qualify them for partnership.

A Christ-centered evaluation of anything is not segmented. For Christians, the total package of who or what something represents is under consideration, at all times! The people of God should not overlook or minimize aspects of a person's personality or behavior, regardless of whether the behavior is positive or negative. Also, partnering with an organization or entity is not limited to the entity's charity work.

For business, friendship or marriage, all aspects of a person, group or organization are always under consideration when contemplating partnership. Just as Paul advised fellow Christians in **I Corinthians 11:1** to follow him as he follows Christ, so should a Christian's consideration for partnership be followed. Christian partnerships are embedded in each partner's willingness to submit to and allow God to govern him or her through the teachings of Christ. It is not enough to say partnering with another or a group makes one feel better about one's self. Nor is it enough to say it looks like the person who is a candidate for partnership has a positive outlook on the things of God. The people of God have a vested interest in knowing that a potential partner is truly God-centered and Christ-driven.

Although positive feelings about a potential candidate for partnership are important; the characteristics of an appropriate partner in God will be evident in the way the person, organization, and/or entity functions daily over an extended period. Hello! These evaluations will seek to discover whether the person or entity in question will openly pray for, encourage, and help their partner(s) work through issues, which may hinder the partner's ability to follow Christ. These evaluations will also focus on the potential partner's ability to listen. These individuals should be able to listen to their partner(s). They should not only be able to listen to their partner(s), but also have an ability and willingness to listen to the truth of any situation and be able to accept biblical feedback and feedback about their life issues and their personal perceptions in Christ. It is also important to observe an individual during stressful and joyful periods in their life. Someone once said, "The true character of a man is seen in how a person deals with stress and with success." So, get to know a candidate that is being considered for partnership in multiple settings.

While encouraging and helping another in their Christian walk, a candidate for Christian partnership will be more than willing to help their partner accomplish the goals of their partnership, whether it is for business, friendship or marriage. These partners will not just do their part/job in the partnership and then look to the other partner and say: "Where is your input?" These individuals are more than willing to help their partner pick up the slack. Christian partners are diligent workers **(Ecclesiastes 9:10; Romans 12:11; Colossians 3:23-24)**. There is no such thing as a lazy Christian. Laziness is a **Red Flag! (Proverbs 10:4; II Thessalonians 3:6-10)**. There are also no big egos in these partnerships (another **Red Flag**), just God-fearing individuals working together to achieve individual and group goals in Christ.

These partners recognize that their union is not only about them and the goals they can achieve within their partnership. They realize and accept that their union is also about the body of Christ. These partners seek to be in tune with what God has willed for them and others. Although Christians are not busybodies, they are concerned about others and the environment. This is because they are highly aware of the fact that the condition of others and the wellbeing of their environment (home, social structure, and ecosystem) is a defining Spiritual and health factor for all. This is a mission statement in the body of Christ, which means **Christians are socially conscious and environmentally friendly**.

There is no such thing as a mind-your-own-business, self-centered Christian. Christians are always curious about the people around them because they know what is at stake, the wellbeing of their soul, and they are acutely aware of the fact that Satan is looking for ways to cripple their ability, for them and others, to live for God in peace. So, **do not be offended if you feel a little nosey, or if someone calls you nosey. Just be nosey unto the Glory of God** and not for the sake of being a busybody. These are some of many qualifying characteristics for potential partners.

Although there are many notable powerful people in this world who are making interesting statements about business, friendships, marriage, and/or who one should partner with, Christians must stay focused on God and His plan for our lives. **Colossians 2:8,** warns the people of God to beware of philosophies and deceits that were constructed according to the traditions of men and the basic principles of the world. If followed, they will deceive His people into walking away from the teachings of Christ.

This is a warning that beckons Christians not to allow anything or anyone to cheat them out of their gift of salvation and the liberty of Christ's redemption. Those committed to the things of God must not forget that their salvation is about Christ's redemption and the example that Christ gave Christians to follow. When the word of God stated in **Revelation 22:17,** "Whosoever will, let him or her come." The interpretation of this calling may best be seen in **Mark 8:34,** which states that whosoever will come after Christ should deny himself and take up his or her cross and follow Christ. In **Revelation 22:17** God is calling for whosoever will come and be governed by His authority according to His word as displayed by Christ.

This simply means Christ came not only for mankind's redemption, but Christ also came as an example of how mankind is to present themselves and allow themselves to be governed by God. Jesus' life was also an example of how mankind should resist sin and address sin through the power of the Holy Spirit. Christ came to free us from the curses that were a byproduct of the original sin in the Garden of Eden. He also came to show us how to live a **sin-free lifestyle through grace under the governing of God as whosoever will choose to follow the example given by Christ**. Note: many will become cynical when discussing the notion that mankind can live a **sin-free lifestyle**. (More will be said on the concept of living sin-free later).

Colossians 2:6-7 reports, everyone should walk in the ways of God through His Son Jesus Christ. Also, **Ephesians 4:14** reminds us that, we should not allow ourselves to be tossed back and forth carried about with every wind of doctrine and thinking but adhere to the truth of God found in God's word. Therefore, the question for a Christian concerning all things is: "What does God's word have to say about the thing or behavior in question?" Amen! This leads us to the question at hand: What does God's word have to say about partnerships? *Also, why has God scripted partnerships the way He has?

Just as God is a complex being, the answers to these questions are also complex. They are multi-faceted and compounded with elements that address one's ability to stay rooted in God and the ability to live a Godly lifestyle. Don't get it twisted! The answers to these questions are not loose fitting and in some cosmic state. The answers to these questions contain multiple elements, with separate and defined characteristics.

Decision-Making and Problem Solving in Christ

The characteristics of the above elements fit together like a well-braided rope and are built precept upon precept **(Isaiah 28:9-10)**. Every element/principle has a name and a purpose. Such as the act of applying the principle of questioning whether one's choices line up with the word of God, prior to making a choice. The principle of questioning, prior to choosing, is intricately connected to the principle of one needing to have understanding. Usually, when someone asks a question, he or she is seeking to gain a better understanding. Having a better understanding supports the principle of making good choices. This is because when the question of what the facts of the situation and/or what God has to say about a move or action is asked, prior to implementing the act/action, a Christian makes an informed choice/decision.

Informed choices in God help Christians in their ability to act appropriately in Christ. Acknowledging that one should make informed choices is intricately connected with the fact that a Godly lifestyle is one that functions according to the truth of the situation within the context of God's word. Christians should not make moves without considering the facts of a situation and without consulting God about how one should, as a Christian, operate and/or address the situation within these facts.

Yes, you freeze! God made this clear in **Isaiah Chapter 30** when He scolded Israel for going down to Egypt without asking Him. A Godly response to oncoming choices is always that of caution. Christians do not jump into anything without investigating the situation and consulting God and His word, there is nothing rash about a Godly approach to problem solving or decision-making. A Christian's approach to problem solving and decision-making is always a **prayerful cautious approach in Christ because a Christian should always be mindful of how his or her decision-making will operate in the Spiritual warfare of Satan.**

A cautious approach to problem solving is not resolved with ignorance. The Christian's state of caution is remedied through an assessment of the situation with consideration of biblical commands and principles, and Spiritual guidance from the Holy Spirit. All Spiritual guidance of a Christian is endorsed by biblical commands and principles **(Romans 3:21-31)**. Everyone should act and react purposefully and within the will and word of God. Without an appropriate understanding of God's will concerning any matter, Christians should not move. The people of God learn to wait on God and no word from God is an answer of no.

Therefore, Christians should uphold the laws of God and if there is no answer within the word of God concerning the matter at hand, they should not act upon the matter in question. Also, if there is no Spiritual answer coming from within you or from any other source, which cannot be confirmed within God's word, according to the teaching of Christ, the Christian rejects the notion presented **(Galatians 1:8-10)**. However, the notion for many Christians is: If something is not explicitly addressed in the Bible to their satisfaction, they conclude it is appropriate to engage in that behavior.

Once again, if there isn't any confirmation from God in His word, the answer is a resounding, No! No, you should not be taking part in that. No, you should not support that. If the question is, should someone partner with another who is operating outside of the word of God? The answer is surely, "NO!" The word of God instructs us to "be not unequally yoked" **(II Corinthians 6:14-18; Ephesians 5:11)**. Although there may be other considerations, like age, equally yoked for a Christian is rooted in each partner's commitment to the teachings of Christ. Yes, you should walk away from things that are explicitly denounced by God's word, as well as, things that are not explicitly denounced by the word of God but can be deciphered within a cumulative evaluation of God's word and the history of His actions and creations.

Walk away, just walk away. Amen!

Many people, including Christians, do not respond to an answer of "NO" very well. This may have a lot to do with early training and/or poor parenting styles. Understanding that an answer of "NO" can be an appropriate and acceptable answer is a learned process. During childhood, most of us are self-centered beings. Children want what they want. However, a reflection of personal maturity and Christian growth is seen in one's ability to accept "NO" for an answer without the individual feeling that their character is under attack. Mature and healthy perceptions and mental processing will always leave room for situational differences and fact finding when assessing any situation. Also, Christians should be truth seekers, especially when it comes to the things of the Lord. Therefore healthy minded individuals, receiving an answer of "NO" should evoke inquisitiveness and a desire to understand a situation better and not resentment toward the concept of being told "NO". An inability to accept or give the answer of "No," when necessary, is a **Red Flag** for immaturity, lack of Christian growth and most likely is an indication of poor impulse control.

One must began to understand, to be given a response of "NO" to a request is not necessarily an attack and should not always be perceived as one. Now, one may question why they are receiving a response of "NO," but this does not distract from the fact that "No" may be the appropriate answer. For a Christian, "NO" is the appropriate response or answer to all things that do not line up with the word of God. Mature Christians are comfortable with giving and receiving the response of "NO", even if others have a problem accepting it. This is because as truth seekers, we can only address the nature of a situation as it exist within the reality of the facts that define it and as it exist in the word of God.

The **Red Flag** is accounted for when it is acknowledged that an individual is not willing or is incapable, for whatever reason, of examining the possibility that their perception of a given situation is not appropriate when the facts of the situation are considered. It is not our job to change the minds of such individuals. It is our job to note the lack of flexibility and possible dysfunction in the thinking of such individuals. Meaning, one should question such a person's judgments and advice; advice and judgments that could endanger you and others. It is our job to accept that partnering one's self with such a person is risky. Therefore, we should avoid such relationships or partnerships.

In one's decision to exclude individuals who cannot take "NO" for an answer from their intimate circle, one must acknowledge most would rather be told "No," when unknowingly entering a dangerous situation. When one is considering involving one's self with elements not governed by God or elements not willing to accept "NO" for an answer, that person is contemplating entering a danger zone. In many cases, an investigation, prior to making demands or approaching a task, will help one accept the fact, the answer "No" may be the appropriate answer for a given situation or relationship.

Intelligent beings, Christian or not, do not jump into a boat then ask the question: Can the boat float? Such behavior is not intelligent, nor is it Christ like. Insightful and wise people fear the hazards of traveling over water in an unsafe boat. To avoid this hazard, they will have the boat inspected. When applying this analogy to the concept of partnership, it must be said; the people of God do not jump into partnerships then ask: Will the partnership work? With the same breath, surely, they do not jump into a clearly inappropriate partnership, then ask God to make an inappropriate partnership work.

The act of beginning something or engaging in acts that are clearly inappropriate and then asking God to make it work to one's good could be considered by many as trying to test or tempt God. When God governs you, God is your boss. You don't test or tempt your boss on your job and expect it to go well for you on that job. When you go to work, you don't engage in actions, behaviors or contracts that are clearly inappropriate according to your job description and boss's expectations, and then ask your boss to make it work. If it is the norm to respect and honor the rules and judgments of earthly authorities, what is it that makes many think God deserves any less respect and honor? Is what an earthly authority proclaims more important than what God has commanded? No, not for the Christian.

Everyone should study and search the word of God and seek God's face for an understanding of what are appropriate perceptions, behaviors and partnerships in Christ **(Acts 17: 11-12)**. However, the norm for many appears to be jumping into behaviors that have been judged inappropriate or maybe questionable according to the word of God and/or partnering themselves with inappropriate self-willed individuals. Upon

22

discovering that the ungodly behavior and/or partnership is not working to their advantage in Christ, which it will not, then they will turn to God and ask God to cleanse them of the mar and stain of the ungodly behavior and/or make the inappropriate partnership work.

Many do not acknowledge the notion of questioning or thinking before engaging. Instead of not partnering with inappropriate parties, these individuals appear to think the acceptable approach is to engage and then ask God to make an individual who is unwilling to be governed by God submit to being governed by God, for the sake of the disobedient Christian. It does not work like that.

A committed Christian who studies God's word understands that the Christian lifestyle is a lifelong journey bound by a personal commitment to be governed by God, through His word and the power of the Holy Spirit **(Romans 8:8-14)**. They also realize or seek to accept the meaning of personal choice. They know that mankind has a free will that was given to them by God and unlike many humans and negative entities, God will not take back a gift. God has given all mankind the free will/choice to use the gifts He gives them to the glory of God or not, including the free will to choose to accept His word and gift of redemption or not **(John 12:47-48)**. They also understand that God is committed to His word and to ask God to oppose His word is not appropriate.

When the people of God realizes God's serious position on allowing mankind the free will to choose his or her destiny, they should seek to acknowledge and accept this fact. The Christian then accepts: To ask God to take away another's free will to choose not to live within the will of the Lord, is not an acceptable prayer in God. God will not make an individual accept His word and gift of redemption. Nor, will He make a person accept the vow of salvation **(John 12:47)**. However, God will hear prayers that seek to deliver an individual from strongholds and demonic influences that hinder their ability to submit to God. Therefore, a knowledgeable and insightful Christian understands not to partner with a person who is not willing to be governed by God. These Christians acknowledge that partnering with a person whether it is for business, friendship or marriage [with someone who] refuses to be governed by God is like walking into a danger zone or getting into an unsafe boat. It is a hazardous act.

Marriage, Partnership, Divorce, and Free Will

Understanding God's view of partnership and God's strong opposition to a Christian being unequally yoked with others, who are not governed by God, is highlighted in **I Corinthian 7:14-16**. Here, the word of God details allowing divorce as a result of one's partner choosing to not commit to God and accept the other partner's commitment to the governing of God. This is one of only two reasons God allows divorce between a husband and a wife. This Scripture also clearly depicts God's commitment to the free will of mankind. It explains how a person of God may be better served accepting the free will of a partner's rejection of the Christian lifestyle.

This is one of the strongest examples given by God showing His people the importance of accepting "No" for an answer, in some situations. **I Corinthian 7:12-17** describes God's willingness to allow the splitting off of a partnership and union (divorce) that He ordained to last a lifetime. God's willingness to dissolve such a partnership demonstrates His serious commitment to His people being in partnerships with others who are governed by Him.

Although, **I Corinthians 7:12-17** is an established part of God's word and vividly reflects how God feels about His people being unequally yoked with unbelievers in marriage, many will not accept this position. They insist on arguing the question of God's disappointment in believers marrying and partnering with unbelievers. Upon reading **I Corinthians 7:16** closely, one will learn that divorce is allowed because of what the word of God states: No one can predict whether a person will choose to submit to the will of God or not, which means that both partners' commitment to God is important to God. These scriptures also show us how a Christian partner's prayers will not take away the unbeliever's free will to choose not to submit to being governed by God.

God is aware of the hazards of His people being in a partnership with an unpredictable person who may never accept salvation. However, Christians beware! The privilege of divorce in cases like these are not granted to the saved partner. The unsaved partner is granted the privilege of divorce because he or she does not want to be governed by or does not respect the governing of God. However, God does not grant the Christian partner the privilege of divorcing under this circumstance because it is expected of them to obey the word of God in the first place, not to be unequally yoked. God expects the unsaved to be lawless, not the saved.

Therefore, the Christian partner is bound to the troubling marriage, unless their unsaved partner engages in adultery, betrayal, or abuse as God allowed Moses to grant. Note: Betrayal and abuse can take more than one form. Also, God would not have His people continue in a partnership that insists on, encourages, or force the believer to engage in sinful behavior. This includes sexual immorality. How do we know this to be true? In **Joshua 24:15,** God asked everyone to choose this day who he/she will serve. Mankind cannot serve God and willfully submit to engaging in sinful behavior. Also, a person who is asking the Christian to submit to ungodly behavior is displaying disrespect towards God and the Christian's commitment to God. Therefore, the Christian can and should move on from the partnership, regardless of whether it is for business, friendship or marriage.

Although God will forgive mankind for almost anything, God does not condone a Christian divorcing from a marriage with a self-willed, self-centered individual just because of the difficulty associated with having to deal with such a personality type. As long as your marital partner is not abusing you, encouraging you to resist the will of God, and/or engaging in adulterous behavior, the Christian must suffer through, for better or worse, and try to hold on to God. What kind of life is that? This is serious, people!

If the unsaved partner is not committed to his/her partner in Christ, the unsaved partner is not entitled to walk in and out of the marriage or the Christian partner's life. That would be considered a form of abuse. Once the unsaved partner makes the decision to move on, whether by behavior or filing for divorce, the Christian is free to move on. Likewise, God does not condone lukewarm limbo partnerships. Either the unsaved partner is willing to accept and respect the vows of the marriage and accept and respect the Christian partner's commitment to Christ or not. The answer to the posing question is clear: the unbelieving spouse will accept and respect the vows of the marriage and their partner's commitment to Christ or move on. Several scriptures depict God's relationship with mankind to that of the bride and groom for this reason. Those entering into a vow of salvation with God must understand that [they] must adhere to the commitment of this vow and accept God for who and what He is or you are free to move on. This is why God stated in **Revelation 3:15-16**, "…because you are lukewarm and neither hot nor cold, I will spit you out." God set the example for His partners to follow.

This precedent set by God, which allowed divorce, further confirms God's position on equally yoked marriages and relationships and His people being in equally yoked partnerships. It also reinforces the understanding that the goals of Christian partnership cannot be fully accomplished between Christians and those who are not governed by God. God is a just God **(Isaiah 30:18)**. God is aware of the fact that humans are not without flaws; therefore, He allows divorce for those individuals who, for whatever reason, have partnered/committed themselves to individuals governed by God and are unwilling to be governed by God themselves. This ruling/judgment also depicts God's mercy in cases where a marital partnership took place while both partners were unsaved and later in the marriage, one partner chooses to accept the vow of salvation, but the other partner is unwilling to do so. It also acknowledges cases when both marital partners were saved at the onset of the marriage and one partner chose to or is duped in to walking away from God and the marriage.

One cannot leave this discussion without addressing the concerns of many people found in **I Corinthians 7:14,**

concerning the common belief that a saved partner shall save their spouse. Many misinterpret this scripture to mean a saved partner in marriage can save the other partner unto salvation. The scriptures found in **I Corinthians 7:16** helps us to know that the verses in **I Corinthians 7:14** are not referring to one's ability to ensure salvation for their partner. The concept of being saved in this context is most likely addressing the issue of protection/sanctification or one's righteous prayers acting as a covering for the unsaved partner. It cannot mean one's prayers will make another accept the vow of salvation, because God's word does not contradict itself. If His word says accepting the vow of salvation is a personal act of repentance and no one can predict if a person will accept the vow of salvation, which it does say, this is the way it is. Salvation is about personal acceptance, repentance and submission to the word of God according to the teachings of Christ **(Acts 17:30; Luke 13:3; II Peter 3:9)**.

The prayer of the righteous profits much, but repentance, loving God, and accepting and submitting to the vow of salvation is a personal choice. **Acts 7:30-31** reports, Jesus' role for the salvation of mankind was to call sinners to repentance, not to make them repent. A Christian can only pray that God presents the unsaved partner with multiple opportunities to accept the vow of salvation. One can only hope that the unsaved partner will see the beauty of God and the workings of the Holy Spirit in the life of the Christian partner and accept God's gift of salvation, but there are no guarantees.

In many of these cases of unequally yoked marital partnerships, the Christian partner spends many years of their life praying for a partner's salvation only to receive in return, resentment and hostility from the unsaved partner. As a result, the Christian partner endures years, maybe even a lifetime of a partner who is constantly manipulated by Satan into tormenting their Christian partner with resentment and hostility.

Once again, the prayers of the righteous offer a covering of God's grace and mercy to a committed Christian's household. These prayers do not necessarily lead to salvation in the life of those the Christian is praying for. This is why **John 8:32** informs us the truth is liberating. This is also why the word of the Lord in **Colossians 4:5-6** instructs the Christian: **"to walk in wisdom toward, not with, those who are outside of the will of God,** using the time with them to encourage them in the Lord' operating under temperance of grace and grounded in the word of God that God may reveal the nature of an individual and that you may know how you ought to communicate with them." This truth may be hard to bear; however, accepting it will free many from a lie that oppresses, binds, and can cause depression in those who allow this lie, that the prayers of a saved marital partner can save the unsaved partner, to consume them.

A lack of understanding, lies, deceit, and secrets oppress and bind. It is God's hope that His people will seek to gain a sound understanding of who and what they decide to spend time with or partner with. This is because a sound understanding of the truth of an individual, group, organization or situation, will reduce the possibility of His people and others developing perceptions, interaction, relationships, and partnerships that are faulty and/or laced with falsehoods.

Attempts to communicate and commune with others outside of the truth of who and what the person or entity is, will fight against the truth and liberty God has for His people. Christians should pray always, especially for our children and those we hold dear. Although, righteous prayers cannot make a person accept the vow of salvation, there are times when these continuous prayers may move God to assemble stumbling blocks and afflictions in the life of a backslider or unsaved individual **(Ezekiel 3:20-21)**. These stumbling blocks and afflictions serve to gain the sinner's attention and act as God's way of hindering the individual from engaging in soul-destructive behavior(s). This is most likely why the old saints would say, "Don't let God have to bring you down before you realize you need Him." The use of these Godly stumbling blocks can be seen in **Acts Chapter 9**, when Paul was blinded on his way to Damascus.

Although these Godly stumbling blocks are not designed to force a person to accept salvation, they do serve as periods of reflection for the unsaved individual. In many cases, these stumbling blocks slow the unsaved person down and weaken their ability to continue in sinful habits. Such stumbling blocks also serve as an opportunity for Christians to minister to the unsaved individual. These periods may also offer an opportunity for Christians, who may not be aware of the fact that he or she (a proclaimed Christian) is behaving badly, to correct themselves in Christ. This is not an opportunity to "save" the individual because only God can "save" through personal repentance in Christ **(Luke 5:32)**.

For those in sin who were raised in Godly homes, Godly stumbling-blocks may serve to evoke a type of **Prodigal Son Experience**. Such periods may cause the unsaved individual to reflect on the Christian lifestyle, which they were raised in. The individual may begin to be visited by reassuring, safe, and calming memories of childhood and growing up in a well-founded Godly home. These nostalgic memories may remind them of the hope and joy of God's grace and mercy they experienced and/or observed while growing up with Christian parents, family members, guardians or neighbors.

The feelings and emotions associated with their childhood memories of growing up in a well-grounded Christian home may cause the individual to acknowledge the mercy and blessings of God operating in his or her life. Experiencing such acknowledgment in Christ can lead many unsaved individuals, with such a history, to Christ. Also, the stress associated with Godly stumbling blocks can evoke thoughts, associated with Christian teachings, of the negative consequences that can befall those who continue in sin. This Godly frame of fear may also act as a spear that leads some to make the wise decision to, repent, submit, and answer the call of God or, as some will say, led them to the Cross. However, no one can say if these stumbling blocks will change the heart of a person. This is because salvation is a personal choice that allows an individual to choose to ignore and/or neglect acknowledging the positive or negative consequences of being in an appropriate relationship with God.

CHAPTER TWO

Embracing a Christian Lifestyle through Understanding the Dynamics of the Divide

The story of the Prodigal Son highlights the importance of having a foundation that is rooted in Christ. When an individual has a history of being in an environment where the Spirit of God is allowed to govern, he or she has observed and experienced the power and effectiveness of God's Holy Spirit and has a basis/foundation or reference in God. Although these individuals may not credit God for the supernatural experiences and Godly manifestations they have been exposed to, this exposure forces them to acknowledge that there is more to living than what meets the eye. These memories of Godly experiences are Godly seeds planted in the life of the individual and will never leave them and will affect the way they perceive the world. These are also seeds that God will use to help the individual connect with Him. Such seeds will serve as the beginnings of the development of a moral compass, whether the individual is aware of it or not.

Raising a child in a Godly environment through appropriate Christian partnership is a part of what it means to, "Train up a child in the way he/she should go ..." **(Proverbs 22:6)**. Christian parenting and guidance give and expose the child to the necessary building blocks needed for the child to acknowledge the calling and governing of God. This type of parenting also exposes the child to the meaning and benefits associated with appropriate Christian partnership networking. This does not mean the child will acknowledge

God and the things of God when a parent or guardian would like them to. It does, however, mean your child will have Godly building blocks in his or her heart and mind and have a history of being exposed to the benefits of growing up in an environment of people with the mindset of Christ. This type of history and Godly building blocks will help drive the child's actions throughout life, fulfilling a promise of God in **Proverbs 22:6**, concerning the values and structure that will help define and frame the course of the children's life.

An adult with a history of being taught the things of God and experiencing and observing God's protection, love, hope, joy, grace and mercy will also have an advantage when it comes to dealing with stressful issues and developing a willingness to accept salvation. These individuals have physical and supernatural references, like the Prodigal Son, of God's love, grace, mercy and redemption. On the other hand, adults without historical references of God and His nature will find it difficult to function outside of his or her own personal visual or tangible reality and are more likely to be overwhelmed by things they cannot explain or understand and by life stressors. They are also more likely to be deceived into thinking that their weaknesses and failures define them and are less likely to be grounded in self-awareness and self-worth, subjecting them to being tossed about buy multiple forms of doctrines and influences. This may explain why research reveals that faith-based individuals are more likely to cope better with stressful circumstances than those without a faith system **(Inzlicht, Tullett, & Good 2011).**

Proper training and child rearing in Christ will lay a fertile Christian foundation in the heart of a child that will not leave them when they are older. Appropriate Christian parenting serves as a defining and supportive element in God's efforts to humble, strengthen, and evoke change in the lives of all mankind. These building blocks associated with appropriate Christian child rearing will stage the framework of behavioral and cognitive operations in the life of an individual. This training will operate in the individual's life, even if an individual appear to be detached from the principles associated with this training in their day-to-day operations. This is because these developmental references are rooted in the individual's subconscious.

The pain of longsuffering associated with Godly stumbling blocks in combination with the history of appropriate child rearing can, and most likely will, cause many to engage in introspection. This is a type of introspection that will cause the basic principles of one's training and life history to emerge. This training will become more a part of their conscious state of mind and present existence. This is an experience which can position an individual to feel a need to search beyond the general or conscious frame of reference they are currently operating within to find relief from life stressors. In other words, a history of appropriate parenting and periods of struggle, pain, and suffering can cause many to convert back to their developmental foundation and become more susceptible to Christian outreach and adherence to the word of God. This is especially the case with those who have been exposed to the truth of God in their early developmental stages. However, due to personal choice and freewill, there are no guarantees. Note: Remember, those who have dysfunctional developmental histories are more inclined to convert beck to their dysfunctional training, when addressing stressors. They are also more susceptible to adhering to less constructive theories or theories that align with their dysfunctional conditioning when dealing with stress.

Therefore, the acknowledgement of one's developmental history must be considered. This is because a person without a Christian foundation can be more resistant to Christian outreach. Therefore, causing attempts by Christians to help their unbelieving partners work through periods of pain and suffering to be emotionally frustrating and painful for the Christian. As a Christian partner tries to help their ungodly partner or family member work through these periods in Christ, they may suffer emotional and psychological frustration that can lead to anger, depression, and ungodly stumbling blocks in their faith. In addition to this, the efforts of most Christians trying to help and minister to a sinner/unbeliever in distress who is committed to living his/her life by their own standards are met with resentment and rejection. Partnering with unbelievers can be overwhelming and partnering with an unbeliever who does not have a Christian foundation can place the Christian in a frustrating and vulnerable position. The question then becomes, why would one put him/herself unnecessarily in a stressful and burdensome position by partnering oneself with those who may never appreciate the love of God the Christian has to offer them? Why would one give their pearls to those who will trample them?

One can never forget that those who continue in sin or do not accept Christ as the redeemer are in a state of sin. This is a state that renders them more at risk of being selfish and defiant towards the discipline needed to make constructive decisions and choices. Many uncommitted individuals do not understand the vulnerability of their sinful state of existence.

They also may not be aware of or understand that this state of existence places them at odds with God **Matthew 12:30; Luke 11:23; Revelation 3:16-18**. As a result, many may not understand that this oppositional state can manifest itself in the form of unexplainable resentment towards the things of God and the people of God. These people are most likely clueless as to the role their sinful state plays in the spiritual warfare of Satan.

Believers cannot afford to overlook the reality of and unbeliever's existences. They need to be in tune with the fact that much of the resentment and rejection of most unbelievers who must receive help from a believer is not necessarily rooted in purposefulness, but in selfishness and in the spiritual warfare of Satan against God and His people. The help offered on behalf of a Christian is crafted in Godly worship and ministry. As a result of these characteristics, the Christian's offer of help and outreach to the sinner or those who are unknowingly in a state of sin will embody openly sharing the love of Christ. The love of Christ has been rejected or not acknowledged by many of these individuals. Therefore, it is most likely natural for them to reject any offer of help that acknowledges the need for mankind to reference the word and ways of the Lord through the power of the Holy Spirit when working through issues and problem solving.

However, it is sad to say that many, and most likely most, unbelievers in need do not want to acknowledge God or to be ministered to or to be put in the position of possibly having to examine their selfish thought patterns and behavior within the context of the word of God. Remember, **Romans 8:7-8** reports, "the carnal mind is enmity (an enemy against) to God; for it is not subject to the law of God, or indeed can be." These individuals may find it especially offensive when confronted with examining inappropriate or deviant thought patterns and behavior that may be the reason for their imposition. Also, Satan will manipulate other sinners to and command his imps to keep the individual in a state of agitation about the possibility of considering that he or she may be the primary cause for their problems. Satan will also try to keep an individual agitated about having to be helped by a person governed by God.

Do not get it twisted, these individuals want the Christian's kindness and loving assistance; however, most sinners do not want to acknowledge or give credit to God and the power of God working through the believer who is assisting them in their difficult times. Many unsaved people in need may also not want the Christian to openly acknowledge and give thanks to God for their ability to assist them or for the improvements gained in the life of the sinner under the watchful care of the Christian. This may be due to how these individuals have positioned themselves in their commitment to follow their own path. This type of resentment can also be seen in the public realm when political groups and many organizations do their best to hamper the voice of God's people and the message of Christ, while gladly milking them for their kindness, patience, time, support and finances.

Many sinners, worldly groups, and organizations, regardless of their state or position, are not willing to be governed by God. They just want help with overcoming their afflictions or achieving their goals, so they may return to or continue in their sinful ways. Also, they do not want to feel obligated to others and many may not want to feel condemned about any self-centered conduct or sinful behavior that may have led to their imposition. Mind you, Satan will also do his best to keep the unsaved in an unthankful selfish state of mind and uncomfortable with considering the role his or her sinful behavior may have played in their current state or disposition.

A Christian partnering with or assisting such a person may experience feelings of disappointment and grief after pouring their love, concern, commitment, and ministry and energy into a selfish or suffering person, just to receive resentment from the individual or entity in need. Many people committed to Christ will experience heavy feelings of disappointment, sadness and even depression when having to watch a partner/s return to their sinful behavior upon recovery or watch an entity they have supported use its' resources to undermined the things of God. This is why God would not have His people partner with those who may never accept support and kindness for what it is; God-sent love and God's desire to fulfill His calling in their lives. Nor, would He encourage partnership with those who place themselves in the position to be destructive toward themselves, their partners and the things of God. God warned His people in **Matthew 7:6** to not give what is Holy to those who cannot appreciate or respect it. One can conclude from this that Christians are required to be loving and kind to all mankind, including the unbeliever. However, God does not want His people to join themselves in partnership with unbelievers. Matter of fact, God commanded His people to come out from among all who are not willing to be governed by God **(II Corinthians 6: 14-17)**.

God has command His people to come out from among the unbeliever because these individuals are not subject to the will of God and are very much subject to the manipulations of

Satan. Much of their resistance and/or resentment toward God, will express itself as resistance and/or resentment toward the closest thing to God (Christians). Meaning, many who are not committed to the ways of Christ will show resistance in general towards the things of God and Christians. Their resentment toward Christians will become more and more obvious over time and manifest in many negative forms, in many cases without a cause **John 15: 18-27; Matthew 10:22**. A Christian who partners with such a person is positioning him/herself to receive the resistance and/or resentment that many unbelievers have toward the governing of God. These individuals will most likely twist and misrepresent the Christian's perspective and their love and kindness for something negative.

After receiving hate filled accusations that attempt to twist their acts of support and loving kindness into something negative, like trying to judge and/or control the unsaved partner, the Christian partner may be plunged into a state of feeling used, abandoned, and lonely in their partnership with such a person. The prayers of the righteous are the unsaved partner's saving grace, not their salvation. The prayers of the Christian partner may offer a temporary shield of protection to the unsaved partner from the curses and penalties associated with their partner's sinful behavior, not deliverance. Deliverance unto salvation and from sin, the afflictions of sin and Satan's manipulations can only come through the sinful partner's repentance, acceptance of Jesus Christ, and a willingness to be governed by the authority of God. So, if a believer has a physically abusive and/or adulterous partner, the Christian partner's righteous prayers may temporarily shield the unsaved partner from the immediate consequences of engaging in such sin. However, it will not necessarily lead to the salvation of or deliverance of the partner from the negative consequences and possible eternal damnation that can befall those who refuse to denounce and refrain from sinful behavior. Additionally, it will not cause the unbeliever to share in the appropriate love and partnership that should be shared between partners, whether it is for business, friendship or marriage.

The prayers of the Christ-driven Christian partner will keep an unsaved partner healthy and strong, while the sinful partner continues to engage in sinful abusive behavior. Continually having to pray for the sinful partner and deal with this partner's sinful behavior becomes a distraction for the Christian. This is because much of the Christian partner's life and ministry becomes primarily limited to or primarily centered on trying to commune with and encourage the growth and salvation of a sinful oppositional partner.

The sinful partner's rejection of God's will for him or her and the partnership will most likely manifest in the form of him or her striking or lashing out against their partner and/or those closest to him/her. The sinful partner's lashing out can go on for many years, because the sinful partner may never be willing, no matter how kind and loving the Christian partner is, to **reciprocate this love or to** be governed by God. **The life of growth, liberty, unity, and love God has for the Christian and their partners and others is much greater than that of one whose lifestyle is focused on an individual who has proven through the history of who he or she is that he or she does not want to be governed by God. Amen!**

Those who are partnered with individuals who engage in sinful behavior may not know it, but their prayers for these partners are most likely interpreted by God in the following way, when it comes to marital partnerships, "I know he beats me God, but I loooooove him so much. I forgive him for abusing me, let him alone and please do not hurt him." And for a man with an unsaved hell-raising abusive wife, as follows: "Lord, I know my wife does not really want me. I know she is divisive and causes problems between my family (parents, sisters and brothers) and me and she is verbally abusive towards me, but I love her. Please make it right between us, Lord!"

Understand this, all of you Christians! God's mercy will not last forever, when it comes to addressing sin. Also, God is not impressed with such prayers or requests. If you would like to know what type of prayer or request God is impressed with, read **Isaiah 38:1-5**. God is impressed with prayers that are a byproduct of what He desires for mankind and is substantiated with a lifestyle that is committed to being governed by Him. God is not impressed with a Christian's praying for or hoping for something He does not want for him or her. Amen! **Hezekiah** is an example of a man who lived for the Lord. He was committed to doing the things of God. Also, **Hezekiah** requested something (long life) from God that God has stated in His word and made evident in the history of who He is, He will give to the righteous. God is committed to blessing, keeping His promises to and giving favor to those who are committed to being governed by Him.

God's judgments will be implemented

You may not care how your partner treats you, but God does, and His judgments concerning your partner's sinful behavior will be implemented **(Numbers 12:1-15)**. God's love for you does not change His word or judgments. God's mercy may allow your sinful partner many opportunities to repent and change his or her wicked ways, but His word and judgments will be fulfilled concerning sinful behavior. God's judgments are not just for the end times. God's judgments are for the right time and the right time may just well be now when it comes to addressing your sinful partner's behavior. There comes a time when every individual will and must answer to God for his or her lifestyle, in this lifetime and in the life beyond. This is why *The Lord's Prayer* states, "*On earth as it is in heaven* (**Matthew 6:9-13**)."

When it is time for a sinful partner to answer to God's judgment concerning sinful behavior, the tragedy of this consequence may bombard the house or structure of the family or entity. As a result of your sinful partner's unwillingness to repent and turn from his or her sinful ways, God has had enough of the unsaved partner's sinful behavior and mercy has run its' course concerning his or her sinful behavior. Remember, although the prayers of the righteous profits/ availed much, these prayers cannot exempt an individual from receiving the consequences of continuing in and/or insisting on engaging in sinful behavior. Also, be aware that the judgments and promises of God will manifest themselves in our lives long before that great day of crossing over. We see this in the book of **II Samuel, Chapter 12** when David had to answer to God's judgment and consequences for David's sinful behavior toward Uriah's wife (Bathsheba) and for murdering Uriah.

It is during times when God's word of judgment is manifested that underdeveloped, immature or self-centered Christians cry out against God. This is because the wages of sin can heap upon the sinner and his or her family members, partners in business or friends' great losses and/or physical death to the sinner, their family members, business and/or their loved ones. Those who have an underdeveloped understanding of God will find it difficult to accept this reality. The underdeveloped Christian's lack of understanding or refusal to accept the truth of God's nature concerning His word and His disposition toward sin, may evoke selfish emotions and feelings of resentment toward God during the times when the judgments of God are manifested as a result of the sinful behavior(s) of loved ones and partners.

These Christians may make statements like: "Why has God let this happen to me and my family or business?" They express anger or ambivalence toward God, because the time has come for their sinful loved one, friend or business partner to reap the consequences of their sinful behavior. Just as the Christian partner's ministry has suffered for their disobedience of partnering themselves with a sinner, their physical wellbeing, children, family, and business may now reap even more consequences of such an unholy partnership. **God does not unite/join His people to the unsaved, because He is never removed from the workings and consequences of sin**. We see this in **II Corinthians 6:14-18** where God commands His people to come out from among them who are not willing to be governed by Him.

Yes, this is a tough bite to chew and swallow. However, many must face the reality associated with partnering themselves with those not willing to be governed by God and putting sinful partners and loved ones before their commitment to God. Christians cannot make these individuals the object of their affection(s) over God and His will for them and others.

To do so is an offense to God. **Deuteronomy 4:23-25, Exodus 34:14, and Mathew 6:33** warn us that God is a jealous God and to put nothing before Him.

God, and what God has to say, should be the primary object of affection for all. Those who inappropriately apply their affections toward anyone or anything above God, may lose touch with the fact of who and what God is and the fact that God will not make void His judgments. This disconnection or unwillingness to accept the truth of how God operates is directly related to the desires of many to cater to their selfish dispositions and their unwillingness to grow and develop in God. Much of this unwillingness to grow is due to emotional and psychological pulls and ties associated with partnering with and committing themselves to individuals and entities not governed by God and their desire to be comfortable with making choices that are contrary to the word of God.

An alignment with ungodly entities and the unwillingness to respect the will of God will serve as a distraction and hinder growth and development in God. It is not that the distracted or underdeveloped Christian does not love God. However, due to their lack of insight, the energy and focus it takes to address selfish desires and/or maintain partnerships with elements not governed by God; the Christian is limited in his or her ability to grow in God and to grow in their love for God. They are limited in their ability to grow in their understanding of the things of God and in his or her ability to accept the fullness of who God truly is; how He truly operates; and how to truly love God and others.

Those who allow themselves to lose focus of God and the things of God are more inclined to insist on God being an entity that operates primarily within their obscured perception of God's love, grace and mercy. These individuals' high regard for self, their ungodly partners, and other ungodly entities have lulled them into thinking that God's judgments and commands are cancelled out or will somehow work around them and their ungodly partners or loved ones. Many have even been duped into thinking that God's judgments will not occur until the day they die or until the coming of Christ. **Not!**

Everyone should know and not forget; God's perception of love, grace and mercy is much more than and is greater than the forgiveness of sin. It is also about restoration and mankind accepting Him as the Creator; teacher; loving Father; and nurturer He is. It is also about mankind acknowledging that He is **the Judge, the Reaper, and the Avenger** and the one who will give out the wages due for righteousness and for sin. God is about being all that He is in our lives and not what some, maybe many, think He should be. **Psalm 148:8 & 103:8; Exodus 34:6; Numbers 14:18** discuss God's lack of implementing speedy execution (mercy to sinners) to those who sin. Perhaps God's unwillingness to bulldoze over those who oppose Him may explain why many people fail to consider the consequences of sinful behavior. Also, the fact that God will implement His judgments in due time, may explain the lack of concern by many that many of God's judgments will be fulfilled while they are on earth. Due time for God is when He says that time is. Believe it or not, God will have His say. This is for the saved, lukewarm, backslider, unbeliever, the indifferent, the agnostic, and the sinner etc.

If a Christian does not understand the need to avoid unnecessary relationships, partnerships, behaviors and/or

45

hazards that can cost him or her their partnership with God, it is high time to learn. It is time for all to know and acknowledge that engaging in or being involved with sinful behavior or sinful people is costly. To insist on embracing elements that are not governed by God can cost the Christian the ability to live a lifestyle that is pleasing to God and one that ensures them God's favor. Also a sinful lifestyle hampers God's release of His promises of peace, love, protection, long life, and prosperity. Christians please, understand that aligning yourselves with entities that are not governed by God can ultimately cost you your eternal salvation.

Some may ask, "Where in God's word is it confirmed that ungodly alignments are acts of playing with fire?" The word of God found in **Luke 11:23 and Matthew 12:30 report God stating, "You are either with me or against me."** Here God makes it clear how being sinful, being involved with ungodly people and ungodly elements, cross the line with Him. This is because sin and an ungodly relationship and partnership are an attack on the Christian's ability to stay committed to the things of God. God knows Satan well. He also knows that it is Satan's plan to manipulate any weak points in a person's life to Satan's advantage. Elements of a Christian's life or partnerships that do not operate within the will of God are a weak point in the Christian's life. As will be discussed further, these elements also weaken the Christian's ability to stand for the things of God.

It is through weak points in a person's life that Satan manipulates men and women into walking away from the things of God or their salvation. God can have nothing to do with sin and will have little or nothing to do with strengthening an individual who is not committed to resisting sin. In **James 4:7-8,** the word of God commands mankind to resist evil (engaging in sin) and evil will flee from (the desire to engage in sin will leave) him or her. In **Galatians 5:16-17,** Christians are encouraged to not walk according to the selfishness of the flesh, but by the Spirit of God. These scriptures ask all to make personal choices that depict one who is trying to live according to God's will for them. They also define one who is under grace and behaving according to Holiness in the sight of God. When a person operates in Holiness he or she is allowing/inviting God to strengthen his or her desire to do the things of God/live in God. **Conducting one's self in Holiness also gives God permission to hold Satan at bay for all who obey the word of God and to stand-down Satan in the life of all who obey Him and believe in Him according to the teachings of Christ.**

Satan is slick and clever and he will make every effort to use the emotional, psychological, and physical pulls associated with being involved with sin and ungodly ties to fog and confuse the mindset of an individual, including the Christian. Satan's attacks on the thinking of a person who associates with sin and sinful entities are focused on undermining the core values of an individual in an attempt to dupe the Christian and others into thinking, living a Christian lifestyle is not fitting for them. Satan also uses ungodly ties to lure, manipulate, and trick Christians and others into believing that one can live a Christ-driven lifestyle outside of the word and nature of God.

Knowingly or unknowingly, ungodly individuals can be manipulated (willingly or unwillingly) in Satan's efforts to kill, steal, and destroy what God has for them and what God has for those who submit to the authority of God **(Mathew 27:**

17-25, Acts Chapters 16 & 17). As seen in these scriptures and throughout the Bible, Satan works through any means possible and/or necessary, this includes encouraging and/or manipulating those who are not willing to be governed by God to dismiss, undermine, and/or attack the will of God and the people of God. Two of Satan's primary tools used in his craft of destruction are manipulating the actions of ungodly individuals through their commitment to pave their own path within their own comfort level. The other tool of Satan is embedded in his ability to use the lure of selfish thinking and fleshly pleasures, especially those associated with sinful behaviors to bring down mankind, the saved and unsaved. Satan uses these tools to move mankind further and further away from the things of God and to uproot the Christian from his or her Christian values and the commandments of God.

Satan uproots and lures mankind into his web of deceit by consciously or subconsciously manipulating them into entertaining a self-centered disposition, sin, emotional and psychological ties that an individual may have to ungodly people, groups, acts, and material things. He also has an uncanny ability to lure individuals into participating in ungodly behaviors through perceived or the very real pleasure effect these ungodly behaviors can have on the flesh.

The flesh has a mind of its own and is highly suggestible to things that pleasure it, whether the pleasures are godly or ungodly. **Romans 6:16** informs us, if you obey the demands of the flesh you become a slave to the flesh. Therefore, what you subject yourself to, you become a slave to. Knowing this, **Satan is working overtime to get mankind to engage in selfish and/or lustful fleshly acts/behaviors and to fixate on lustful behaviors and material things in an attempt to**

enslave them within the workings of material things and sinful behaviors.

The demanding pull of the flesh is addressed in **Romans 7:20-25 & Romans 8:1-14; Galatians 5:16-17**. It is only through the renewing of one's mind through the Spirit of God, as one operates in the things of God, can one discipline oneself to transform or release the flesh from the affects that sin and the iniquities of the world has on the flesh. **(Galatians 5:16; Romans 12:2; Ephesians 4:22-24)**. Therefore, **Romans 6:16** is trying to alert mankind to the reality, the more a person operates within a behavior, one becomes more and more subject to or more committed to or more apt to feel comfortable functioning within the confines of that behavior. Also, the more one will begin to own a given behavior or own various thought patterns as a part of one's sense of identity and the more one will become hardened or resistant to moving away from that disposition, mentally and physically.

What you practice is what you will perfect **(Romans 6:12-23)**. When God instructs His people to resist sin, He is asking them to operate within His word. The word of God is empowering and when one operates within His word the power and promises of God's word adorns and empowers an individual to continue to operate within the word of God. Also, as one operates in God, these Godly acts purge the flesh of impurities and sinful impulses that are operating within it. Additionally, operating within the commandments and judgements of God will help prevent sin from becoming an established part of who or what a person is. It will hold Satan at bay and open the door for God to extend His empowered Hand of deliverance. **Operating within the word of God is an empowering act**, especially when you do it with the consideration of Christ.

The difficulty of walking away from sinful behavior and ungodly elements is made even more burdensome because just as Godly behavior is empowering, **ungodly behavior is seductive and debilitating**. Sin and ungodly elements weaken all who participate in them and in their ability to live within their calling in Christ and to have a closer walk with God. Sin and ungodly elements can carry with them ungodly strongholds, curses and demonic spirits that attach themselves to many sinful behaviors. In other words, as one operates in sin, the workings of sin is strengthened in its ability to operate within one's mental, physical, and spiritual makeup and interfere with and dictate the natural operations of one's mind, body, and spirit. Sin becomes an established part of who and what a person is. Operating in sin allows sin to grow and take charge of one's natural God given operations, desires, and thought patterns.

Satan uses ungodly distractions, sinful behavior, strongholds, and demonic attachments to subdue and pressure mankind in every way possible. Satan believes in the philosophy and saying that, "All is fair in love and war." The pressure of ungodly distractions and strongholds work against the Christian and others and their ability to think clearly, consider the truth about Christ, and stay focused on the things of God. His goal is to keep mankind in a drunken fog of distractions. Satan is constantly beating those bongo drums of self-gratification. As a result of Satan's efforts of manipulation and many Christians unwillingness to discipline themselves to stay focused on the things of God, many Christians behave and function in ways that are not indicative of a committed Christian. Their mental state is hazy and their behavior is iffy and unstable in Christ.

A Christian's mental state and behavior should not be iffy, hazy, or unstable. The Holy Spirit is not iffy, hazy or unstable and a Christ-driven Christian's thinking and behavior is ordered by God through the Holy Spirit. Thinking clearly in Christ is important for the Christian because thinking clearly is not just a process for the Christian, it is an examining and decision-making tool. The ability to think clearly in Christ is used to give and receive appropriate introspection, commune with God, and for assessing partnership characteristics. Therefore, the people of God cannot afford to be blind, hazy, iffy or unstable in their thinking or behavior. This style of thinking is also a **Red Flag!**

James 1:5-8 reports, it is the double-minded man who is unstable in all his ways. Committing or partnering one's self with something or someone that operates outside of the will of God can cause a Christian to function in a double-minded state. This is because the mindfulness and consideration for their partner can become a distraction. This focus on elements that are not considerate of God will cause a Christian to lose their Christian focus. In many cases, these types of partners can cause the Christian to be at odds with God. The Christian can become mentally and spiritually torn between a commitment to God and a commitment to a partner who is indifferent and/or disrespectful towards the things of God, setting into motion a double-minded mental state. A double-minded mindset will fluctuate between embracing the things of the world and the things of God. A Christ-driven Christian should not be, and cannot afford to be, double-minded. As a matter of fact, Christians should work on staying focused on the things of God. Such focus will help discipline them and prevent them from functioning in a double-minded state. A focused mind will also help the people of God resist coming into agreement with elements not governed by God. The mind of the Christian should be fixed on God and the will of God. Therefore, a Christian cannot afford to allow him or herself to be put in a position that will cloud their thinking and distract them from their commitment to God.

Faith vs. Godly Faith; The Distinction

A Christian's behavior should always focus on being purposeful. Their behavior should be fixed on God and God's will for the situation at hand and for all parties involved. A Christian's thinking and behavior is a direct reflection of his or her faith in God. A Christian's faith in God should not be blind, hazy, iffy, unstable or reliant on the support of others. The support of others is helpful and is more than welcomed, but not a must in the life of a committed Christian. **Hebrews 11:35-40** reminds us that those who believe in God, their faith is in God and God's will for them. Therefore, our faith is not in our will for ourselves or in what others may want for us. Then the question of faith becomes, not what we think or want or what others think or want for us. The question is, "How can we have a better understanding of how God will address the needs and desires of His people in any given situation?" This means our faith is in what God is going to do for His people according to His will for them and His word, in a given situation **(Hebrews Chapter 11)**.

When ungodly entities are at work, the first thing they do is to uproot the believer and others by distorting or hampering their understanding of God and Godly faith. Satan does not want us to understand or adhere to the truth of God's word or the truth of what it means to have Godly faith. This is because

Satan is at a disadvantage when our expectations of God operate within the appropriate knowledge and understanding of God and Godly faith. It is when a person operates within the realm of fiction and not in God or fact (the truth) that Satan has an advantage. **One's fictitious thinking in God is Satan's playground.** It is through lies and fictitious thinking in God and life events that Satan enslaves and binds an individual.

Simple Minded Thinking

Satan knows that if he can keep a person chasing after a lie or if he can engage an individual in a multitude of lies, he can keep them void of one of the fundamental principles of God; having an appropriate understanding of God's truth and the truth and reality of a situation. This is why **Proverbs 12:22** states that lying lips are an abomination to God. Without an appropriate understanding of God and the truth of God, one generally functions as a **simple-minded person**. Simple-minded people tend to operate through basic instincts and selfish desires. One's advanced level of education does not rule a person out of this category of simple-mindedness. This is because simple-minded thinking, in this case, has little to do with one's level of education and has more to do with a way of thinking when assessing oneself, others, and world issues.

Simple-minded individuals tend to have a mindset that focuses on personal survival, personal achievements, and personal pleasure seeking. Their mindset is not necessarily concerned with the truth of a given situation. This type of thinking can happen at any educational level. **"I" is the "god" of a simple-minded person.** To keep it simple, "I" is their focus. Their communication style and lifestyle is defined by the definition of "I". They don't want to know the truth of any matter outside of what they think or feel. Their concern and belief system is primarily focused on how the situation at hand will affect them first and foremost. Such a mindset will cancel these individual's ability to think logically, to understand, accept and consider how mankind must work together in respectful partnerships in order to sustain the fiber of our humanity. The selfless concepts of Christ will be foreign to such individuals and submitting and committing to the will of God and others in Christ is a difficult concept for such a person to accept.

God-focused thinking and truth-based thinking promotes a desire to seek the truth about a matter and encourages objective thinking, which aids in logical thinking. This simply means, when one's thinking is based upon or is guided by truth/facts, one's decision making is less likely to be defined by personal perceptions and opinions. What "I" think and feel is not the basis for decision-making for a truth seeker but uncovering the truth of the matter is the defining factor.

Logical thinking assists in one's ability to make appropriate and good choices. According to **John 8:31-32,** it is God's truth that frees us from the lies of sin and enables mankind to live the Christian lifestyle. God's truth also allows us to understand the realities of life, as they should be understood. **When addressing humanity, the realities of life cannot be just about "You" or "I."** Nor, can the realities of humanity be defined by one individual's personal needs or pleasures.

The selfish nature of a simple-minded mindset promotes divisiveness and hinders the productivity and growth of an individual and the people the individual may partner with.

The truth of God teaches and has shown mankind through the united efforts of the Father, Son and the Holy Spirit, the reality of the human existence is about a united effort working together to achieve common goals. Therefore, this truth (God's truth) is about partnership. Also this tells us, God's truth concerning partnership is an expression of His people operating within the confines of partnerships that are about unity and partnerships that are founded in God, through Jesus Christ.

Christians are Truth Seekers

Committed Christians are truth seekers **(Ephesian 5:9-11)**. This is because knowing the truth is empowering and freeing, also because the truth of God's word is life to all that take part in it **(John 6:63; Proverbs Chapter 3)**. The truth of God and the truth of Godly faith generate teamwork that is not selfish or self-serving. Satan is aware of this. Satan is also aware of the fact that the greater one's understanding is in God, the stronger one's faith in God becomes and the stronger one's relationship/partnership is with God and others who are committed to being governed by God. Also, Satan is fully aware of the fact that a sound understanding of God weakens Satan's ability to manipulate the mindset of mankind.

Therefore, Satan uses all of his worldly wiles to distract and hinder a Christian from knowing and understanding God's truth, a truth that unites and ties us together. Satan is well aware of the fact that united we stand and divided we will fall. Therefore, Satan's goal for mankind is to keep them focused on living a lie and functioning as simple-minded self-indulgent persons. His primary way of doing this is by distorting one's ability to connect with appropriate Christian partners. This is because appropriate Christian partnerships strengthen all parties involved in their ability to accept, commit, unite, and grow in the truth of God and in the truth of God's expectations of mankind.

Desires, Choices, Judgment, and Faith

Once it is clear that the Christian's thinking is not iffy and Godly faith is about having a better understanding of God and His truths, all should seek to obtain a sound understanding of the truths about God and Godly faith. To have a better understanding of how God addresses our needs and desires through faith, we must first seek to gain a better understanding of God and the nature of God. Understanding the character and the history of the way an entity or individual functions/operates/responds will help define how the entity or individual may act or react in any given situation.

Do not fear. It is okay to examine God, because one should always question who or what they are dealing with. This is a principle of God. **Matthew 11:29** tells us that God invites us to learn of Him. **Romans 1:20-23** informs us that although we cannot see God physically, who God is and what He supports is evident in the things which He has created, His principles, commandments and in His judgments. Truth is, "Yes," God has made judgments and elements of who God is are seen in His judgments. As displayed by God in **Romans 1:20-23, who a person really is, is found in the history of one's judgments and choices**.

The revelation found in **Romans 1:20-21** allows for the following conclusion: God endorses the belief that the choices of a person will reveal the true nature of one's character.

Therefore, if we are operating by faith in God, we believe God for the manifestation of His will for us, based upon the evidence of who He is (a Being seen through the history of His actions). Accordingly, faith in God is the state of expecting God to address our situation(s), whether it is deliverance, blessings, judgments or partnerships, according to His word and His former precedence (the history of the choices He has made for His people and this world).

If adhered to, this perception of faith in God will lead one to conceptualize Godly faith as something much more than a person believing God for one's needs and/or heart's desires. One may begin to understand that Godly faith is rooted in and grounded in God's expectations and will for mankind and not just in what an individual desires of God. We see this in **Romans Chapter 4** when God attributed Abraham's faith in His will for Abraham as righteousness. Abraham's faith was not idle or passive. Abraham's faith was rooted and grounded in the workings of acceptance, submission, and obedience to the word and will of God. Abraham accepted God's will for him. He submitted to God's will for him and in the process of acceptance and submission, Abraham obeyed the will of God. Therefore, it was Abraham's obedience to the will of God that nailed/secured God's acknowledgement of Abraham's action and credited the totality of Abraham's action (his acceptance, submission, and obedience) to Abraham as righteousness. This acknowledgement and contribution caused God to move on Abraham's behalf in every way.

*Sincere faith/trust in God that is rooted in obedience will move God to act on behalf of an individual in every way. Abraham obeyed because he believed in God and trusted in God to do right by him, based on the history and nature of who God is. This type of belief and trust in God is Godly faith. Based on the history of who God is Abraham knew of God's faithfulness and dutifulness to those that trust in Him and obey Him. It was this understanding of God that allowed Abraham to submit to the authority of God without focusing on what he would get for his obedience to God. He knew his walk in God would always work for the good of those who love and obey God. It was this understanding of God and God's history and nature that evoked the Godly belief and trust that was acknowledged by God and attributed to Abraham as righteousness. Abraham had studied God and showed himself approved. **God's acknowledgement of a belief and trust that was rooted in understanding and obedience opened the door that made way for the blessings, favor, and promises He has for all who trust in Him and are willing to be governed by Him**.

II Corinthians 10:3-6 reports, **God will address warfare/problems, issues, troubles, and disobedience of others as His people submit to being obedient to Him.** While this scripture is addressing God's judgments visiting the disobedient; the fullness of this promise of God addresses God's promise to address/punish the disobedient and all forms of lawlessness, warfare, issues, and troubles that offend or hinder His people, when His people submit to obeying His will for them. In other words, when a Christian choose to submit to the will of God, the justices, promises, and blessings of God will unfold. This promise is also affirmed in **II Chronicles 7:12-22** when God address the leadership of Solomon and God's willingness to heal the land of His people. The land of a Christian starts in the home and extends throughout the world as Christians submit to the authority of God and unite in partnership.

The scriptures that refer to Abraham do not reflect or indicate Abraham ever asking to be the father of mankind. Neither do they suggest that Abraham or Solomon ever asked for riches, health or long life. However, when they both performed their reasonable service of operating within the Godly faith of obedience, God addressed them according to the blessings, riches, and glory He has for those whose faith brings about the workings of obedience unto Him. Abraham and Solomon had no worry for material things, health, and long life. Their focus was on God and God's expectations of them, with the understanding that God will take care of them according to His promises and His former precedence.

Therefore, God's people must begin to understand that the true nature of Godly faith is not about God doing what an individual would have Him do. **Godly Faith is about His people knowing and understanding what to expect of Him when they love him, acknowledge, honor, submit to and obey Him, as they love one another in Christ**. It is also about His people acknowledging and submitting to God blessing and delivering them according to this knowledge and understanding. Therefore, one of the primary responsibilities of a Christian is to work on having appropriate expectations of God and their ability to acknowledge and submit to God's will in Christ.

God blesses, delivers, curses, and unites in partnership, according to His laws, judgments, and former precedence. There is nothing blind, iffy or unstable about it. A Christians' hope/faith is in God and the evidence they seek should also be in God. Therefore, if a person's faith is in God, their faith is not blind because he or she knows that God will bless them according to His word. God will also discipline, curse, and command according to His word. He will also judge according to His word (**Romans 2:2-16 & John 17:17**).

The question then is not about one's faith, but about knowing (do you know) and about accepting (do you accept) that God will fulfill His promises, according to His truth (His word). Therefore, a mature/insightful Christian expects God to address their faith in Him, according to His truth/word and former precedence and not according to their personal perceptions of what he or she thinks God should do. Therefore, it is clear in God's truth/word and established precedence, concerning partnership and Christians partnering with those who are not governed by God, that God is directing, encouraging, and/or commanding Christians to come out from among them (all who are not willing to be governed by Him) **(11 Corinthians 6: 14-18).**

Although, God is the one who makes the crooked road straight **(Isaiah 45:2 & Luke 3:5)**, it is not the goal of God to fix, mend or correct situations or partnerships that are not condoned by Him. God's goal is to present the plan He has for His people and have them submit to His governing (trust in Him), so that He can implement His plan (a perfect plan) in the lives of His people, according to His grace through Jesus Christ. Accepting the vow of salvation is an agreement with God to submit to His plan for us. A Christian cannot partner with those, which are not governed by God and are operating outside of the plan God has for His people and expect God to be pleased. These individuals cannot also expect God to bless or deliver them as He would those who submit to being governed by Him and are committed to operating within the plan God has for His people.

A person operating outside of God's will (sinner) can be blessed and will receive many blessings from God. **Matthew 5:45** tells us that God blesses whom He will. However, the history of who and what God is does not bear witness to God blessing a sinner with the fullness of what God has for those who are committed to Him. A relationship with God, safety, security, rest, and the peace that surpasses all understanding is reserved for those who honor God **(Isaiah 32: 16-19, Matthew 10:26-29)**.

When a Christian's faith operates outside of who God is, according to His word and the history of His actions, the manifestation of what the individual believes God for may not come forth. Therefore, Christians should always question what they ask God for. If God does decide to bless an individual with something, He does not necessarily want the individual to have, due to their stiff-necked disposition and persistence to have what they want, the fulfillment of the blessing will most likely carry with it outcomes/results that could weaken the individual's ability to stay focused on God.

This potential to weaken the individual's ability to stay focused on God is most likely why God did not want the individual to have the object of desire in the first place. Therefore, a person's faith or expectations in God for the manifestation of a desire should be mindful of the things of God. This is why Jesus rebuked Peter in **Mark 8:31-36**. Jesus was trying to convey to Peter and all Christians that they should not have or harbor expectations of Him or God for things that are outside of the workings of God, according to His word and history of that which He has created and commanded.

Once again, one's heart and desires should operate within the will of God. When one's desires are not the focus of what God has to say concerning them and all things, the individual's focus may be leaning more toward the desires of the heart than the will of God. Focusing on personal desires more than on what God would have for you will lend itself to carnal-minded thinking; thinking which moves a person further and further away from the ways of God and limits the anointed blessings of God. Anointed blessings are those, which keep His people focused on Him and offer the protection, safety, love, and the peace of God. **Keeping one's heart and desires focused on God is a growth process that is established in training and maintained through discipline and is nourished by appropriate insight and understanding**.

It is carnal-minded thinking that demands of God something that is not within the plan God has for a person or situation. It is also carnal-minded thinking that causes one to ask God for something not acceptable in God's word or history of who and what He is. Now, God's rejection of one's request does not necessarily mean God does not want the individual to have what he or she is asking for. It may be a timing issue or God may want the individual to experience their request in another form.

For example: A woman or man is asking God for a spouse and the person would have God agree with a marriage taking place between them and a candidate. However, after much prayer, examining the history of who the candidate for marital partnership is in God, things are not coming together in spirit (feeling comfortable in your spirit about the concept of marriage to this person) and truth (there are a number of things about the person and you that are not clicking) for a marriage to take place. This lack or inability for the relationship to move toward marriage in God is most likely the result of one of the following: (1) God is trying to get an individual to see the imperfections of what is hindering the union, **He does not approve of the union**; (2) The candidate for marital partnership is a Christian and will make someone an appropriate Christian partner, but **he or she is not the one God would have you partner with in marriage**; or (3) **You might not be ready for marital partnership in God**, due to your lack of Godly maturity or willingness to submit and allow God to strengthen you in the partnership you have with God through Christ.

Whatever the reason, the progress toward marriage is not taking place or the peace that comes with knowing God has condoned your relationship for marriage is not there. This possible marital partnership is most likely not to be, at the very least, not to be at this time. The imperfection of the possible union will be evident in the word of God and the history of how God operates. Therefore, a Christ-driven Christian will end the relationship, as it relates to possibly being a marital partnership. Christians should be careful of what they ask God for. They should also be willing to trust God when He makes it evident in His word, in one's spirit, and in the history of who a potential candidate for partnership is, this is not the one for partnership may it be for business, friendship or marriage.

However, God will sometimes allow or give a person the desire(s) of his or her heart that He does not necessarily condone. **We see God's disappointment in His people requesting something He would not have them have and granting the request in spite of His disapproval in 1 Samuel**

8, when Israel asked for an earthly king. An earthly king was something God did not want for His people. The fact that God allowed Moses to grant a petition for divorce is also an example of God giving His people something that was not within His will for them. Both concessions have worked against the people of God staying focused on Him and accepting and following through with what God has for them.

The problem with the faith of many is their lack of understanding in what it means to have faith in God. Another problem with the faith of many individuals is found in the fact that many of them do not want to accept that their faith should be within God's will for their lives and the things that God has for them and others. Many do not appear to understand; one's faith should not be all about believing in God for whatever one wants from God but applying Godly faith in a way that considers what God also desires for them. Meaning, one's faith is not just about one's personal desires, but should also consider God's desires for you. Such consideration is an expression of love toward God. Israel's lack of consideration and insensitive disposition toward God's desires for them when freed from Egypt, seen in **Exodus chapters 32 and 33**, caused God to be disappointed with Israel after He bought them out of Egypt.

Many of the people of Israel had faith and trusted in God for a type freedom, which did not consider God's desires for them. They fail to understand that their relationship with God was a partnership and their hopes and desires should have considered their partner (God). **Therefore, when one is making a choice that does not consider the importance for unity and cohesiveness in a partnership, it is not a choice that is good for the individual or the partnership.** Christian partnership is about love and love does not exist without consideration. So, **if you love God, you will consider Him in the midst of your desires, hopes, dreams, and faith for yourself and others**. **Proverbs 3:5-7** states that we should acknowledge God in all our ways. The way you apply your faith is a form of acknowledging God.

Christians should commit to acknowledging God in their faith as God performs a good work in them and their lives. However, **believe it or not, many Christians do not want to operate within the plan God has for their lives and others**. These Christians refuse to accept that their relationship with God is a partnership and they must accept the will of God as defined in His word and the precedence set by His actions seen in His history. This acknowledgement is what fine-tunes one's perception, approach to Godly faith.

The refusal to apply one's faith in God for who and what He is as the authority of one's life is crippling the ability for many to acknowledge and accept what God really has for them and the type of relationships/partnerships God has designed for them and others. This resistance appears to be in some respect, due to a lack of appropriate leadership and understanding in God. With that said, it must be stated that separating from those who are not committed to being governed by God's will does not mean one should go off and join or develop a cult. **Luke 14:23** tells us to go into the highways and byways. **John 17:14-16** informs us that we are in the world, but not of the world. These Scriptures are reminders that the Christian's lifestyle and the partnerships that God has for His people is not about going off to some isolated place, but their lives and the partnerships God has for them are similar to the life of Christ and His fellow partners in God.

Christ and His disciples lived and did the work of God among all mankind throughout the nation, according to the Spirit and will of God. Living the life of God and God's plan for Christian partnership is not about isolation. *Christian partnership and a Christian lifestyle is about knowing that God would have His people live lifestyles and have partnerships with others that are governed by God. Christian partnership is also about knowing that when one operates outside of God and partners oneself with those that chose to function outside of the will of God, one is in a hazardous zone and it could cost them in very destructive ways.

Everyone should try to understand and accept that God will not speak/put anything into their lives or put anyone in their lives for business, friendship or marriage, which does not embrace His word, according to His divine nature (the history of His actions) and purpose. So, when people begin to speak on who or what God has partnered them with or who or what God is going to partner you with, the following questions must be asked; (1) Where is such a partnership found in God's word? (2) Where can this be confirmed in the history of God's actions? (3) How does such a partnership relate to God's divine purpose for mankind and for you? Ask the question; Is God known for doing, accepting, condoning or engaging in the partnership/relationship in question; as it pertains to partnership or any other matter?

Some may be feeling a little overwhelmed with these discussions and the idea of living a Christ-driven lifestyle, but **Matthew 11:28-30** informs us that God's yoke is easy and His burden is light. It is also stated in the word of God, it's your reasonable service to seek to operate within the will of God **(Roman 12:1)**. Concluding, while there is much wisdom, knowledge, and understanding to gain, when it comes to the things of God, God's commandments are not burdensome **(I John 5:3-5)**. Living a life in God is first about repentance in Christ and accepting the love of God. Once one is willing to embrace God's love and the redemption of Christ, salvation is accepting one's need to learn of God and seek understanding of God through Christ and the grace offered through Christ. One must be willing to work towards accepting, submitting to, and becoming comfortable with God's established commandments and judgments. In the process of loving God and receiving love from God, it is vital that the people of God press toward accepting His established commandments and judgments that were established for the good of them and the nation. Simply stated, living a Christian lifestyle is primarily about the acceptance of the living God of Abraham for who and what He is (the all mighty authority), according to His word and the history of His creations, decisions, and judgments through the redemption of Christ.

Once one's acceptance of God has been established, a Christ-driven lifestyle is about the individual's submission, commitment, and trust/faith in God with the understanding of God's word found in the teachings of Jesus Christ. This is accomplished in conjunction with the guidance of the Holy Spirit and the statutes of God's grace. A Christian's ability to press toward loving God, acknowledging God, repentance of sin, trust in God, submitting to the authority of God, and follow the word of God in Christ through grace, with the guidance of the Holy Spirit, crafts a yoke of God that can be worn with ease. A yoke crafted of anything less or more, is a yoke of salvation that is difficult to wear and is a yoke that is not condoned by God.

It is when an individual becomes bogged down in theological formulations of men concerning the things of God and what these formulations report that God should be or one's life in Christ should be that the simplicity of the Christian lifestyle is distorted and becomes complicated. These formulations move one's focus away from the simple truths of God, and more toward the misleading perceptions of mankind. This shift in one's focus creates conflicting thought patterns and stressful feelings in the Christian (**Mark Chapter 7**).

Conflicting thoughts and feelings associated with philosophies scripted by men has convinced many, the yoke of God is too much for them to bear. Also, the stressful and difficult emotional ties a Christian may experience in their relationships/partnerships with the unsaved can make the yoke of God difficult. These ties to unsaved individuals and uncommitted Christians (believe in God and His salvation through Jesus but are not committed to Christian growth and being governed by God) play a significant role in complicating the Christian's lifestyle. Dealing with unbelievers and uncommitted Christians, as stated, is distracting, stressful, and complicates the Christian's ability to focus on the things of God and live comfortable in Christ.

CHAPTER THREE

An Even Closer Examination of Relationships with Ungodly Partners

The stress associated with ungodly relationships can hinder one's ability to strengthen one's self in the Lord. This is because associations of any type are time consuming. However, ungodly associations are not only time consuming, these associations, as in all associations, also force Christians to establish the legitimacy of such relationships. The lifestyle of a Christian should operates within the plan of God and what He has for them, according to the mentoring of the Holy Spirit. This is a lifestyle that seeks to move further and further away from sin. Therefore the mentoring of the Holy Spirit, which lives within the spirit of the Christian, will tug at the heart of a Christian concerning being involved in ungodly behaviors and/or relationships. This mentorship will require/force those who are involved with an unbeliever to consider a number of factors. A person who is committed to a Christian lifestyle and is concerned about what God has to say about their lifestyle is forced to address the following questions:

> *(1) How does being involved in ungodly behaviors and/or establishing myself with this unbeliever fit within the Christian lifestyle and God's plan for me?*

> *(2) How does a relationship or partnership established with a person not committed to Christ and*

Christian values fit within or is maintained within
their commitment to God?

These two questions will haunt the life and relationship/partnership that exists between a Christian and one not governed by God. This is because the thinking associated with the Christian's ability to address these two questions will not be comfortable for the Christian. The Christian's inability to comfortably address these two questions within the word of God, will most likely start the beginnings of a chipping away at the Christian values that lie in the heart and mind of the Christian. Such thinking will also chip away at the relationship/partnership that exists between the Christian and the unbelieving person/element. The Holy Spirit's mindfulness of how God would have the Christian live his or her life and establish relationships/partnerships in Christ will also chip away at how these individuals may see or define him or herself in Christ. It will also chip away at the Christian's ability to clearly perceive and accept the truth of God's word, who God is, and how He truly operates.

Note: As noted, Christians who engage in relationships/partnerships with those not willing to be governed by God will place themselves in a compromising position. Also, those who have been exposed to or grew up in Christian environments that minimized or watered down the word and truth of God will be even more compromised in relationships with those not willing to be governed by God. Their diluted history in Christ will put them at risk and cripple their ability to effectively deal with the complications of being in such a relationship/partnership. They are at risk because their insight, knowledge, and understanding of God and the truth of God is compromised. This compromise puts them at risk of

70

rejecting the mentoring of the Holy Spirit. Their poor training has also put them at risk of not making appropriate choices in Christ. These are choices that will help them avoid being compromised by the values of those not governed by God.

Christians with poor Christian training may miss the importance of being in partnership with others who share their Christian beliefs. Understanding the importance of respecting and being in relationships/partnerships with those who embrace Christian values may evade them. The shared beliefs of two or more Christians and the Spiritual connection between the two, provided by the Holy Spirit, foster the stability of each person's commitment to Christ and the stability of the partnership. The supportive nature of Christian relationships and partnerships also allow and encourage partners to embrace a Godly lifestyle with ease. Just as Christian relationships require their partners to be present, relationships with unbelievers also require their partners to be supportive and present. These relationships and partnerships also have emotional, psychological, and in many cases, physical pulls associated with them that require all parties to be present in the relationship. However, pulls associated with these relationships work against God's plan for mankind. This is also the case when people of God connect or become involved with groups and organizations not governed by the word of God.

The general elements of communication, association, and compromise associated with maintaining a relationship or partnership between two or more Christians are also needed to maintain a relationship/partnership between a believer and non-believer. The primary difference is, the Christian finds him or herself needing to communicate, associate, and compromise with a person or element that has made it clear, by the history of their lifestyle and operations, they are not committed to being governed by God. This is a problem, because the Christian must engage in a type of dance with someone that opposes or is indifferent to their values in Christ in order to maintain a relationship/partnership with them.

In addition, for there to be a need to be present in an unequally yoked partnership, the average partnership requires some kind of commitment by all parties. The idea of one committing one's self to anything is normally backed by some type of reasoning. Additionally, it takes a type of justified commitment to develop an association with anyone or anything for a significant period of time. It is this justified commitment that is backed by the Christian's need to reason or rationalize why it is acceptable for him or her to maintain a relationship/partnership with an unbeliever that leads to the Christian's fall from grace.

This is because it takes a type of justified reasoning to get someone to commit to anything. It is this type of justified reasoning that hinders one's ability to put forth their best efforts in Christ, and the statutes of grace are in place for those who put forth their best efforts in Christ. Whether the reasoning behind the Christian's choice to engage in sinful behavior or develop and continue in a relationship/partnership with an unbeliever is small or large, it is this reasoning that serves as a distraction from their commitment to Christ. This is also the reasoning that renders the Christian emotionally, psychologically, and possibly, physically vulnerable to the party/parties in question and the Christian's fall from grace. The Christian has decided to justify their commitment to something or someone that works against the will and word of God. The Christian is going to attempt to justify the wrong of not putting God first. This justified reasoning also renders the Christian vulnerable to the antics of Satan. This is because reasoning that justifies one's willingness to disobey God is rooted in rebellion against the commands and principles of God. This type of reasoning works against the Christian's commitment to God and His authority, a disposition that not only binds the hands of God, but also weakens an individual's ability to resist Satan's antics and mind games.

It takes a type of reasoning that is not God-focused to justify commitment to elements not governed by God and this type of reasoning weakens one's ability to stay committed to the things of God. A lack of Christ centered focus will create a mindset that places a Christian in a vulnerable position. This is why Christian should stays focused on God and what God has to say about all things. The Christian should not try to force a connection between them and anyone, anything or between other concepts, especially when God's word and the history of who God is do not support the connection.

The reasoning and justification that would cause a Christian to connect him or herself to individuals or groups unwilling to be governed by God will put this individual in a stressful headspace and make room for the workings of Satan. This is because the Holy Spirit that lives within the Christ-driven Christian will challenge their reasoning and justifications for engaging in sinful behavior and/or maintaining such a relationship or partnership. This challenge will manifest as reminders of God's word that contradicts such reasoning. Also, Satan will evoke every oppositional thought pattern and action of the unsaved or an entity not governed by God in an attempt to get them to oppose and work against the Christian. These entities will try to cause the Christian to question God's truths and His desires for an individual's life. These unsaved entities will attack issues in the life of the individual and the little unsolved issues in an individual's life to cause distraction and emotional destress in an individual's life. These "little foxes" are used to try to shake and shape the individual's state of mind and draw them away from Christ **(Song of Solomon 2:15).** Note: You see, Satan wants to use the unsaved and elements of entities not governed by God to create a crack in a Christian's faith. This is a crack that he will use to wiggle his way into an individual's life. A believer's connections to unbelievers and sinful elements may just be the wiggle room Satan needs to cause the Christian to question their faith and move them further and further away for the will of God.

The Holy Spirit's Role in Unequally Yoked Relationships

As a result of the Holy Spirit's push to not allow the Christian to be comfortable being committed to or with elements not governed by God, a Christian can become irritable, depressed, express anger, and/or become hardened to listening to the Holy Spirit, other Christians, and the written word of God. Either way, a Christian who justifies being committed to engaging in sinful behavior and/or partnering him or herself to elements not governed by God will not function in Christ as they should and are involving themselves in a deadly mind game. Therefore, the Holy Spirit's urgings will quickly turn that dance of value differences between the believer and an unbeliever into a wrestle of wills.

The Christian will try to stand up for his or her values in the relationship and the unbeliever will make it clear as to what he or she stands for. Now, the question becomes: Who will be the victor? This wrestle of wills between two or more partners with different value systems will open the door to Satan's crafty ways. Believe it; Satan is an old soul with thousands of years of experience on how to manipulate others, especially when they are operating outside of the will of God or are involved in conflict without the support of the Holy Spirit. Satan will use these value differences to exploit every little perceived break in the life of a Christian. This is why God informs His people to abstain from every form of evil/sin and to come out from among those who are not willing to be governed by God **(I Thessalonians 5:22; II Corinthians 6:17)**. Also, this is a position a Christian can avoid, by avoiding engaging in and/or resisting sinful behavior and relationships and/or partnerships that are indifferent or resistant to the authority of God.

One's Associations Will Make and Impact

*The closer the connection or the more extended the association, and the stronger the commitment, the more vulnerable one is to another or to a group. This means that giving your time to an element or allowing a person or element into your world, will have an impact on you. To allow a person to have an effect on you is not always a conscious experience or choice. This is because dealing with another person on a continuous basis will generate a form of commitment, whether you are conscious of it or not. It is this commitment, which causes an individual to seek to justify and legitimize their relationship with another, whether it is for business, friendship or marriage. It is also this commitment that Satan uses to manipulate his way into the lives of all individuals, Christian or not. When a Christian's associations, relationships or partnerships operate outside of the will of God, Satan can use these associations, relationships, and/or partnerships to operate (to implement his antics) in the life of the Christian and others, with or without the individual's conscious consent. This is why **Satan is called a serpent/viper. He will slither his way into a person's life anyway he can**.

Therefore, as a result of a Christian's ungodly associations, relationships or partnerships, Satan can blindside the life of a Christian who is making a diligent personal effort to live for God. So, when a person keeps company with or develops partnerships with individuals and/or groups or organizations that engage in behavior that is in conflict with God, these individuals are at risk. Christian and others are at risk of being affected by the fallout of Satan's manipulation and of curses that are attached to the workings of sin. These individuals are at risk of succumbing to attacks from Satan, mentally, physically, and spiritually.

Satan will attack these individuals through the workings of the sins that the individuals and/or groups they are associating with or partnering with or are involved with. Many of Satan's attacks are not physical, but mind games that cause Christians and others to question their values. These mind games are designed/aim to push the mind-set of the Christian and unbeliever further away from the things of God and more toward becoming sympathetic and accepting of values that are not Godly and Christ centered. **Satan does not care if you are a Christian or not**, his goal is to kill, steal, and destroy the beauty of God that exists in all mankind and the partnership and unity that God has for mankind.

The negative fallout of sinful behavior and Christians being involved in inappropriate relationships may also be the result of the consequences of God's judgments, as much as they are of Satan's maneuvers. These are judgments of God that address sin and one's willingness to continue in an association/relationship and/or partnership with persons or groups engaging in sin. The consequences of opposing these judgments will work against the wellbeing of an individual, group, organization or society. They can even be detrimental. In the middle of Satan's antics and a Christian's commitment to continue in inappropriate behavior and/or relationships/partnerships, the Christian can lose focus of the things of God and distance themselves from God (his shield of protection) **(Psalms 91)**. This is a state that will not only make them vulnerable to Satan' antics, but subject them to the wrath of God **(Colossian 3: 25)**.

Mind you, the wrath of God is not always swift and Satan's attacks do not always feel like attacks. These attacks can feel quite pleasing to the flesh; a night out with the girls or guys may end up at a strip club or perhaps dinner and dancing that leads to too much drinking. As a result, the Holy Spirit and other Christ-driven-Christians will press the Christian to address sinful behavior or actions displayed by the Christian, the unsaved or uncommitted. As the result of the tempered nature of God and the manipulative unpredictable actions of Satan, an individual could find him/herself enjoying life and feeling really good in the midst of sin. Therefore, one could be living a sinful lifestyle and feeling really good about their lifestyle and what is happening with them. However, due to the reality of the consequences of sin, the individual can be blindsided and all hell breaks loose in his/her life.

This is why the Holy Spirit of God compels the Christian to behave according to scriptures, which addresses unacceptable behavior and help them avoid engaging in things that have negative consequences **(John 16:7-29)**. The Holy Spirit is always conscious of the fact that the consequences of participating in sinful behavior(s) and inappropriate relationship/partnerships are hazardous and can blindside an individual. Although the Holy Spirit's urgings are not aggressive and negative, they are quite clear as to what God's position is concerning a matter. These urgings are not going to let the Christian feel comfortable with sin and/or partnering with or hanging out with those who are not governed by God.

In many cases, even the unbeliever will question the Christian's willingness to continue in an association or relationship with them. This is because the spirit of the unbeliever will not come into agreement with the spirit of a believer. Note: Many Christians may turn to self-medicating with drugs, alcohol, partying, sex, thrill-seeking, and achievement building in their efforts to block out the Spirit of God's reminders of their danger zone existence. In combination with a wayward Christian's effort to define their own path in Christ and ignore God's calling on their life, Satan will do everything he can do to manipulate and keep them moving away from the things of God. So, believe it or not, a fall from the grace of Christ and blindness to the things of God is a twofold effort; you doing your own thing; "You doing you!" and Satan doing his thing (working to bring you down). **Satan cannot accomplish his goal(s) without your help**.

Therefore, when we choose to associate ourselves with sin and those not willing to be governed by God, we are developing commitments with sinful or carnal-minded company who cannot be fully committed to the Christian. This is because the Spirit of God within the Christian cannot come into agreement with the unbeliever and the Christian's commitment to the unbeliever, is distancing them from God **(Roman 8:7)**. Also, the Christian's lack of focus is giving Satan ammunition that will assist him in accomplishing their demise.

The Holy Spirit's way of informing us of the ungodly association's threat to our commitment to God is by erupting feelings of discomfort within our spirit. Many of us may identify with these uncomfortable feelings upon our initial contact with someone that we later discover is an unsavory person. Committed Christians are not comfortable in the company of sin; so do not ignore feelings of discomfort when dealing with others. A person who operates in the flesh and outside of the will of God is far from God and the Spirit of God is not with them **(Romans 8:6-14; John 3:6; Isaiah Chapter 59)**. Therefore, Christians should assess their comfort level when in the prolonged company of those not willing to be governed by God. Their ability to feel comfortable in these inappropriate situations may well be a reflection of their lack of commitment to God and His will for him/her.

Uncomfortable alerts from the Holy Spirit are due to the critical nature of a Christian's need to distance themselves from sin. The Holy Spirit's alerts will not end with mild feelings of discomfort. As the Christian continues to move away from their Christ-driven path on a daily basis, the Holy Spirit's alerts of discomfort will become stronger and more compelling until it is clear in one's intent and actions that he or she does not want to be governed by God. At this point, the Christian is in a backslidden state. A prolonged backslidden state can cause God to turn the individual over to a reprobated/depraved/unprincipled mindset as He did with the disobedience of mankind in **Romans Chapter 1**. This is a mindset that is severed or completely separated from God. God has removed His hand from the individual and left the individual to his/her own doings or to walk after his/her own devices and plans **(Romans 1:21-32)**. A state of existence that allows Satan free rein in the life of the individual and we know what that means. Without the conscience of God, the individual becomes comfortable with sinful behavior(s) and/or comfortable with unsaved individuals they have positioned themselves with. Without the conscience of God, these individuals become convinced and hardened to their carnal or sinful way of thinking. They become comfortable operating in sin and with their sinful lifestyle.

The alerts of the Holy Spirit can also take the form of dreams and feedback from others. These alerts are in place to compel the Christian to address the issues of ungodly behavior/s in their lives and as seen in those in their company. The Holy Spirit is trying to get the Christian to conform to the word of God that instructs us to resist wickedness and to come out from among those who refuse to be governed by God **(James 4:7, II Corinthians 6:14-18)**. This is a command that is concerned with the danger such interaction poses for Christians and others they associate or partner with.

You Cannot Afford to be Passive

God also requires His people to address and devise a plan to avoid and/or rid themselves from those unwilling to be governed by God. This is seen in **I Samuel** when Eli's sons behaved sinfully in the house of God and with the young women of the church. Eli spoke to his sons about their unacceptable behavior **(I Samuel 2:22-25),** but Eli did not take action to end the wickedness of his sons in God's house, after his verbal confrontation with them failed to have a repenting effect on them and bring an end to the sinful behavior.

As a result of Eli's inaction, God removed His hand of mercy and protection from the house of Eli and allowed the curse of sin, loss, destruction, and death to take its course. **Romans 6:23** informs us of the judgment of God, which says the wage of sin is death. This curse of sin addresses all forms of death, not just the physical death associated with human life. Note: Death can be defined spiritually, mentally, physically, and financially, through the death of relationships, partnerships, and the death of one's status. Eli's downfall also tells us that **you do not have to be the one who engages in the sin to reap the consequences of sin**. Beware of those who you are associating with, have relationships with, or those you are partnering with who are engaging in sinful behavior(s). You may be just a little too close to sin when the judgment of God strikes. Oh, and it will strike!

In the Garden of Eden, death came in the form of a lifestyle and in the form of man's days being numbered on earth. In Eli's case, death consumed the life of Eli's sons, the life of Eli, and the status of Eli's family line in the priesthood of God. God has made it evident, in the history of His actions, that He is not pleased with the people of God or anyone being passive about sin.

Accordingly, the story of Eli warns all who have ears to hear what God has to say about the results of sinful acts or behavior. **God does not care if the person who needs to be addressed about sinful behavior is your child!** The curse of sin is still in effect. This point is highlighted because many Christian parents and others are observing the sinful actions of their children and being passive about their children's sinful behavior. Some parents are taking it a step further and condoning their children's sinful behavior. In this case, **Proverbs 17:15 reminds us that he who justifies those who operate against the things of God are an abomination (is rejected by the Lord).** Such a parental approach can be devastating to the wellbeing and life of the child and their parents.

A State of Marginality (the gray zone)

A Christian's willingness to engage in or develop associations with those who take part in sinful behavior not only compromises his or her relationship with God and the potential safety of that Christian, it defines the state of their existences in Christ. These individuals are functioning in a state of marginality (living on the edge) or living below the standards of God. As noted, the Holy Spirit will not be comfortable with, nor will He allow the Christian to operate in a state of marginality comfortably.

Satan also will not allow an individual to comfortably operate and function in a prolonged state of marginality. This is **a gray zone of existence** and there is little or no protection in God for those who function in this area. The little protection that exists for these people is found in the prayers of the righteous and in the possibility that these people may experience an awakening to the fact that they need to repent and refocus on God, as David, and follow the teachings of God according to Christ. This gray zone of existence is also not acceptable to Satan because Satan prefers his subject to be in a state of a sure fall.

He would have his subjects to be so fallen that they have no mind to think of God or God's truth's and surely not be in a position (state of mind) to long for God. Satan would have all mankind in a reprobated state.

Satan wants to keep mankind on a straight and narrow pathway to hell. When mankind is operating in the gray zone, he or she may and can have those moments that make them long for improving their walk with God. Christians operating in this zone are even more likely to have these moments because they have a history with God. These individuals may and can experience periods in this hazy gray zone that may cause them (for whatever reason) to acknowledge elements of God's truths about them, humanity, and the need for Christ's redemption.

As a result of someone acknowledging any element of God's truths, the Holy Spirit can fall upon that person, awakening them to the reality of their gray zone existence. It can also awaken them to the reality of who and what God is and to the reality of their need to do better toward others and God in Christ. It is in this moment of spiritual wakening, as seen in the prodigal son, through the moving of the power of God, a type of restoration can be evoked that can lead to salvation (repentance and a willingness to recommit and submit to God). It does not take a person acknowledging all of who God is, for God to cause a change in them. Just coming into the acknowledgement of God, understanding, and the acceptances of elements of God's truth and authority through Christ can breathe life and resurrection into a troubled or dead soul.

Therefore, Satan will use every trick in the book to pull and tug at an individual in the gray zone to move them further and further away from God until the person completely falls into a state where he or she does not think about God and the things of God or does not think they are good enough to be considered by God. As a result, an individual may experience prolonged feelings of hopelessness, depression, and/or is too weak and distraught to cry out to God due to possible self-indulgence, ignorance, shame or guilt. A person in a fallen state can repent and return to God; but Satan will do everything within his wicked power through his imps and minions to manipulate the individual, his/her environment, and others in his attempts to get the individual to submit to their fallen state and forgetting about God's love and offer of redemption.

Satan can manipulate individuals better when they are in a fallen (in opposition with God) state. It is when one is in a fallen state that Satan gathers his ammunition for the deadly mind games he uses to attack and keep an individual in bondage. Satan takes pleasure in reminding a person of earthly and fleshly pleasures, the negative perception for the need for discipline in their life, how they fell from grace and of all the sinful things they have engaged in during their fallen state and throughout their lives.

Torturing an individual and manipulating them into staying bound by their imperfections is one of Satan's last hoorahs before he is sent off to his final destination, eternal damnation. A Christian who is comfortable with behaving sinfully and with partnering or hanging out with those who behave in ways that are in conflict with God, is one who is putting him or herself in a vulnerable position. This is one who should question his/her commitment to his or her personal vow of salvation. This is also one who should know, they are in the clutches of Satan's game plan to seek their demise, which is **in the mouth of an eeeevil dragon!**

Do not forget **Ephesians 6:11-20.** It informs us that our time spent on earth is in the midst of Spiritual war with two defining sides, for or against God. An individual is either on one side or the other. There is no in-between with God. An unsaved individual should question the role they are playing in this Spiritual warfare. Most likely, an unsaved individual is a pawn of Satan, willingly or not **(Mark 15:10-13)**. And, their lifestyle is working against the things of God, whether the person is aware of how Satan is trying to use them or not, even if their lifestyle appears pleasing. This is because the only thing that interrupts the hand of Satan, in the life of mankind, is the power of God through Christ, not one's willpower or positive thinking. When a person is operating outside of the will of God he or she is greatly weakened in his or her ability to resist Satan's manipulative antics, which will bombard his or her life, in one way or another.

The Empowered Act of Repentance and Obedience

*However, it is the empowered act of repentance and one's willingness to submit to the authority of God in Christ, who can stand-down Satan, which protects us from Satan's elaborate manipulative pranks. Also, if a person is saved or not, when an individual conducts him or herself in accordance with God's word, Satan is held at bay. This is because **God's word of instruction is empowered with assurances**. Just as one's continual disobedience to the instruction of God will ensure eternal damnation, obedience to God's instructions

85

breathes life into all that abide in them. This is why the word of God reminds us that obedience is better than sacrifice **(I Samuel 15:22-23)**. Obedience to the word of God, although in itself is not deliverance unto salvation, can create a type of safe zone that work against Satan's antics for all who abide in the word of God.

There is life in the word of God **(Proverbs 4:20-27)**. This means that there is life when one lives according to the commandments of God, Christian or not. However, **there is no salvation found in a lifestyle that is committed to the commandments of God but does not answer to the calling of repentance found in Jesus Christ**. Those who are committed to obeying the laws and commandments of God can find peace in knowing the laws and commands of God are in place for their protection. People who operate within the laws and commandments of God are operating as kind and dutiful people who are committed to the structure of God but are not committed to the plan of God through Jesus Christ. They live in the unsaved zone of life.

There are some benefits and mercy in conducting one's self according to the laws and commandments of God, but there is no redemption, complete deliverance or salvation. **(John 5:39-44; Romans 3:19-23)**. Therefore, these individuals are not in the body of Christ and are not empowered with the power of the Holy Spirit. This missing element leaves them void of the ability to rightly divide the truth form a lie and command the hand of God who can stand down Satan **(Isaiah 45:11)**. As a result, Satan's efforts of manipulation can blindside these individuals and beat these kind and orderly people down mentally, emotionally and spiritually. Satan does not care if you are not a "bad" person. He likes "gooooooooood" people.

Note: When a partnership, group or society is operating according the word of God, the empowerment of operating within God's word will offer a significant amount of stability, peace, and hope to that entity.

The Mission of the Holy Sprit

God's relationship with mankind, as well as the offer of His partnership of salvation to mankind are established and exist in Spirit and in the truth of His word, not just in following His commandments. God will gift the Holy Spirit to all who repent of their sins, accept the vow of salvation, and is willing to receive, submit, and abide within the truth of His word, to the best of their ability. The Holy Spirit is the power of God, which can operate from within us and on our behalf through the grace of God, which was enriched through Christ Jesus **(Romans 8: 26-27)**. The Holy Spirit works on behalf of the Christian to mentor and help the Christian learn the true meaning of life, love and how to find peace **(John 14:26-27)**. It is also there to help the Christian understand and embrace the truth of God. Through the power of the Holy Spirit, Christians also learn how to submit to and obey the word of God as they are strengthened in their ability to resist the manipulations of Satan and the temptations and weaknesses of the flesh. The Holy Spirit introduces mankind to the true meaning of living. He does this by introducing the Christian to the love and truth of God and by breathing life, hope, strength, and fight into the lives of all who seek/press to operate within the will of God. The Holy Spirit is the power that helps the word of God to effectively operate in those who believe **(Thessalonians 2:13)**. Without the power of the Holy Spirit in Christ, the individual can do little to stop Satan from working many, if not all of his ills to eat away at the will and wellbeing of that person.

An unsaved individual's desire to do good things and be a "good person" will be challenged by Satan on a continual base. Satan is relentless in his aggressive approach to destroy the will and wellbeing of mankind and he has no mercy. **John 10:10** states that Satan comes to kill, steal, and destroy. Knowing this, we all need to ask ourselves – the saved and the unsaved – does God's word and His divine nature operate in our lives, and is it expressed through our conduct? This is because the operations of God through the Holy Spirit are expressed not only through belief and faith, but also through one's conduct and works in Christ **(James 2:14-26)**. If one's conduct and works are not a reflection of the Holy Spirit operating in one's life, one may be unknowingly walking down a path of destruction, no matter how many wonderful things may happen to them or how many sunny days they may have.

The press of the Holy Spirit for the Christian to address the ungodly behavior of loved ones and partners, combined with Satan's manipulations of such relationships, will create anxiety and frustration in the life of a Christian who refuses to stay focused on the word and will of God. In trying to cope with the anxiety and frustration associated with the need to address the Holy Spirit and the emotional pulls of ties from the unsaved, many Christians can become emotionally overwhelmed, conflicted, torn, and drained. This may explain the overwhelmed and depressed feelings expressed by many Christians in their daily walk in Christ.

One of the biggest agonies for the people of God is learning how to appropriately appreciate and love those they hold dear within the context of God's truth and God's will for them. Learning how not to let family members and other loved ones, who are not committed to being governed by God, set priorities for one's life is a task. This is a task which one works through by strengthening one's partnership with God and His truths about how Christians should live their lives. The strength needed to accomplish this task can only come by spending time with God, His word, and fasting and praying. Yes, sometimes one must turn down the plate to gain Spiritual strength to work through emotional and family issues and the ties one may have to those who are not governed by God.

The Parenting Relationship

It is critical that Christians put their feelings and emotions associated with groups, organizations, and people, who are not governed by God, into perspective during the early stages of their salvation. When it comes to children, Christians should recognize that their children are individuals with their own will and with their own soul salvation to work out. Yes, one day your child will have to work out his or her own soul salvation. Therefore, parents and their partners cannot become so committed to a child that they neglect the fact that God is their first priority and strength. This is because God is the one the child will have to answer to one day. Also, parents and guardians will need the strength and guidance of God to assist them in helping their child work out the child's soul salvation when the child is of age. **So, parents, in the midst of loving your child, do not forget God**.

A parent's commitment to God and appropriate actions in Christ can shield, protect and help their children receive the calling of God and become effective survivors, helpers and warriors in this Spiritual warfare of Satan. However, helping children become overcomers in Christ starts with adopting a parenting style that is Christ-centered. Christian parents must accept that their primary role as a parent is to empower their children in Christ. A parent can empower their children in Christ by empowering the child's ability to partner with the parent/s in the parent's and the child's ability to live a Christ-driven lifestyle. Such partnership between a child and its parent is established through **proactive parenting in Christ**.

Proactive parenting in Christ starts with open prayer and communication that embodies the word of God. This prayer and communication is with and between the parent/s and child/children. Openly praying and sharing the word of God with the child will help develop a partnership with one's child in Christ and will help teach a child how to be resilient in Christ, through God's word and prayer. Openly praying and singing songs of praise in one's home and over one's children and having unity prayer and singing songs of joy and praise with one's children will also help establish a good foundation for the spiritual development and growth of the child. Children learn through these experiences, that one must spend time communing with God and family. These joyous times create heartwarming templates that can ground the child in the Christian faith for life, consciously and/or subconsciously.

These Spiritual periods of communion, praise and worship with one's children are a good foundation for the parent-child relationship and their relationship in Christ. The child may not have a sound understanding of salvation or Christ, but the child is learning through the word of God, prayer, song, loving on God and communing with a parent, Christ and the authority of God is important and valuable. However, parents should keep in mind, family prayer, praise, and worship with a child is about exposing the child to the parent's relationship with God, creating loving memories, planting seeds of wisdom in the heart of the child and not about making the child saved or making the child accept the redemption of Christ. Once again, these experiences are about parental leadership, sharing your faith with your child/children and exposing your child/children to the Christian faith. In due time, God will address the salvation of your child/children because **God is the one that saves and not the parent**.

Proactive parenting is rooted in the parent's ability to communicate to the child and teach the child the parent's position in Christ. This teaching includes helping the child understand that the parent-child relationship is a partnership that works to help the parent and the child live a more productive life in Christ. This style of parenting is not about being the one who knows it all or the one who never make mistakes. Christ- centered, proactive parenting is primarily about acknowledging the fact that the child is a free will agent who needs to be equipped with intellectual and Spiritual tools to resist the antics of Satan. Now, raising one's child in Christ is not about the parent and not about the child being the parent's cute baby. It is also not about trying to raise a perfect child because no one is perfect. Once again, raising a child in Christ is about equipping a child with the tools and skills needed to face the world and the antics of Satan through the efforts of personal choice, discipline, gaining appropriate knowledge and understanding in Christ and Christian partnership **(Proverbs 13:24)**.

The parent's acknowledgement of the fact that a child is a free will individual encourages parents and guardians to spend the early developmental stages of the child's life sharing the truth of God's word. This is a truth that shares the love of Christ and helps the child learn to discipline and structure his or her life within the freedom of personal choice. This is also a truth that exposes a child, through example, how to live for and commune with God. Proactive parenting clearly frames the picture and is the training ground for the child's understanding of the meaning of having a partnership with God and the meaning of how to maintain an appropriate partnership with others in Christ. Christian proactive parenting is also about exposing children to life lesson that will help them become overcomers in Christ, through personal experiences and through the life experiences of other.

Proactive parenting starts while the child is in the womb, by reading the word of God, praying and singing songs of praise daily in spirit and in truth over the unborn child. Praying for one's child in the womb protects a child and helps the child's spirit become resilient in Christ from birth. **Job 1:6-7; I Peter 5:8** reports, Satan is seeking to destroy all mankind. As a result, one can conclude, Satan is present even at the birth of our children seeking to destroy or distort that which God has for the child. This is why it is so important for Christian parents and their Christian partners to be on high alert and united in prayer during the conception, gestation, birth and life of their children. Also, frequent expressions of open prayer and praise throughout the home create an atmosphere that encourages the operations of the Holy Spirit. Believe it or not, this type of praise and worship in the home sets the stage for your child's ability to accept and appreciate the importance of godly praise and worship and communing with and loving on God, loving on their parent and other family members in the spirit of partnership.

Parents should also make it clear to their kids from birth, in their communication with the child and the parent's lifestyle, the parent's position on ungodly issues, behaviors, associations, and partnerships. Although parents should not nag their children, they should be persistent and consistent about their Christian beliefs, throughout the child's life. One cannot impose their beliefs upon an adult child, but one can make clear to the adult child that God's word does not change by standing up for the word of God in one's Christian walk with one's child. The proactive parenting process is a loving balance of appropriate teaching and communication in Christ and discipline that helps the child develop appropriate Christian understanding, insight and boundaries. The earlier a child learns that there are given boundaries in Christ and are encouraged to operate within these boundaries, the more comfortable these boundaries become for the child. This parental style is marked by clear patterns of communication and behavior that seek to stomp out ambiguity concerning God's position on topics and God's plan for His people in Christ. Meaning, parents do not leave the discussions of topics open or to the discretion of the child but are willing to confront issues head-on.

Proclaiming, living, and teaching God's will in a child's life will rain down the promise of God, which is found in **Proverbs 22:6. This Scripture informs parents that they have a leadership role in their children's lives and directs parents to bring up a child in the way the child should function in Christ**, according to the word of God. It also informs parents of God's assurances associated with appropriate Christian parenting. These are assurances, which promise parental partners in Christ, their child will not stray far from their upbringing when they are old. Assurances that also gives the parent and child the understanding, there is always hope in God, no matter how dire the situation may look or be at a given time.

Many experts insist that parenting stops at a child's specific age; however, those that are governed by God acknowledge that parenting is a lifelong process. Remember, Eli's sons were adults. Don't get it twisted; being a parent is very serious business for anyone. However, the leadership role of Christian parenting is twice as extensive, intensive, and comprehensive as general parenting and will require the partnership of the extended body of Christ to succeed. As someone once said, "It takes a village." Appropriate parenting in Christ through appropriate Christian partnership will help reduce negative ties in a Christian's life and in the lives of their children. In spite of the growing pains associated with a child's developmental stages, proactive parenting, and discipline will help reduce the possibility of one's children falling into worldly and satanic pitfalls and becoming a negative entity in the parent's life **(Proverbs 13:24 and Proverbs 23:13)**.

Stress-Based Dysfunctional Thinking and Pitfalls

Once again, emotional pulls and ties on those who operate outside of the will of God can create stress and deceive many into thinking it is acceptable to overlook the word of God. **Matthew 6:24-33** tells us to put God first. When one does not put God first, he or she compromises his or her commitment to God. This is an act that is not acceptable in the sight of God. Also, when a Christian puts the needs of others or the needs of a loved one before God, it may mislead loved ones and others into thinking God is pleased with the unsaved person's conduct. A Christian valuing the needs of others more than

God's constructive and divine will and desires for them and others, will make it difficult for the unsaved person to see Christ in the Christian and for them to submit to the calling of God.

As stated earlier, the Christian's commitment to sinful partners and loved ones can cause the Christian and others to rationalize and dispute the word and nature of God. In the process of questioning God's word, Satan can slip in and deceive or fool the Christian and others into believing that God will excuse their sinful behavior and/or the loved one's sinful behavior, in spite of the fact that the word and the attributes of God do not support individuals engaging in the given behavior/s. In many cases, these stressed-out Christians begin compromising the word of God by trying to justify their sinful behavior and the sinful behavior of their loved ones, associates, partner, or the organizations they are engaging in.

Normally, justification of sinful behavior begins with questioning the truth of God's word and judgments. It is acceptable to ask God questions about His plan for mankind, as a student, but questioning God's wisdom and authority is completely different and unacceptable. When a Christian begins defiantly questioning God's position on matters, emotional pulls associated with their ties to ungodly elements have weakened their commitment to the commandments, judgments and principles of God. As a result, many Christians may begin to be less willing to accept the truth of God's word concerning the sinful behavior(s) of themselves, sinful behavior(s) of family members, associates, and partners. At this point, the Christian's desire to question the principles of God and define their own path and live peacefully with sinful individuals has rendered them vulnerable in their commitment to Christ. This is a disposition that leads to a fall from grace and works to the advantage of Satan's craftiness.

In the midst of a chaotic headspace and emotional conflict, these Christians lose their footing, and their faith in God suffers. They are not happy and may become angry with God and react as a child having a tantrum. The emotional pulls associated with their ties to sinful behavior(s), people and/or activities can press these Christians to flip the script on God. In this fogged state of thinking, they will find themselves searching for answers as to why it is unacceptable for God to reject their sinful behavior and/or the sinful behavior(s) of their loved ones or partner(s). Now, **Romans 9: 20-21** calls in to question the boldness of questioning what God has decreed.

Defiant thinking toward the things of God will lead to rationalizations that are not supported by the word of God. Such thinking is most likely expressed in statements similar to the following: The acceptance of God's gift of salvation renders a person eternally free from eternal damnation; how one conducts him or herself from the point of embracing the gift of salvation is not a condemning factor or a factor that will cause them to fall from grace, as long as the person loves others and loves God. This is a rationalization that is not supported by the word of God. As a matter of fact, in **John 14:15 & 14:23-24** God states: If you love me, you will obey/keep my commandments.

One may also defiantly ask: How can a loving God condemn anyone to hell? The question is then posed, what does love have to do with God being what or who He is? The Judge with responsibilities, Amen! Mankind appears to understand the important role and authority of an earthly judge but refuses to accept the role of God and His authority as the Judge of this universe. Matter of fact, most would encourage an earthly judge to be impartial. God is the Judge, the Commander and Chief authority of the universe and with this title comes responsibilities and these responsibilities have nothing to do with His love and kindness **(Isaiah 30:18)**. There is no hooking a brother/sister up outside of the commandments of God. Christians and all who have ears must hear and recognize they cannot usurp God's authority and His established plan of salvation. It does not work like that! Christians should deal with the truth of God and the truth of who God is, which is found in His word and in the history of His actions and not in the traditions, philosophies, doctrines, and personal desires of mankind.

When dealing with God, one must deal with the facts and truth of God as He has presented Himself in His word, His creations and in His actions and not according to manmade philosophies, traditions, and doctrines **(Matthew 15:3-9)**. Nor, can those who are considering following Christ afford to allow worldly sympathies and trends to beguile (trick, flatter or hoodwink) them in to compromising this commitment **(Ephesians 1: 21-22)**. Meaning, God has established all truths and they will not change, not for sympathies, trends, doctrines or traditions. God's truths and core values and what God has for mankind does not change or evolve (Malachi 3:6). Many will apply the principles of running a business and what they will or will not accept in their lives, but when it comes to the things of God, it is all about taking a fictitious, romantic or unrealistic approach to addressing issues. The same individuals refuse to discipline and structure themselves to apply Godly principles to achieve success in their spiritual lives in the same way as they do in other aspects of their lives. As a result of their refusal to accept and be governed by the truth of God's word, these individuals risk moving further and further away from living the lifestyle God has for mankind. Christians with this state of mind, not only move further away for God's plan for them but will move closer toward a fall from God's grace.

Christians and others who insist on ignoring the truth of God, as seen in His word, are functioning in the gray zone, which is addressed in **Isaiah 55:8-11.** Here, Isaiah speaks to the thought processes and behavior of men being different from the ways of God. The thinking of God and His behavior are different form mankind. Christians operating in this gray zone are not focused on the word of the Lord but are more focused on being good people and defining their behavior in a way that addresses worldly principles and behaviors that are pleasing to mankind. Although it is important to be a sensitive and kind person, it is more important that one become an effective Christ-driven individual. Some may ask, are not the two one in the same? No! One can be a kind person or someone that appeases the call or demands of many and yet exist in a state of opposition against the word of God. Remember, living a Christ-driven lifestyle is first and far most about following the principles of Christ in obedience to the word and will of God. Christians who think and develop resolutions that are not Christ-driven, will live lifestyles that lend themselves to one who is operating within a **form of Christianity**.

In the process of trying to make right, their wrong behavior, and the wrong behavior of their loved ones, a partner and/or organization's sinful behavior(s), unfocused and undisciplined Christians will begin to overlook and/or ignore

God's word and judgments that have determined the sinful behavior(s) in question unacceptable, as well as the unacceptable nature of other behaviors. Many Christians will lash out when confronted with God's judgments concerning the issue in question or the need to accept the true meaning God's word. This type of rationalizing and justifying is done to help ease the alerts of discomfort from the Holy Spirit and the stress associated with honoring sinful behavior or partnering with a **person whose spiritual salvation hangs on the gallows**.

Rationalizing, ignoring or denying God's word may ease some of the stress associated with one's unwillingness to accept God's rejection of their behavior, that of their loved ones, or that of their partner. However, this approach will not change the truth of God's word or judgments, nor will it change how God will deal with those who are in conflict with His word. Accepting God's truth is what being a Christian is about. This is what Jesus was referring in **John17:14-19** when He reported, Christians are not of the world as He is not of the world. Christians operate within the truth of God and not within the context and expectations of how mankind would have them.

The cloudy thinking of a Christian who is experiencing emotional conflict and wrestling with God's position concerning the sinful behavior of themselves or their partner(s), may also cause that person to forget that **feeling comfortable with a given behavior or loving someone does not mean it is okay to neglect or abandoned his or her Christian values**. This person may also misunderstand the concept of unconditional love **(a concept that will be discussed later)** and are unable or unwilling to acknowledge that love for another person or thing is not the "end all" or "be all."

The Christian's emotional conflict will cause him or her to lose the awareness that the love one has for God and His will for him or her is what defines and perfects the efforts of one in Christ. He or she has a mindset which can cause him or her to lose sight of the reality that his or her ability to love God and put His truth first will ease the stresses of life (bring peace), simplify the issue at hand, and give them the favor of God. This favor will move on the Christian's behalf, putting him or her back on course with God and giving him or her victory in any situation. This victory will stand down Satan and help the Christian overcome any form of abuse, rejection, dysfunction, strong hold, and even cause the negativity of others to work on his or her behalf.

A Christian whose focus is not on God will eventually forget that God's truth is empowering. These Christians are also not aware that a Christ-focused commitment supernaturally imparts a seed of faith into the life of the unbelieving loved one, partner and all observers. This is a seed that will present Holy obstacles in the path of Satan's quest to destroy mankind. These obstacles are seeds of righteousness, which offer hope to the soul of the individual and all observers by acting as anointed points of reference to that person. These are points of references that are empowered by the Christian's commitment to the things of God and the Christian's prayers concerning the matter.

The prayers of the righteous will profit much, because they rain down roadblocks against Satan and his antics. The believer's faith and commitment to the things of God will move God to act on behalf of the Christian and those they love and partner with. Therefore, a Christian's faith and commitment to the things of God strengthens the prayers of the Christian and plants an empowered seed of life, protection, deliverance, hope, and discipline into their lives and the lives of others.

CHAPTER FOUR

Appropriate Christian Witness, Insight, Knowledge and Understanding, Strengthens the Soul

The Christian's committed lifestyle to being Christ-driven serves as a strong testimony to the unbeliever and pours living water and strength into all that witness it **(John 7:38)**. A person who is a witness for God in his or her ability to stand up for the things of God brings alive the word of God to all observers; the believer and unbeliever. Their witness offers living water of hope to those who love the Lord and for those who are dead in Christ. Does this mean the unbeliever or underdeveloped Christian will approve of the believer's commitment to the things of God or the Christian's resistance to their refusal to be governed by the word of God? No! But, that is not the point. The point is, the Christian's commitment to the authority of God is addressing the soul of the individual and planting a Godly seed or is watering an existing seed of God within the makeup the observer(s).

It is vital that Christians live in their truth in Christ, because addressing the souls of others is a process that requires the truth of God. This is similar to when a person gives mouth-to-mouth resuscitation to a person who is in a state of crisis and has stopped breathing. The person who is trying to revive the unconscious person will take action only acceptable in times of crisis. A person in jeopardy of losing soul salvation is in a similar state of crisis. Therefore, treatment of the individual in an uncomfortable way, in an attempt to save his or her soul, is acceptable to God. **II Corinthians 7:8-12** reports that it is acceptable to make a person feel sorrowful unto righteousness. Just be mindful, all you who are in the trenches of trying to address such a crisis, this is not a spiteful process. This is a process that is done according to the authority of God and is about one's commitment to the salvation of mankind and is flanked with consideration and love **(II Corinthians 13:9-10)**. The fragile nature of the ministry of salvation and Christian outreach is why it is always important to live the Christian lifestyle, in spirit and in truth, as one consults God and His word, prior to addressing the salvation of others.

Therefore, the sincerity of a Christian's life and commitment to the things of God waters the seed of God's word at the appointed time of God's calling upon a person's life. When God's people resist going along with and/or rebuke or denounce sinful behavior, they are strengthening their position in the Lord and helping other Christians and unbelievers, making it easier for the unbeliever (although it may not be apparent at the moment) to receive the calling of God. The Christian becomes a living witness and plants a permanent Godly seed and pours living water into the life of all who observe their commitment to the things of God. A Christian's commitment to God also moves God to act on behalf of the Christian and the spirit of the person the Christian is opposing. This is the message confirmed in **I Corinthians 3: 6-13** when the word of God clearly states that the men and women of God plant seeds and water the lives of another, but it is God who gives the increase.

Appropriate Christian partnerships are seed builders and an oasis in a dry land and they will not take positions that may cause their partners and others to suffer internal conflict about the commandments and judgments of God. Committed

Christian partners will not feel, nor will their partners make them feel, a need to condone sinful behavior. Insightful Christians know and acknowledge that Christians do not compromise, when it comes to submitting to God's commands and judgments. They are familiar with the Scriptures found in **Deuteronomy 4:2 and Proverbs 30:6,** which instruct us to add not, nor take away from, the word of God. These partners are also familiar with the consequences of and curses associated with denying or rejecting God's word. These Christian partners have learned to do right by God first, and to stand by this decision. They do not condone sin (things outside of the word of God). They also do not try to justify sinful behavior. Committed Christians know or should know the importance of God's will for the saved and for the unsaved.

Overt and open display of an individual's commitment to God

God's word is the seed of righteousness and the committed convictions and actions of a righteous person in Christ tills the ground (soul) of the unsaved to receive the word of God. As noted earlier, When Christians stand up for the word of God, this act bears witness to the souls of others about God. The devil knows that a righteous man's open commitment to uphold the word of God is a powerful act that moves God to act on their behalf and on the behalf of others. This is why Satan makes it his mission to silence the voice of God's people. **When the voices of God's people are silenced, the works of Satan blossoms**. This is why the word of God instructs the people of God to cry loud and spare not **(Isaiah 58:1)**. The silence of God's people may be the primary explanation of the sinful state of our society, today. This is why it is important for Christians to position themselves against elements, organizations, and agencies in our society, and throughout the world, whose mission is to silence the voice of God's people in Christ.

This is also why it is important for a Christian to become rooted in the fact that a Christian does not fixate on, focus on or demand things that are outside of the word or will of God. They also do not demand things of God that God has made evident through His creations, laws, and principles that He rejects. The people of God must learn to take "No" for an answer and they do not seek to tempt God as the tribes of Israel did in the wilderness. This is because what God's word says about anything or any situation serves as the building blocks for the Christian's approach to decision making and the success of God's plan for mankind. Christian decisions, conclusions, and goals should be based upon God's word. God's word is the foundation, construction, and definition of appropriate decision making in Christ, conclusions, and lifestyle. Do not turn your head now; all should know that Christians should not make a move without understanding what God has to say about the matter and they and their partner (s) do not allow others to sway them otherwise!

It is the insight, understanding, and acknowledgement of knowing that one should internally and openly put God's opinion first, prior to making a decision, which lays the foundation for a Christian's most prized partnership, a partnership with God. God's word is rooted in His commandments and principles that are designed to draw all near to God. It is these principles and commandments that help mankind live a lifestyle that is pleasing to God and one that will help the person fulfill his or her destiny in God. The path of constructing one's Christian lifestyle in God is paved with His commandments and principles. **One's Christian lifestyle and their partnerships are as solid as** one's ability to acknowledge and accept that he or she should do his or her best to love God, and others, and live by the word of God through God's grace found in Christ Jesus, according to the history of who God is. Meaning; a Christ-driven lifestyle and partnerships are about the press of all parties' and each parties' willingness to pick up their cross and follow Christ, in love and obedience unto God through His word and the history of God's creations.

If a person has problems with the need to accept and follow the word of God, that person surely has problems with God and understanding God and what God has for him or her. A poor understanding of God and how He operates will hinder the believer's ability to be committed to the Christian faith, lifestyle, and appropriate partnerships in Christ. According to **John 1: 1-5,** God is the manifestation of His word. This is why God finds joy in His Word. The word of God is an expression of who He is. A rejection of portions of God's word detracts from God. One would have to change God in order to change His word, and **Malachi 3:6** explains that God never changes. **John 1:1** also says, "In the beginning was the Word and the Word was God." This leads to the conclusion that you cannot get away from the Word of God, when attempting to please God or trying to be committed to God and others in Christ. This also informs us that the word of God cannot change, not for tradition, not for doctrine, nor for trendsetting, because the **Word and God are one in the same and God is unchangeable.** There is no such thing as an old or new word in God. God's Word is the eternal and the final conclusion from God and will never change, because it is the physical manifestation of an unchanging God. **(John I: 1)**

God Set and Made the Precedent and Christ was the Example

John 1:1 reports, the word of God and God is one in the same. Therefore, when a person makes the suggestion to God that He (God) should accept or expect less of them than what His word requires of His people, one is asking God to question or reject the very essence of who God is. Now, who would want to be in a lifelong relationship and/or partnership with someone who requires them to be something other than who they are? Or should it be said, what intelligent person would want to be in a lifelong relationship/partnership with a person with this view? With the understanding that the word of God and God is one and the same, we learn the first principle to apply when contemplating a partnership. This principle addresses one's ability to acknowledge who or what a person or entity is in its entirety.

Appropriate partnerships are built upon the truth of whom or what a person really is. The reality of who or what a person, group or entity is can be observed in the history of the principles and actions that govern their lives or existence. The expression of this principle is seen when the word of God states, the nature of God can be seen through observing the things that He created and through the history of His actions **(Romans 1:20)**. Because God and His word is one in the same, one's ability to accept and adapt to the word of God or not will not change the effectiveness of God's word. This means that God and His word (truths) may be difficult to accept, understand, or adhere to, for unbelievers and for many Christians, but an inability to conform to and/or a lack of understanding does not cancel the intent, meaning or effectiveness of who God is, what God has to say about His expectations of mankind, partnership(s) and how one should live a Christian lifestyle. When God's word asks mankind to make conclusions about Him by examining the totality of His actions, God was setting a precedent: The history of one's actions is an expression of who and what the individual represent. Stated more plainly, one's actions are expressions of what they are committed to.

According to **I Thessalonians 5:22,** the Christian's lifestyle should be void of any concept, act, or appearance of engaging in behaviors that God has commanded men and women not to engage in. One's ability to stay focused on God and on the things of God is found in one's commitment to the word and/or principles of God, through Jesus Christ. A Christian will go out of their way to know that a candidate for partnership is committed to being governed by the principles and commands of God.

It is only when a person acknowledges God and has a history of being committed to obeying God's commandments that the individual is equipped with the basic tools needed to develop and maintain an appropriate relationship/partnership with God and others. Everyone should know that a person's commitment to God is further found in his or her ability to repent and accept God's offer of redemption through Jesus Christ and in his or her willingness to grow in God through Christ (press to do their best to follow the word of God). We see this in **Luke 18:18-25** when Christ had His conversation with the rich ruler.

To grow in God is to become more and more like Jesus. John prophetically made reference to this concept of growing in Christ in **John 3:30** when he said, "He (Christ) must increase, but I **(John)** must decrease." **Matthew 16:24** advises Christians that they must repent of their sins first, deny themselves and discipline themselves to take up their cross and follow Christ. Also, Paul advised fellow Christians to follow him as he followed Christ **(I Corinthians 11:1)**. Therefore, to be connected to God, one must respect and accept His offer of redemption through Christ and grow in God through a willingness to follow Christ's example. These scriptures further confirm and support the belief that salvation and living a Christ-driven lifestyle is a process and a process that embodies a lifestyle, not just a proclamation, a statement, deep feeling or acts of kindness. Paul in **II Corinthians 13:5-14** ask Christians to examine and test themselves as to whether they are in the faith. He went further to conclude that unless one can conclude that Christ lives in them through self-examination and testing, they are not complete in their faith and are possibly disqualified in their faith as a Christian .

Jesus was not just a good and kind man who proclaimed He loved God. His walk on earth was the supernatural manifestation of God's presence in human form **(I Timothy 3:16)**. Jesus was God's way of drawing closer to mankind and demonstrating how He would help mankind fulfill His commandments and principles in the flesh. Being the just God that He is, He wanted to let mankind know He acknowledges their fleshly issues and give mankind a tangible example of how to live a pleasing life before Him. God told His people what He expected of them in His word. Then God showed mankind how to fulfill His word through the teachings and life of Jesus Christ.

Jesus' life on earth was God's effective nature operating in the flesh. God and Jesus are two, but one in the same. We know this by Jesus' statement in **John 14: 9-21,** "When you see Me, you see my Father and my Father is in Me." Therefore, the test of Jesus' realness was seen in the manifestation of God in Him. This was a manifestation that is devoted to the love God has toward mankind, towards the word of God, and towards the discipline that is devoted to the will of God. This was a will that was not only good for Him, but also for the good of the nation. The manifestation of God in Christ made Christ complete and ready to take on the role of redemption God had for Him. Christ's ability to adhere to the Spirit of God that lived in Him by following through with the word and will of God prepared Him for the crucifixion that made way for God's gift of redemption and the grace that covers a multitude of faults for those who are willing to receive and commit to the will of God.

Jesus is an extension of God and when we partner with God our lives become committed to the word and will of God through Jesus Christ. As Christ was an extension of God, Christians also are extensions of God through Christ. As followers of Christ, when others see a Christian, they should see Christ in the lifestyle of that person. Meaning, others should see Christ's mannerisms in the Christian. They should also see an extension of the glory of God who sent Christ to redeem mankind **(John 17:21-23: II Corinthians 3:18)**. This is the test of salvation. The character of Christ and the manifestation of the Spirit of God should be seen and is what we are looking for in ourselves and others. When the Word of God informs us in **Philippians 2:12** to work out our own salvation, it is telling us that we must make sure that the Spirit of God, the word of God, and the discipline needed to fulfill God's desire for us to be ready for Jesus' return is, shown to be operating in us daily.

Jesus made it clear that He was all about God and the word of God when He said in **Matthew 5:17-18,** "I come not to destroy the Law/Word of God but to fulfill it." The totality of Jesus' lifestyle was one that walked within the word of God and within the will of God. This was a lifestyle that was pleasing to God and a lifestyle that commanded the attention and favor of God. Christ's ability to live a lifestyle with the support of God, focused on the word and will of God, defined Him. Operating within this framework maintained Jesus' sin-free status on earth. This is also true with mankind. An individual operating within the word and will of God, to the best of his/her ability under grace, will also be an expression of who the individual really is. This is also an expression of someone who is living **a sin-free lifestyle**. Likewise, it is the spirit-filled Christian's ability to live a lifestyle, **in its totality that** follows the teachings and life of Christ that empowers the Christian to live sin-free through grace.

Living Sin-Free is Not about Perfection

Staying focused on the word of God, being committed to the will of God, and making a daily effort to do God's will is a Christ-like walk, and **a walk that is free from sin** in the sight of God. **Romans 4:3** reports that Abraham believed God and his faith and obedience were counted as righteousness. It was Abraham's obedience to God that affirmed or made evident his faith in God. One's diligent efforts to obey God is tangible evidence that the individual has faith in God. **Obedience is the evidence of one's faith in God**. Meaning, obedience is evidence of one's press to grow in God and will affirm an individual's faith and lifestyle in God as sin-free under grace.

Did Abraham make mistakes? Yes! David made a number of mistakes and paid for them, but God's word in **Acts 13:22** reports that David was a man after God's heart. God's word also reported that God loved David. If David made a number of mistakes (sins), why then did God give David favor? Because, when confronted with his sins, David did what all mankind must do. He did not make excuses or try to justify his sins, and quickly repented of the sins he committed. Also, David did not continue in sin. He repented and strengthened himself in God and refocused himself on allowing the word and will of God to govern his life. In spite of the consequences, David had to endure for his sins. He worked on making it right with God by striving to operate within the will of God, according to the word of God. To make it clear, David answered the call of God, which is expressed by Paul in **Romans 6:1-2,** "Should a person continue in sin? God forbid!"

A sin-free lifestyle is not about perfection nor is it about God looking the other way when a person sins. Nor, is it about God's grace affirming the lifestyle of one who insists on choosing his/her own path (choosing to continue in sin). **Romans 6:14-23** report, a sin-free lifestyle and perfection in Christ are founded in the constant efforts of a Christian, choosing to continually walk in the word and will of God. One who is living sin-free is a servant of God whose lifestyle is focused on operating within a state holiness. Paul depicts this effort/press to stay focused on the word and the will of God in **Romans 7:21-23** where he said, "When I seek to do the right thing, the devil is always present." Here Paul is informing us, the devil is always present, but Christians are commissioned to press forward in their efforts to do the right thing in God. In **Philippians 3:10-17** Paul also depicts his lack of perfection and need for him and other Christians to continue to press toward the upward call of God. This press is also discussed in **Colossians 1:23-29** when it uses the phrase **"If". "If", a Christian continues in the faith, being grounded and settled, and not being moved away from the hope of the gospel, then the perfection of Christ shall be fulfilled in the Christian**. You see, perfection is in the "IF". If an individual press to do the right thing, through grace, they will find themselves in the midst of perfection in Christ. Therefore, Christians should not worry about being perfect. They should just stay focused on doing the right thing in God, to the best of their ability.

A sin-free lifestyle is not just about acknowledging God and His word. **Romans 7:13-25** shows us that living a sin-free lifestyle may be a struggle at times, but this lifestyle is seen when a person makes every effort in his or her being to love God and others and live and function within the will and word of God through Christ. A sin-free lifestyle is about loving God with all one's mind, heart, soul, and strength. The weakness of the flesh and Satan's antics causes mankind to make daily choices, choices that bring the flesh in to subjection to Christ (disciplines the flesh in Christ), encourages the flesh to resist sin and the devil and openly affirms his or her position in Christ.

Affirming one's love and commitment to God is not about perfection or an ability to perfect daily expressions of love toward God. No one can say: A Christian will not falter. Matter of fact, all have fallen short and all will face many milestones in their efforts to follow Christ. **(Romans 3:23)**. However, a Christian who loves God and is living a life that is pleasing to God is one who **repents when he/she falters and makes every effort not to engage in sin again**. They will definitely try not to continue in the same sinful act(s) over and over again. This type of Christion will make every effort to get it right in God. A sin-free lifestyle is making every effort to learn what is considered sinful in the Lord, according to God's word, and making every effort to avoid sin according to God's word. In other words, **Colossians 1:23-29** is informing us, **the grace of God established through Jesus Christ affirms (qualifies) your best efforts in Christ**.

The diligent efforts of a God-focused Christian's willingness to love God and others, learn of God, and try to understand how to submit to and honor God through the teachings of Christ is affirmed by God as, not only perfection in Christ, but also a lifestyle of Holiness. This affirmation process of God, under the statutes of Christ's grace, will count as righteousness the lifestyle of all who are committed to operating under the authority of God to the best of their ability. Therefore, no one should try to define one's own personal state of perfection or righteousness or another person's state of perfection or righteousness. God is the one who knows when one is putting forth his or her best efforts and he will give account for each Christian's efforts in Christ.

Therefore, once again, a Christian should walk in the ways of God by faith to the best of his or her ability, according to God's word and the teachings of Christ, and should not focus on perfection. God has committed Himself through the statutes of grace to meet the Christian in the middle of the Christian's best efforts to love, embrace and submit to His authority. A Christian's mindset should be focused on seeking to love God and embracing the things of God with all his or her heart, mind, soul, and strength and not focused on how perfect or righteous he or she or others may think he or she is.

It is God who defines perfection or righteousness, as He did with Abraham. The evidence of faith in God that leads to righteousness is seen in mankind's heart and behavior. **Matthew 7:16-23** reports, you will know them (the Christian) by the fruit they produce. These are fruit that may not all flourish at one time or may look malformed at times but are present just the same and will endure and flourish over time, in the life of all who are committed to being governed by God.

Ezekiel 18:4-9 clearly explains God's perception of His expectations of mankind toward Him. These Scriptures also depicts how God views the operations of mankind and an individual's ability to be viewed as a just and righteous being in His eyes. These Scriptures are calling for the people of God to follow the commands and principles of God in the spirit of faithfulness. The question then is not: Is God expecting the Christian to be perfect? The question becomes: Are you (the one proclaiming he or she is saved) putting forth his or her best efforts to love God the way He would like to be loved, with all your heart, mind, soul, and strength and to love others as yourself **(Matthew 22-38; Mark 12:30)**? According to the Scriptures in **John 14-23**, to love God in this manner is an "act" (form of conduct/behavior) of being committed to obeying and submitting to the word and authority of God. One's commitment and obedience to God, is an act of faithfulness to God and a depiction of one's trust in God for His will for them and others.

The grace accomplished through Christ's sacrifice is God's way of helping mankind perfect their ability to accept their responsibility to press towards loving God, understanding Godly faith, fulfilling their faith in God, and trusting in God's original goal for mankind's lifestyle of partnership on earth.

You see, God has always known of mankind's limited ability to understand their personal responsibility/partnership role concerning a relationship with Him, and how to perfect His calling for them. The forbidden tree was placed in the garden and Adam and Eve were forbidden to eat the fruit from the forbidden tree, because God wanted them to know and accept that they had a role in maintaining an appropriate relationship with Him and living a lifestyle of prosperity. Also, their respect for this role was to be seen in the expression of their actions (i.e., obedience). This expression of obedience was done to show that they trusted in His will for them and they understood that they had a responsibility/role to fulfill in order to maintain an appropriate relationship with God and receive the fullness of His blessings.

The unblemished animal blood sacrifice was originally required for atonement in the Jewish culture to help mankind understand and accept that they had a personal responsibility for maintaining their relationship with God. This ritual was also in place to help them acknowledge their partnership role with God for the fulfillment of their position in God. God first tried to address the weaknesses and self-willed disposition of mankind with instruction and punishment alone. We see this with Adam and Eve. Then His approach was to embrace mankind with the assistance of a personal offer (this was God's desire for His people to accept personal responsibility for their actions) of an unblemished animal sacrifice, under the watchful eyes and prayers of His righteous prophets. This combination of an offering and the prayers of a righteous prophet for mankind's atonement became a distraction for many.

The distraction was the result of multiple factors involved in the acknowledgement and atonement process. This approach to atonement appeared to work against God's original plan and goal for mankind to be sincere, accept personal responsibility and put forth one's personal best efforts to live within the design God has for His people. Finally, through the sacrifice of Jesus Christ and the statutes of grace, God eliminated factors that may have distracted or hindered many from personalizing and understanding God's plan for mankind to take on a partnership role with God for their protection and prosperity on earth.

God's original design for mankind was always about personal responsibility and partnership. It was also never God's intention to create a perfect being. If His intention was to create a perfect being, capable of following His every command without His support, He would have done so. God also would have never spent so much time trying to help mankind work through imperfections with prophetic teachings, if His desire for His people to understand their need to accept personal responsibility for their relationship with Him was not a factor **(Isaiah 30:20)**. It appears that God's design for mankind is about Him joining in partnership with His creation (mankind) to enjoy the beauty of an earth He created in its' fullness in the beauty of Holiness (in a state that allowed mankind and God to enjoy His creations together), as He did with Adam and Eve prior to sin.

Upon understanding that God does not have an expectation for mankind to be perfect when a person has done all that he or she can do to honor God according to the principles of Christ, there should be no stress. A Christian's sincere efforts allow Jesus to take the wheel and empower the Christian through the statutes of grace and the power of the Holy Spirit to meet the mark that God will justify, not mankind. This is why a Christian who has put forth his or her best efforts in Christ can say, **"I am covered under the blood of Christ**." Christ's sacrifice paid the price for God's grace. Grace strengthens mankind's ability to re-establish a relationship with God and make way for God to re-establish His original design of partnership with mankind. Grace is a set of statutes that beckons mankind to be at peace and not worry about what is lacking in them when they put forth their best efforts to do the will of God.

About Free Will, God's Will, and Moral Choice

Being covered under God's grace has nothing to do with a person choosing to continue in sin and not being held accountable. It is in the devotion of a Christ-driven Christian that the grace of God is understood and flourishes, not in one's belief in God, proclamation of salvation or in the idea that one is always saved and cannot fall from God's grace. Even the demons believe that there is one God **(James 2:19-24)**. One can fall from the grace of God. Satan is the primary example. Satan lived in Heaven under the authority of God but became so focused on his personal perceptions that he chose to be rebellious against the will of God **(Revelation 12:7-12)**.

Satan clearly had the ability to choose to submit to the authority of God, even in Heaven. As a result of his enchantment with his own perceptions, he was no longer willing to submit to the authority of God. This act of defiance plunged him into a fall from God and into a state of eternal damnation. Judas also fell from grace. Judas Iscariot was one of the twelve original Disciples of Christ. He walked with Christ, but he lost focus or was distracted and turned from Christ and fell from grace to eternal damnation. He that has ears, please listen to the words found in **James 2:24-26: A person is justified by works and not by faith only**. A Christian must take responsibility for their partnership role in their relationship with God and in their salvation in Christ.

*Therefore, one cannot buy into the theory that one's belief in God through Christ is enough to justify one's lifestyle unto redemption/salvation. Nor can one afford to partner oneself with those who buy into the theory that someone who is "truly saved" in Christ, is somehow immediately released from their ability to sin or desire to continue in sin. Many who buy into this perception also supports the theory that condones a perception of God's grace offered to mankind, which is not concerned with mankind's desire or willingness to sin. This theory suggests that grace creates a state of existence which appears to exempt a Christian of his or her responsibility to stay committed to God in Christ. Those who condone this theory believe a person who is "truly saved" are somehow transformed in a way that causes him/her to lose their desire to sin or oppose God, which is rooted in God's gift of personal choice. This is not biblical. Paul's discussion in **I Corinthians 15 30-31**, where Paul {man of God}, is telling God's people that they stand in jeopardy every hour and he die daily by moving further away from his own perceptions and focusing more and more on God's will for him and mankind, and in **John 3:30** where the word of God through Paul clearly reports that Christ must increase, but he (John) must decrease. This teaching and confession by Paul and John clearly suggests that mankind's submission to and existence in God, according to the teachings of Christ is a process. This is a process of surrender, submission, commitment, and devotion. Salvation is a fluent/ongoing expression of faith. The concepts used in these scriptures such as, time, increasing, decreasing, and death indicate this process of submission is a challenge that requires mankind to discipline himself/herself to choose to commit to God's calling and will for them over time, every hour of every day.

There is a transformation that is activated in a Christian when they accept the vow of salvation, but this transformation will never exempt a person from their God given gift of personal choice. This is a transformation of awareness, acknowledgement, humility and the need for repentance, submission and discipline. This is not a transformation that take away mankind's human characteristics, which include their free-will.

A person does not transform into some type of robot when he/she accepts the salvation of the Lord. Christians are human, with human characteristic that will stay with them until they die. These are characteristics that require them to deal with the operations of the flesh, including sin and iniquity that the flesh is subject to. The word of God, in **John 17:16,** informs Christian believers that they are not of the world. It does not report that a Christian is some type of celestial being or angel who can mount up and fly away from the realities of their human state of existence. This scripture is addressing a state of mind, a disposition, and one's committed devotion to humble themselves to the things of God. This is why Paul, who professed to be a slave of Christ **(Romans 1: 1-15)**, struggled to do the right thing in God **(Romans 7:19-25)**. Here, Paul was "truly saved" and having issues with doing the right thing. He was having issues with making appropriate choices in God because he was human with human characteristics that are subject to sin and the iniquity of this world.

Paul's struggle was the result of existing in the flesh, existing in a flesh that had been exposed to sin and shaped in iniquity. This is why Jesus came in the flesh (took on human characteristics). This is why God commanded Him to show Himself to be and overcomer/ do the will of God in the flesh. In other words, to discipline Himself to follow God's desires for Him and others in the flesh, in spite of doctrines, traditions, the social trends of the time, and His empathy and sensitivities to the command of others, trials, tribulations and suffering. Jesus had to make choices hourly and daily, as all Christians must do, to stay the course, "in the flesh", assigned to Him by God. In spite of His human characteristics, that would be with him until death, He had to discipline himself to stay humble and committed to the will of God. Christ set the example for mankind to follow.

Note: One can be "truly saved" and become distracted, causing one to lose his/her Godly focus and as a result, fall from God's grace. This is the definition of a backslider. A backslider is a person who was once "truly saved" but turned from God to pursue his/ her own path. If the definition of salvation was defined within the concept of; once saved always, there would be no need for God to address the concept of one being a backslider.

Individuals who embrace a perception that rejects the concept that a Christian can choose to reject God's will and fall from God's grace, due to an unwillingness to press to choose to submit to and obey God's authority daily, would have to have an underdeveloped understanding of Christ's redemption. These individuals would also have to have and underdeveloped understanding of human nature, the ability for sin to embed and dwell in the flesh and the demanding pull the iniquity of the world has on the flesh, as discussed in **Romans 7: 19-25 & James Chapter 4**. These individuals also do not really understand the traumatic effect of negative or dysfunctional environmental factors, dysfunctional or poor child rearing, and/or how abusive experiences in the early stages of development can interrupt and/or hinder one's ability to make appropriate choices in Christ or anything, even when one is awakened to the truth, whether the individual is saved or not.

What it means to be born in sin and shaped in iniquity has evaded/escaped the understanding of those who fail to accept that one can fall from grace, due to an inability to choose to stay the course with Christ beyond accepting the vow of salvation. They also do not have an insightful understanding of the true nature of the baptism of the Holy Spirit or the growth process of salvation, how the statutes of grace operate, and the supernatural warfare of mankind's spiritual existence. Compounded with a lack of understanding of how human nature exists and is molded, individuals with this belief system appear to reject or overlook God's command as seen in **James 4:7-8** and Paul's discussions in **Romans 7: 14-25**. In these scriptures, God instructs His people to submit and draw close to God and resist evil and Paul discussed waging war with fleshly desires. These scriptures are informing us that the flesh is an independent agent. It is an independent agent that operates in an interactive manner with the world. This is an interactive manner that subjects the flesh to the positive and negative elements of its environment. This includes subjecting the flesh to the influences of sin and the iniquities of the world.

Fleshly desires are normal and natural. However, in these scriptures, and as seen in **Galatians 5: 19-21,** God is focused on mankind understanding that they must discipline their natural desires. He is focused on mankind knowing that they must address their natural God given desires in a way that resist sin and the iniquities of the world. We must also address desires and behaviors that manifest in us that have not succumb to Godly discipline. God's instruction and Paul discussions acknowledges mankind's ability and freedom, saved or not, to choose to pull away from God and engage in evil or not. This acknowledgement informs us that mankind can fall from grace and lose their redemption, even after repenting and accepting God and Jesus' true status **(Romans 11:20)**.

The word of God also tries to convey that a person can fall from grace in **Galatian 5,** when some of God's people chooses to prioritize their own perceptions of His word more than the need to have faith in God and be committed to God's word according to the redemption and liberty of Christ. This is the definition of a backslider. Meaning, a person can fall from grace after salvation. Also meaning, God introduced a new covenant in Christ and the old covenant of how mankind can maintain a relationship with God before Christ has passed away. God is not dealing with the sin of mankind in the way He did in the past. This new covenant in Christ is about one's commitment to God and His laws under the redemption of Christ and not about one's ability to perfect the laws of God through rituals. This is a covenant that does not exempt the laws of God, but informs all, grace abound or outweigh the consequences of not being able to adhere to the law for those who are committed to God and press to operate in His will and His laws in Christ.

Sin Nature

Individuals who refuse to accept that a Christian can fall from grace to damnation, fail to understand the true meaning of the privileges associated with mankind's freewill. They have most likely given little or no thought to what it means to be an entity who truly has the free will to make choices that can define his/her destiny. Also, they most likely have not considered the true nature of the human flesh. They have not considered, the human flesh is one of several important human entities/tools working together within the intricate makeup of mankind. These are entities/tools working together to accomplish the goal of allowing mankind to exhibit the gift of free will.

These individuals have not considered the possibility that the flesh, along with a number of other human characteristics, are most likely tools that are in place for human survival and each characteristic has the capability of functioning as an individual mechanism with its own intellect. The flesh, brain/mind, heart, and the spirit of mankind are all, most likely, high functioning elements/tools of mankind with defined characteristics, with different duties, and responsibilities that are independent yet inter-dependent at the same time.

Accordingly, the healthy growth and development of the brain/mind, physical makeup/flesh and the spirit of an individual enhances the proficiency of personal growth and the individual's ability to move forward and make personal life choices. The role of the flesh appears to primarily focus on ensuring the physical survival and tangible motivation of mankind. When God asked mankind to love Him with all their heart, soul, mind, and strength, maybe He is defining independent life forces that exist within mankind's design. These are life forces that are needed for intricate higher order operations associated with mankind's freewill.

The notion that the flesh and the desires it evokes are the byproduct of it being a life force/drive that motivates, strengthens, and presses an individual to move forward to thrive and live is not given much consideration by many. The makeup of our human flesh may just be a life force that is expressed in the form of emitting needs and desires that strengthens and force mankind to move forward and make choices. In other words, the elements of the flesh make up a life force that is in place to foster mankind's motivation, strength, and biological survival. This is a life-force that compels and propels mankind forward. This is a forward march that requires mankind to make choices. These choices operate within mankind's free will and addresses the livelihood, comforts, and equilibrium of the human body and the human existence.

This fleshly force is neither evil nor does it have a sin-nature. It is a self-willed organic energy that is good for human survival and seeks to help the body live and develop to its fullest potential. How do we know the flesh and the elements that define the flesh are a good thing? In **Genesis 1: 26-31,** after creating mankind, God reported that His creation of mankind (in its entirety, including the flesh), along with all of His other creations, were good. The perception that nothing about what God created in mankind is bad or evil is further expressed when the word of God reported in **Ecclesiastes 7:29** that "...God hath made man upright; but they have sought out many inventions", and in **Psalms 51:5,** by David, where he addressed the concept of being born in sin and shaped in iniquity. This is a bible verse that suggest that sin is an external element that has an effect on mankind and not the idea that mankind is somehow innately sinful.

At no point did God report in His word that He built a sinful nature into the design of the human flesh. In **Romans Chapters 7 & 8,** the word of God discusses the weakness of the flesh and sin dwelling in the flesh **(Romans 7: 17-25)**. When the word of God speaks of the weakness of the flesh, most likely, it is addressing the natural propensity for the flesh to be selfish and self-willed. When one is in survival mode, selfishness is not necessarily a bad thing and mankind's inherent will to move forward is a good thing. We see this in the training and the development of a good lifeguard. Lifeguards are trained to consider self-preservation first and foremost. However, this training is not about abandoning the considerations and needs of those in need of being rescued. This training is about disciplining a lifeguard to understand that they cannot help another if their life is in jeopardy. Therefore, the lifeguard's will (desire to help) and understanding of what it means to help others is tempered with appropriate understanding, training, and discipline. This is an understanding that applies a disciplinary approach that is good for everyone involved: the lifeguard and the individual in distress.

Just as a long-term state of selfishness cannot work when trying to help others, it also does not work in an intellectual design that addresses the long-term cohesiveness and survival of an individual or mankind. In other words, selfishness is not necessarily a bad thing in times of crisis or as a form of motivation in some cases. From God's perspective, the self-centered nature of the flesh is in place for basic survival and not the depiction of the intellectual lifestyle He has for mankind. Prolonged self-concern is a primal state of existence and does not take into account the higher order of intellectual capabilities of mankind.

The concept of sin dwelling in the flesh, as discussed in **Romans,** could not be addressing the notion that one is born with a sinful nature as a natural part of the makeup of the flesh. Because, if one was born with a sin nature, there would be no need to address the negative effects of living in a sinful environment or a need to resist something (sin) which is a natural part of mankind's makeup. If read carefully, **Romans Chapter 7 & 8** highlights the theory that sin has the ability to embed and dwell in the flesh and not the idea that sin is a natural part of the flesh. In these chapters, the concepts of being in the flesh or sinful and being carnal minded are interchangeable. Therefore, informing us that the sins of the flesh are not a byproduct of the flesh by design, but is associated with how one chooses to conduct him or herself. Informing us that one's submission to fleshly impulses is driven by one's state of mind. Having a sin nature would not be a good thing for mankind and would contradict the word of God found in **Genesis 1: 26-31**. It would also not allow God to partner with mankind, saved or not, because God can have nothing to do with sin.

Romans 8: 3 reports, Jesus condemned sin in the flesh and not the flesh. Most likely Jesus was condemning the sin that had been acquired in the memory of the flesh through the developmental process that occur as a result of being born in sin and shaped in iniquity. These memories influence one's state of mind and spiritual wellness. Highlighting to us, flesh has the ability to adopt, incorporate, and capture memories of sin or sinful acts and other memories into its natural God given mode of existence/operation (mode of survival, strength, and motivation). This concept has scientific support and is discussed in **Romans 7: 13-21** where it addresses the concept of sin producing death in the body **(Mackay, L.K., Stock, A.T., Ma, J.Z., et al, (2012); Schenkel, J.M., Fraser, K.A., Beura, L.K., et al (2014); Watanabe, R., Gehad, A., Yang, C., et al (2015)**. As a result of these captured memories, sin and other memories become housed in the flesh and can be at liberty to operate within the natural desires, urges, and impulses of mankind mentally, physically, and spiritually **(Romans 7: 13)**.

Throughout God's word, His concerns, which are associated with the sinful behavior of mankind, addresses the choices a person makes. God's primary focus is not on urges and desires, but on how one chooses to address the urges, impulses, and desires that emit from the flesh. This is because God is fully aware of the fact that He designed the flesh to emit urges and desires, and these urges and desires of mankind can be influenced by the sin of the world. Therefore, because the flesh/life-force is about one's personal survival and urges and the flesh's ability to house sin, God is on high alert. **God would also have us be on high alert as well, when it comes to one's ability to discipline themselves to resist sin and make appropriate choices in Christ in spite of what they feel or are feeling**. Therefore, due to the propensity of the flesh to be influenced by ungodly influences, **Christians and**

others must learn to discipline themselves to resist allowing their feelings, sensitivities and sympathies to exceed their commitment to the word of God and the teachings of Christ.

The social structure God has for mankind is similar to His design for the human body. The structure of the human body is composed of independent elements working together to accomplish the goal of survival for the whole body. God's plan for mankind requires individuals to move beyond primarily focusing on one's personal needs, desires, feelings, comfort level, and survival. His goal for mankind is about mankind operating within an environment and a social structure that is inclusive, interdependent, and cooperative in Christ. This is an environment that requires mankind to move beyond primarily focusing on his or her personal survival, needs, feelings, and comforts. God would like mankind to grow and learn to see survival as an existence within a social unit of partnership that is disciplined, according to His statutes in Christ.

However, the flesh is a driving force that is not naturally geared towards taking into account the needs of others and towards respecting the cohesive interaction needed for personal survival and the survival of others, when motivated to act or make choices. Once again, the flesh does not naturally operate or reason beyond personal survival, feelings, and comforts. Those who operate in the flesh are carnal minded (operate in a way that is pleasing to self or one's personal perception over God's desirers for mankind) and the Spirit of God is not in them (I **Corinthians 2:14)**. As a result, these individuals are in opposition with God. They are operating in a state that allows them to oppose God and feel comfortable making decisions without considering of God's word. This is why God would not have His people operate according to the commands of those who are governed by personal or worldly perceptions and not governed by Him. Also, the negative influences of sin warps the ability of the flesh to develop beyond being self-centered. This is why God designed the brain and made way for the Spirit of God to live within our hearts and our spirit.

The brain is independent of the flesh, but it is intricately connected to the flesh, because the flesh ensures the brain's biological survival. Meaning, it is difficult for the brain to rule out the needs and/or desires of flesh when making decisions, because of the state of biological interdependence that exists between the two. However, the brain is empowered with reasoning and the ability to make choices that are more comprehensive than those associated with personal needs, desires, and urges. Although the brain must address the body/flesh, because the brain is also about life and living. The brain and the spirit of mankind can communicate and can be communicated with at a higher intellectual level than that of the flesh.

As noted, mankind's brain, spirit, and the flesh are powerful elements and are all required for human survival. However, also noted, the mind, although considerate of the physical, has the ability to operate at a higher order, intellectually and spiritually. It has the ability to reason and function beyond the physical. This is the characteristic of the brain that God uses to harness and discipline the life force of the physical body (the flesh) to overcome sin and the iniquity of the world and operate within the will of God, to the best of one's ability.

The mind and spirit are in place to help the flesh learn to operate with the consideration of personal long-term survival and with the consideration of God and others. **The mind and spirit of a person help discipline the flesh and encourage it to operate within necessary boundaries. If this physical life force (the flesh) is not disciplined, it will not evolve beyond the need to address personal needs, urges, impulses, feelings, and the negative influences the iniquities of the world has on it from a selfish and primitive perspective**. Without discipline, the flesh will be hampered in its ability to address the desires and impulses from a higher ordered intellectual approach. This is a state that can cripple the individual not only in the flesh, but in their mind and spirit as well, because they are interdependent agents. In other words, **undisciplined flesh will function like a wild briar patch** that is self-destructive to the totality of a person and will grow to be dangerous for everyone that come into contact with it.

The flesh is not a byproduct of the essences of God (Spirit). The spirit of mankind is a portion of the immortal Spirit of God. Unlike the spirit of mankind, which was breathed into mankind by God, the flesh does not have a natural connection with God and does not have the ability to commune with God. This is why God ask mankind to worship Him in spirit **John 4; 24**. Therefore, the flesh it is not naturally subject to the will of God and cannot return to God when this life is over. As a result of the flesh's mortal state, it is weaker than the spirit of a person and is more subject to being malleable and corruptible and must learn how to surrender to God for its constructive survival and wellbeing. It also must be made aware of its limitations (mortality).

Because the flesh was designed to motivate mankind and for mankind's survival, the flesh is a natural daredevil. It will try anything, if it perceives what it is getting into will be good for its survival, is pleasurable or will comfort it in some way. The flesh is in place to help mankind survive and maintain a level of comfort. The question for the individual, for mankind and for the individual's relationship with its creator (God) therefore is not: Is the flesh sinful? But the question is: How will the flesh survive and maintain an appropriate level of equilibrium (find a level of balance and comfort) within the social and environmental structure it was born into.

In other words, the flesh must be disciplined to know what is truly good for its survival, for its constructive growth and for the wellbeing of its mortality, whether what is needed to address the flesh's needs are pleasing or not. This is a state that forces mankind to learn to mentally and physically succumb to the reality of the mortality of the flesh (the limitations of a self-willed state). Mankind must learn and come to understand the consequences of answering to feelings, drives or instinct, without question. The flesh is a good thing, but it is untamed. It is primitive. It is not tolerant of the influences of outside forces. Mankind must accept the limitation of the self-willed motivations and actions of a force (flesh) that instinctively answers to the basic/primitive elements of life that embody the human life force. A state of realization that can be difficult for those without understanding, training and the discipline need to walk appropriately in the totality of the design God has for mankind.

As a result of the flesh's natural design to move forward without the consultation of outside forces, the flesh is naturally positioned to resist or be at odds with anyone or anything that it perceives is working against its mission to help mankind thrive. This has a propensity to cause one to lean toward selfish characteristics and create a struggle for mankind that can only be overcome through teaching and acknowledgement that operates within God's truths through the power of the Holy Spirit. When one learns or is disciplined to resist elements and concepts that work against God's truths, work against what mankind was designed to be or to do and one's ability to accept the reality of the limitations of the flesh one's perception of reality is improved. One's perception of reality is important. One's perception and understanding of a situation defines the willingness of the flesh to change/transform or evolve and accept that the concept of survival should extend beyond self, personal feeling, and personal concepts.

The flesh is not unreasonable nor is it some type of overly selfish evil entity. The flesh just needs to be disciplined and introduced to appropriate knowledge and understanding that is empowered with the word of God. This is an empowerment that is able to stand down the adverse/negative effects of sin and iniquity. When the flesh comes into the knowledge that it's design was not only for mankind to live but to live more abundantly with others in Christ, the flesh will be more willing to adhere to principles of life that are not only about personal survival, but are also about a form of survival that is ordered and structured with others in Christ. Therefore, one may say the flesh is an instinctive drive that can evolve and the evolution of the flesh is contingent upon socialization, training and discipline. This is why God would have all seek to study, learn and listen to His truths that they may have an appropriate understanding of all things, especially the things

God. Also that they may know how operating outside of the will of God works against mankind's survival, productivity and mortality, as well as their immortality in God **II Corinthians 5**.

As a result of the flesh's propensity to be selfish and mankind's inevitable need to face their mortality, the organic nature/template of the physical makeup of mankind must be tempered and disciplined to respect one's personal desires and needs beyond the physical and to respect the desires and needs of God, its' Creator, and others. It also must be tempered to conform to the reality of its morality. This includes pressing to do one's best to discipline one's self to conform to the authority and word of God, the word of truth that works for the good of them and all mankind, and to resist sin and iniquity that work against their wellbeing. As noted; this is a disciplinary process that is manifested and formulated through learning and gaining an appropriate understanding of the truths of God and this world. This is and understanding that is gained through personal growth, conditioning, learning, and understanding under the power of personal commitment and effort.

This is a personal commitment that one does with all of one's soul and strength. With all of one's soul and strength, one should commit to embracing the help and instructions of others, the word of God, and the mentoring of Holy Spirit. Disciplining one's self to learn and conform to the truths of God is done with a conscious awareness and reorganization of the vulnerable state of mankind's existence within the supernatural warfare of Satan against God and mankind. Discipline is also a conscious effort, because a person cannot afford to be idle or passive to the realities of the need for personal responsibility and growth in Christ and the consequences of sin. Mankind cannot afford to be idle or passive to the reality that a healthy human being will grow and progress in one way or another (in a constructive, destructive or debilitating manner). Nor can mankind afford to be idle or passive to the reality that sin is a natural part of the structure of this world and it will have an influence on all mankind. Also, we must accept the reality that mankind must learn to thrive in a world that is inundated with sin and iniquity. Therefore, without a conscious understanding of the existence and nature of mankind (the flesh) and the influences of sin and the need for discipline that is rooted in God through Christ, sinful behavior or rebellion toward the word of God and others is inevitable in the life of mankind **(Romans, Chapter 6)**.

Sinful desires, whether physical or mental, are byproducts of exposure to sinful and/or dysfunctional learning and conditioning and not because mankind has a sinful nature organically. The issue with sin is centered on the effective and proficient nature of the flesh, the mind, and the spirit of mankind and their exposure to sin. This is because exposure of these mechanisms to sin and dysfunctional learning and conditioning can allow sin and iniquity to embed in the mind, the flesh, and the spirit of mankind. Christ is mankind's deliverer from all things. When mankind submits to the authority of God in Christ, liberty is in place. All things are possible and the captive is set free. Meaning, sin that has embedded itself in mankind is purged from mankind's existence through repentance in Christ under the statutes of grace **(as one operates in this deliverance)** with the power of personal effort and the Holy Spirit.

Exposure to sin and iniquity will cause sin to embed in the mind, flesh, and heart of mankind in a way that can and will interrupt and defile the natural desires, impulses, and motivations of mankind. This exposure will hinder the spirit, mind, and flesh's ability to move forward and make appropriate choices in a constructive, healthy, and Godly manner. The flesh, mind, and spirit are like Amazon' Echo, Alexa, and Google's Home, they can take in information and build upon it according to their technological ability and design. On the other hand, sin is like a virus which has the potential to invade a system, manipulate the operations of the system, and if not addressed, sin can cause the system to break down, malfunction or function in ways that are completely different from the way the system was originally designed to function.

In other words, the flesh, brain/mind, and spirit of a person can incorporate information and that information can influence and/or change the fundamental operations of that individual spiritually, physically, and mentally. As a result of the capabilities of the flesh, brain/mind, and spirit to take in information and this information's ability to influence and/or change the natural operations of the flesh, brain/mind, and spirit, one must recognize the power of sin and other influences on the human design. Therefore one must acknowledge, respect, accept, and never forget, that sin and other social, environmental, and spiritual influences can and will influence the natural operations of mankind physically, mentally, emotionally, and spiritually.

Sin can even command the operations of the flesh, brain, and spirit, especially when the flesh and mankind's mental processes are made to feel comfortable with the commands of sin. The more comfortable one becomes with sin, the more sin can command the individual. In other words, the more one operates in sin or are made to feel that sinful behavior is the norm, one will submit to sin and be governed by sin with ease **(Romans 6:15-23)**. When you submit to sin you cannot operate in righteousness **(Romans 6:20)**. However, mankind does not have to submit to sin and inequity; mankind can resist sin and iniquity at any point in one's life. In order for one to resist sin and be delivered from the influences of sin and iniquity, one must engage in the following:

(1) An individual must first begin to question who or what he/she is (What is being human and how does being human set him or her apart from God's other creations?) and their origins (Where did I come from?). This includes examining and acknowledging how one is conducting himself or herself. This involves studying to know, to the best of one's abilities, if one's conduct is a byproduct of their human mental, physical, and spiritual design (Are you conducting yourself like a human being and not as a primitive form of life?). Are you using your intellect for the good of mankind and the world? Are you conducting yourself according to God's design for mankind and according to God's design for your personal destiny?

(2) Phase two is entered into when a person acknowledges their human existence and their need to address their creator, (God) through repentance. Repent of one's sinful state in the name of Jesus. This empowered repented state is an acknowledgement and recognition of the fact that you have been operating or conducting yourself physically, mentally, and/or spiritually contrary to God's design for mankind. This Acknowledgement has nothing to do with one's knowledge of

the fact that they are operating outside of the will of God or one's intention to operate outside of the laws of God. This state of acknowledgement and repentance is done as a result of one's understanding of the effects that the sin and iniquity of this world has and is having on them, has had on them, and is having on all mankind in general and on all of God's earthly creations. Your sins may be the result of omission/unintentional or commission/intentional. Either way, mankind must acknowledge and repent of the sinful state of their existence.

One must acknowledge, due to the sin and iniquity of this world, that he/she was born into and shaped in, there are some things about them that are out of sync with their human design. You need to acknowledge that you are, in some part, engaging in forms of conduct that operate according to the sin and iniquity you were born in to. This form of repentance is also an acknowledgement that God is our Creator and He has a design for us that excludes the presence of sin and iniquity and this is a design that He would like to fulfill in all mankind. This acknowledgement should also take into account, Jesus is the Son of God and mankind's redeemer who was sent by God to help us return to His original design for us. This is a design that is embedded in Holiness and is in place to help us overcome the sin of this world. This acknowledgement is the first step toward fulfilling our God given design according to His truth and not according to the sin and iniquity of the world. This is a logical and conscious acknowledgement that should not to be clouded by feelings, emotions and ideologies striped by mankind.

Here it is important to note: **Romans 5:12-15** informs us that the disobedience of Adam and Eve imputed sin upon mankind. Meaning, their disobedience made mankind subject to the sin and the law that governed the world. This scripture reports: Although sin was in the world, sin and being governed by the law that addresses sin was not a part of mankind's existence. Therefore sin was never a part of who or what mankind is. Adam and Eve's disobediences made mankind subject (imputed) to sin and the law that governs sin. Therefore, as a result of mankind's existence, not nature, the nature of what mankind is (biological mental and spiritual existence) is subject to sin and the governing body of the laws that address sin. As a result of Adam and Eve's disobedience, the essence of who and what mankind is, from the point of the first act of sin, mankind became subject to the effects of sin and is subject to being governed by the laws that govern sin. Once again, sin was in the world with Adam and Eve, but mankind was not subject to the sin of the world.

(3) Once one acknowledges the nature of the sin of this world and the truth of God's design for the human race, one should resist the lure of sin and a willingness to conduct one's self in a way that is contrary to the word and will of God's design for mankind. Meaning, one should respect the laws that govern sin by resisting sin. One's state of resistance is accomplished through prayer, studying the word of God, and disciplining and submitting one's self with all one's strength, mind, body, and soul to a willingness to be transformed from what you think and/or have been conditioned to think is appropriate, to what is appropriate in God. This transformation should focus on God's truth found in His word, His creations, and the teachings of Christ. This includes examining fleshly thoughts, urges, impulses, conditioning, and socializations that dwell in you, which are contrary to the word of God. In other words, one should resist and not allow sin to rein or rule and abide in the make-up of how he/she operates **(Corinthians 15:31)**. To

allow sin to rein in one's life, will allow sin to grow in the operations of your conduct, mental status, and spiritual development, unleashing the development of and strengthening of demonic strongholds in your life. **(Romans 6:12)**. These are strongholds that allow sin to flagrantly operate, rule and rein in an individual's life physically, mentally, emotionally, and spiritually.

(4) Seek the filling of the Holy Spirit. This is a desire of the Holy Spirit that is separate from the Holy Spirit's calling on one's life and an individual's ability to feel the presence of the Holy Spirit moving in their life. When one has accepted God as the all mighty authority and Jesus as the Son of God (mankind's redeemer) and is conducting one's self, to the best of one's ability, according to the word of God in Christ, one can invite God's Holy Spirit to come in and live within them spiritually, mentally, and physically and it will. We need the Holy Spirit because it has the power to purge the mind, body/flesh, and spirit of sinful influences that have embedded or established themselves within the life of an individual. The Holy Spirit is also a guiding and empowering force that strengthens one's ability to resist engaging in sin and notifies one of the lurking of demonic influences.

It is the sin and iniquity of this world that warps the natural beauty of our God given design and life-forces and damages the flesh's ability to submit to necessary boundaries and commands of God. These are boundaries that are in place for the good and development of His creation and His ability to partner with His creation. It is also the iniquity (sin) of this world that has shaped the world and negatively agitated and affected the positive nature of mankind's life-forces. Therefore, as a person grows and develops in a sinful environment, they will sin. This is because in a sinful world, sin and engaging in rebellion against God's design for mankind are a part of the learning and conditioning process from birth. This is why everyone must repent of sin, because of the operations of the sin, mankind was made subject to, by the actions of Adam and Eve, all mankind will and has sinned. Sin is a part of the world we are born into and we engage in it either by omission (unintentional) or commission (intentionally) and it plays an intricate part in shaping our lives. This is why God's word places significant value on personal development and growth as seen in **II Timothy 2: 15,** which request that mankind study: **Proverbs 4: 7,** which states, most of all have understanding: and in **I Samuel 15: 22,** it reports that obedience is better than sacrifice: and in **Proverbs 1:5**, which encourages listening.

Although a number of prominent men of God address their struggle to overcome dysfunctional and sinful learning that was embedded in their mind and flesh, such as David and Paul, the struggle is not about the natural makeup of the flesh being sinful. The struggle is more about addressing sinful learning and conditioning that has been embedded in the mind, spirit, and flesh through exposure to dysfunctional and sinful socialization and Satan's antics.

Therefore, the struggle for mankind is about the press to stay committed to the commandments and Spirit of God in spite of sinful urges, desires, impulses, and thought patterns. The struggle is the same as it was for Jesus, making the choice to stay the course of following the commands of God, in spite of the demands of the body or desires of the flesh; in spite of feelings; whether these demands are sinful or not. The question is: How will you address your needs, desires, urges, and impulses? How will you address your feelings? Will you address your needs, desires, urges, feelings, sympathies, and impulses according to the plan God has for you and His people in Christ? This is a plan that is scripted in Holiness and acknowledges the need to partner with God and others in Christ. Or, will you look to your own understanding and devices, void of the commandments and ordnances of God (which is an act of sin)? **As it was with Adam and Eve, our relationships with God and others, our survival and salvation will also lie in our ability to address our needs, desires, urges, feelings, sympathies, and impulses by making appropriate choices in God (Galatians 5:23). However, for us, it is with the help of Christ and the power of the Holy Spirit under God's grace.**

Note: Accepting the concept that mankind has a sin nature has a tendency to distract from mankind's need to acknowledge and accept personal responsibility for all of their actions and responsibility for establishing and maintaining appropriate relationships and partnerships in Christ. This theory also distracts from the notion that mankind has a responsibility to address God and try to understand what God has designed for mankind, as a whole and on a personal level. When one begins to realize that they were not born sinful and there is nothing about them that is innately sinful or evil, one can begin to understand that the negative and/or sinful behaviors they are participating in, is not about who they were born to be. At this point, many may begin to accept the fact that God did not design them to be negative or sinful.

The empowering insight and understanding that one does not have a sin nature can stimulate the inquisitive mind of mankind and cause them to seek the true meaning of life and what God has for them. This understanding can also help and cause many to resist sin and evil behavior, because they now know that sin and negative behavior is not a natural or normal part of their design or makeup. They now know that their lives and destiny are primarily controlled by the choices they make and not by some negative or evil force that lives within them. Their ability to resist sin and their ability to discipline themselves in the ways of God becomes more illuminated. They become empowered with the fact that they have the power to direct and redirect their lives. It becomes evident that living a constructive lifestyle verses a lifestyle plagued by negativity and sinful behavior is within one's personal control through Christ under grace. They begin to understand that they do not have to succumb to sin and the iniquities of this world. All mankind needs to know is that mankind was created and born of the loving and good essence/image of God **(Genesis 1:27)**. A realization that informs us that all of what we are is a byproduct of a good thing (God), the only good being, and there is no sin in God **(Luke 18:19; Genesis 1:31)**. Therefore, mankind was not born with sin in them nor were they born to sin.

CHAPTER FIVE

Believe it or Not!

Note: Many disagree with the concept that the flesh is not inherently sinful. Also, many may ask the question: If the sin of mankind is primarily a socialization process, why would a person living in isolation have to repent of sin? Well, the natural maturation (growth) process of mankind will cause him/her to question their origins and who or what he/she is. As a result of an innate desire to know, a part of mankind's design, a person will be naturally led to seek out his/her creator (God). The natural intellectual development of mankind will also cause them to acknowledge the things of this world such as hate, pollution, and war etc.... The natural inquisitiveness of mankind will cause them to also question the things in their environment, which work against the harmony and balance of the operations of the world and the wellbeing of mankind.

Therefore, even though one has always lived in isolation, the innate nature of mankind will acknowledge God through His creations and long to connect with God, the Creator. Therefore, although Jesus' redemption of mankind has been accomplished and mankind does not have to repent for the personal sins of Adam and Eve (for them making mankind subject to the workings of sin through their disobedience), they must repent of the sin that Adam and Eve have made them personally subject to. Therefore, acknowledging that their state of isolation within itself is questionable in God. In other words, to address God, all are required to personally acknowledge and accept God's offer of redemption through repentance in Christ for one's personal state that may not align with God's will for mankind. This is a state that is not in totality or necessarily a byproduct of their own doing, but needs to be addressed in order to commune with God. When one does this, one is ushered into a place of Holiness.

Existing in a state of Holiness will make way for an individual to commune with a Holy God. Meaning, one is no longer subject to the stronghold of sin and the laws that govern sin. This state of Holiness is erected/exists because the individual has submitted to God and as a result, is now operating under the statues of grace, offered by God through Christ. Meaning, your submission to the authority of God in Christ, now qualifies you to operate under the statutes of grace. These are statutes that blot out your sins, whether they are intentional or not, when you press to submit to the authority of God with all your mind, body, soul, and strength. You are under the covering of grace as long as you are committed to loving God (being governed by God) and others in Christ to the best of your abilities. You are covered under the blood of Jesus and you are now eligible to exist in a state of Holiness through grace. This is a state that allows you to commune with a Holy God. You are in position to commune with God and not just be blessed by God or benefit from His mercy. You can now also qualify for the favor of God **(Proverbs 3: 1-4; Psalm 5:12; Psalm 84)**.

In other words, to accept God's offer of redemption and position one's self in Holiness, one must first acknowledge the invisible God of Abraham as God (the authority). One must also accept that Adam and Eve's disobedience to God was sin and made way for sin to flourish in the world and in the lives of mankind, an act that subjected mankind to sin, put them in a sinful sate and separated mankind from a Holy God. Then one must also, acknowledge their personal role in the perpetuation of sin and iniquity in the world (whether this perpetuation was of omission or commission). In other words, a person's need to repent of sinful behavior or his/her participation in sin. This acknowledgement and state of repentance is not all about one's participation, willingness or desire to participate in sin. However, the focus has more to do with the existence and the operations of sin in the individual's life and in the lives of mankind, due to their growth and development in a world where sin and iniquity flourish.

In this state of Holiness that is commanded through one's acknowledgement and repentance, the Holy Spirit will help an individual acknowledge and accept the negative effects of sin and how sin has affected the individual personally, has affected the world and has affected mankind in general. This is an awakening that causes one to acknowledge one's sinful state, not because they were born sinful or, in many cases, not because most have knowingly chosen to engage in sinful behavior but because they are in a sinful state that is the result of being subject to sin. A state that was imputed upon them by the actions of Adam and Eve and is hammered/formed as a result of being born into a world where sin flourishes and where one's development is shaped by iniquity.

This inequity is inflamed by the demonic spirit of Satan. During this period of acknowledgement, the individual will experience a transition that is spiritual. This is when the spirit of an individual has a spiritual awakening to the spiritual nature of mankind and God. It is during this period of transition from primarily experiencing life from a

146

fleshly/carnal and self-willed perspective or existence to being more sensitive to your spiritual nature and acknowledging the spiritual nature of God and your need to be governed by God. One begins to better understand Jesus' call for mankind to submit to a state of sincere repentance. This state of repentance is a result of one coming into the realization and acceptance of the fact that sin is operating in this world. It is also an acknowledgement of the fact that sin and the iniquities of this world are operating in each of us (him/her). This is a conscious and spiritual transition.

Once again, it is when one accepts the authority of God and the calling of His Son Jesus that one begins to acknowledge and know, just by the state of one's existences in a sin filled world, sin can and is operating in them. They acknowledge that mentally, spiritually, and physically, they are in a sinful state. Through their state of submission and willingness to accept God as the authority and Jesus as the redeemer, the Holy Spirit is empowered with the ability to help an individual address their sinful state and answer Jesus' call to repentance. Therefore, in a state of acknowledgement, repentance, and submission, the grace of God will make room for an individual to operate in a state of Holiness. As a result of operating in Holiness, the door is open for an individual to begin gaining an appropriate understanding of God, an appropriate understanding of what and who they are, and an appropriate understanding of their role in Christ and gaining the ability to enter into an appropriate partnership with a Holy and righteous God. Therefore, an individual begins to understand that he/she cannot have an appropriate relationship or partnership with God unless they are operating in Holiness. Unless they are pressing to do their best, to the best of their ability, to submit to the authority of God, there is no appropriate relationship with God.

Sin and iniquity has prevented mankind from existing in the good and holy state of their original design. As a result of mankind being subject to sin, mankind has been separated from God and is hindered from acknowledging and submitting to the truth and authority of God. This state of separation has most likely led many to choose a life of isolation in the first place. This disconnect, induced by sin, hinders one's ability to accept God's will for them to live and prosper in a social unit of unity and partnership.

Sin has most likely caused many to seek isolation or one may say self-preservation. Many are uncomfortable in the sinful state of mankind's existence. They know something is out of balance, but they can't put their finger on the cause. Therefore, many retreat into a mode of self-preservation. Although this self-preservation can take many forms, for many, it can take the form of isolating one's self from others or the reality of the tragedy of humanity. Many recoil into isolation and/or many other inappropriate patterns of behaviors in an attempt to disconnect with what they cannot process or understand, a sinful world of selfishness, divisiveness, and hate.

The workings of sin has hindered many from identifying with the fact that living in complete isolation or operating in ways that separate them from others works against the plan God has for His people and can be defined as sin **(Genesis 2:18; Proverbs 18:1)**. They cannot acknowledge what their creator (God) declared in **Genesis 2:18**: "It is not good that man should be alone." Also, we are encouraged to "forsake not the assembling of ourselves together" (Hebrews 10:25-31). The question then becomes, how are you going to love your neighbor as yourself, if you don't have any neighbors or any interaction with your neighbors? Also, how are you going to function in the body of Christ, when you are isolated from it? Mankind was made to partner with God and others and to share love. This is something that cannot be done when living a life of isolation or when withdrawing one's self from the realities of life.

The heavenly lifestyle God has for mankind is not one of isolation. A Christian's earthly lifestyle is about preparing for communing with God and others in heaven. Therefore, each individual must come to acknowledge that mankind must learn to come together on earth that we may be prepared for our heavenly destination. God and the plan He has for mankind on earth and in heaven is about unity. This is why God requires His people to go and share His word and the good news of Christ, God's redemptive love and Christian brotherhood throughout the world that all may learn of Him and how to properly acknowledge Him and others in their daily walk. This is an acknowledgement that is Christ centered, has no respect of person and embodies the love of one another through partnership in Christ.

Now for those who are stuck on the concept of mankind having a sin nature, consider the following: God can have nothing to do with sin. Jesus and God are one **John 19: 9; John 14: 9-10**. Now do you really think Christ could have lived in a body that was organically sinful? There was no sin in Christ, nor His fleshly body. We know this because Jesus reported God was in Him. God can have nothing to do with sin. We also know this because Jesus said, His disciples did not need to fast and seek a helper when He was on earth with them, because the helper they needed (Jesus) was with them. He was speaking of His Holy state in the flesh **Matthew 9: 14-18**.

You see, Jesus embodied the definition of Holiness even in the flesh, and Holiness cannot dwell in a sinful vessel. Remember, part of Jesus' mission was to show us how to live holy in the flesh. He came to show us how to live holy in a vessel that has the potential to succumb to the inequities of this world, not one that is naturally sinful. He came to show us how to be overcomers in the flesh when faced with the sin and iniquities of this world through repentance, commitment, discipline, with the teaching of Christ and the Power of the Holy Spirit under grace. He came to show mankind that they had the power in Christ to resist sin and live a lifestyle that was designed for them prior to the sin of Adam and Eve making mankind subject to sin.

Jesus tried to do this by showing us how to submit to the authority and commands of God in spite of the sins of this world, homelessness, loneliness, abuse, persecution, and even in the face of death. Jesus came to show us and empower us as to how to resist evil, sin and sinful behaviors as seen in the world and others. He did not come telling us the flesh has us bound. The good news is, He came to tell everyone, inspite of the workings of sin, we are empowered with the ability, with the help of the Holy Spirit, to discipline the flesh to resist sin and to be subject to the authority of God. He came to show us that we have been set free from the curses of sin. He came to show us how to live sin-free through the power of the Holy Spirit under the statues of grace. Matter of fact, **Romans 6: 14-19** reports, sin does not have a hold on us when we submit to the authority of God according to Christ.

Also, our submission in conjunction with the Holy Spirit, frees us from sin through grace. Jesus came to show us that although we may have sinned and may have times when the sin of this world may get the best of us, we don't have to continue in sin or succumb to sin. In spite of the times or the situation or what you think you need or what you desire, you can discipline yourself to resist rebelling against the path designed for you by God. Jesus was expected to stay His course in God and so are you, to the best of your ability and in spite of the sin of the world and your experiences.

When Jesus asked Christians to pick up their cross and follow Him, He was trying to inform us that we can be like Him (Holy)! He was also telling us that we are expected to take what God has given us in the flesh, by grace and with the help of His Spirit, and move forward with all our strength; mentally, physically, and spiritually. This is why God asked us to love Him with all our mind, body, spirit and strength. This is because a mind, body, and spirit that is disciplined to love and submit to the authority of God in Christ, is an overcomer and is unstoppable in Christ. Also, a mind, body, and spirit that has been disciplined to the things of God, can serve God and live in Holiness through grace, in spite of the weaknesses and imperfections of the flesh and the sin and iniquities of the world.

Individuals who refuse to believe salvation is a process defined by one's ability to discipline themselves to make appropriate choices in Christ are not good candidates for Christian partnership. Christians must learn to choose to make Godly choices and to love God on a daily basis. A belief system that refuses to accept that a life in Christ is a learning process which disciplines mankind to press forward through submission to the authority of God, will add unwarranted tension in the life of the believer and within a partnership in a number of ways:

1) **Unrealistic Expectations**. This type of partner will always be looking for perfection in the salvation of others and finding fault in their partner's ability to be Christ like. For these individuals, salvation is about one's perfection in Christ or a Christian's ability to always produce good fruit. These individuals do not believe Christians can mess up or make mistakes or struggle with following through with God's desires for them. Even when they accept that salvation is a process, many will be unable to truly rightly divide the truth of one being saved and working through issues and the nature of a backslider. This is because their position on salvation is faulty and a solid foundation of understanding cannot be established on a faulty premise.

A faulty premise will cause splintering (cracks and splinters) in any foundation. Therefore, these individuals will always be poking and picking; pointing out how unsaved or imperfect individuals in Christ are. The mentoring of many will not be able to move beyond the point of one accepting the vow of salvation. This is because salvation for them is about perfection in Christ. These individuals will also have problems rightly dividing the word of truth in God. If perfection is not found in the one proclaiming salvation, which it will not be, these individuals will be forced to minimize the effects of one's conduct as it relates to one's salvation. Splinters will be seen in their ability to see imperfections in themselves and other Christians, and in their ability to attribute these imperfections to one who is saved. Also, many of these individuals will be backed into a corner when trying to explain why one who proclaims salvation is still inclined to behave contrary to the word of God on a continuous basis.

One's imperfections will not be seen as an indication that salvation is a growth process or as a reflection of the press to overcome the sinful influences of the world and Satan's antics, as discussed by Paul **(Romans 7:19-25)**. **Isaiah 64:6** clearly reports, there is no perfection found in the actions of mankind. **Colossians 2:14-15** reminds us that **God's grace blotted out the ordinances (His ordinances) of perfection that worked against mankind**. **II Corinthian 3:6** reports that all should acknowledge, Christ's redemption. This is a covenant that does not hold the behavior of mankind, in its entirety, to the letter of the law. This covenant is primarily focused on the spirit and of a person and his/her sincere efforts to fulfill the will of the Lord and not one's ability to behave perfectly within the letter of the law of God.

Statements like: "You are not really a Christian, because you did not do or say this or that just right in Christ," will be the philosophy of many with this perception. Also, because of their inability to rightly divide the word of truth concerning the statutes of grace, many of these individuals will describe a Christian's continual misconduct and defiance in Christ as one whose misbehavior is covered under the blood of Jesus. These individuals may also embrace the theory that a Christian who continues in sinful behavior and defiance against God is covered/saved by the statutes of God's grace. Because of their poor understanding of the definition of salvation and mankind's partnership role in their salvation, these individuals will experience a disconnect or misconstrue the true meaning of

Christ's redemption and how grace truly operates. Many will apply or consider the meaning of the statutes of God's grace out of context. These individuals will be unable to appropriately explain what it means to be saved and live a Christian lifestyle. They will also lack the ability to help others understand the meaning of salvation and how to live an appropriate Christian lifestyle. Because of their limited understanding of salvation, many will not be equipped with the ability to identify many forms of sin and discern the true nature of a backslider appropriately.

Many Christian partners may end up feeling like they are walking on eggshells, trying to live up to the expectations of a partner with an underdeveloped understanding of salvation. Many will feel like they are drowning in agony as they try to live up to their partner's definition of righteousness and may never understand the expectations of God, because they are in a partnership that works against the truth of God. Many individuals may also feel confused about their roles and conduct as Christians, due to the confusing feedback from a partner with a false narrative of salvation. The truth of salvation is redeeming and liberating, not condemning. However, the truth about salvation also embodied a definition that includes feedback, instruction, learning, discipline, and the acknowledgement and submission to the expectations of God found in His word, His actions and His creations. This is something that is not properly understood, acknowledged or addressed by those who refuse to accept that salvation is a process. Individuals who refuse to accept that salvation is a process, defined by a press to move forward in Christ and not a state of existence, can cause stagnation and confusion in the lives of any Christian and in their partnerships.

2) **Cynicism**, as it relates to a Christian's free will. The theory that salvation makes void one's desire or willingness to make choices outside of the will of God, would force one to rationalize or justify the righteousness of one who has proclaimed Christ or who was in Christ, but now is in a fallen state. In other words, many adhering to this philosophy will find it difficult to accept the true meaning of what it means to be saved and what it means to be a committed Christian. This is because their concept of what it means to be saved is underdeveloped and not scripturally based. These individuals will most likely conclude that a backslider was never truly saved. Such conclusions work against the true meaning of salvation and present an image of salvation that is cynical. Therefore, it becomes difficult for many to take the idea of salvation seriously. Christians cannot afford to ignore the following facts: (1) Accepting God requires one to understand that they must focus on living within necessary boundaries. These are standards, laws, and judgments that define holiness; (2) Holiness is a required state of existence in order to commune with God and to return with Christ. Although God's grace is sufficient for our imperfections, it was established for those who are willing to acknowledge their personal responsibility and their partnership role in their salvation by doing the best they know how to walk according to the word of God in Christ; (3) Additionally, these required standards will never change, not for the times, not for friends, children, partners or family members, and not for comfort, feelings or traditions; and (4) Mankind has a free will that defines his or her destiny and one's destiny is defined according to one's daily choices, daily conduct, and personal commitments in Christ, saved or not.

According to the philosophy of salvation that embraces the theory of "once saved always saved", a person who is "truly saved" would not walk away from God. This philosophy does not truly acknowledge that an individual's free-will is irrevocable, change not, and it is the free-will nature of an individual who is truly in control of one's destiny in Christ. These theorist fail to acknowledge God's word found in **Matthew 12:30** that reports God saying to His people, "you are either with me or against me," and in **Joshua 24:15, if serving the Lord is undesirable to you**, "…choose you this day whom you will serve…" In both of these scriptures God is acknowledging and addressing the free-will nature of mankind. Here God is not speaking to unbelievers. God is informing all, He has imposed a command that gives everyone the freedom of choice and this freedom must be respected even by Him (God!). This is a choice that was gifted by God to mankind and God does not make void what He has spoken. This is also a choice that must be expressed through one's willingness to repent, submit to God's authority, stay submitted, and show love toward God and others "daily" or make an informed decision to move on without God **(Luke 9:23)**. This is a daily walk, people, and not just a proclamation.

Individuals who refuse to accept that an individual can choose to walk away from their salvation found in Christ, are more likely to give undue credit to the devil for themselves and/or others willingness to engage in sinful behavior. They would rather blame Satan than accept that the power to choose God is found in their willingness to discipline themselves to choose to resist the selfishness of the flesh, the enticement of sinful behavior, resist Satan's antics, and submit to the authority of God.

Their view of sin will most likely conclude, Satan made them and others sin or the individual was never "truly saved". One with this perception may also conclude, there are people who can't help themselves when it comes to engaging in sinful behavior, or the idea a person is naturally evil will consume their thinking. The concept of personal responsibility and owning up to one's partnership role in their salvation will sound foreign to them. They will most likely fail to recognize that mankind, saved or not, are overcomers in the flesh, when they chose to discipline themselves to resist the selfishness of the flesh and lawlessness and follow Christ's example with the help of the power of the Holy Spirit under grace.

These individuals may not be aware of or may not accept the reality of God's truth concerning mankind's free will and the salvation offered by Jesus Christ. A truth of salvation that defines a Christ-driven Christian, according to one's free will devotion and desire to press toward the mark of obedience in Christ, is what God is calling for. This is a devotion and desire to press toward the mark, through one's act of submission and obedience, to love God with all one's heart and with one's entire mind, body, strength, and soul. These individuals will not realize that salvation is a lifelong growth process, defined by a moving away from sin (things that are in conflict with God) and not by perfection or justifying those who continue to engage in sin.

Once again, the free will of mankind was gifted by God. It cannot be taken from mankind. Mankind can submit or will him or herself to commit to anyone or anything. Satan's goal is to get individuals to submit to his authority. The ability for mankind to dedicate or submit him or herself to anything or anyone may explain, why there are so many different types of religions and cults. **The Bible appears to support the theory that a Christ-driven Christian's state of being is one who wills him or herself to submit to God through Christ and not a Christian who is void of a will of his or her own**.

It is Satan who would have mankind not believe in the concept of having a free will to resist commands. This is because a person without a will cannot resist the antics of Satan and will not be able to command him or herself from a fallen state (a state of Satan's evil grip) through repentance in Christ. It is one's love for God and knowledge and understanding of the truth of God and the reality of the human existence that help the individual to understand that he/she can resist sin, Satan and his antics

(3) **The perception of and possibility for hypocrisy**. The perception that a person who is truly saved will not sin, gives Christians a false sense of what salvation is and may cause many to live lives that are contrary to the word of God and God's will for them and others.

Individuals who hold to the philosophy, "Once saved always saved," will most likely live and/or condone lifestyles that can hinder them and others from living in the fullness of what God has for mankind. Their unwillingness to accept or their poor understanding of the true meaning of free will hinders their ability to understand the true meaning of salvation and the liberty associated with salvation. This limited ability to understand, or rejection of the true meaning of salvation and the liberty associated with it, will challenge, maybe even hamper, the average person's ability to live a lifestyle in Christ full of truth and liberty.

A flawed definition of salvation will force them to reject the true definition of what it means to live sin-free. They will have a problem accepting God's expectation for mankind to be personally responsible for their actions throughout their lives, saved or not, and the fact that this expectation will never change. His expectations for mankind, the unsaved or the saved, does not change. They will also have a problem accepting, one who lives a sin-free lifestyle is a champion for the word of God according to His will and His command. Meaning, Christians who are living sin-free seek to please God the way He has commanded them to do so and not in a way that some may feel is right or feel comfortable with. A sin-free lifestyle is about knowing that your feelings and God's will for you and others are not always one in the same. A sin-free lifestyle is a form of worship. The truth of Christianity realizes that the body is a temple of God and the life lived in that temple is like burning incense before God **(I Corinthians 6:19-20)**. These Christians work to make sure that the scent or smell from their temple is a good smell before God and they know the definition of salvation is defined within a process and is defined within one's ability to discipline themselves put God first as they make every effort/press to fulfill the word of God in their lives and in the lives of others daily.

It Will Take a Personal Transformation

To follow another requires an examination of one's personal walk. The act of following also requires a willingness to possibly change one's personal perceptions or habits. To follow Jesus, will most assuredly require a personal transformation that moves the individual away from viewing the world from his or her personal perspective **(John 3:30-31)**. "I" is not a word that should be frequent among Christians.

159

God and His approach to all things are found in Him and in the expression of His word. Also, God and the things of God, including mankind, is not about anyone's personal perspective, but it is about God and God's will for His people and His intent for this world. This may be difficult to accept for many because "I" dominates in our society and in most cases the "I" has the final say. What "I" feel, what "I" am or what "I" am not comfortable with and what "I" think is the way many make decisions and live their lives.

Some may ask, why is living for God void of one's personal perspective? A Christ-driven lifestyle is void of one's personal perspective because one's personal perspective is limited in its ability to comprehend the layers of physical and Spiritual phases of past, present, and future existence associated with who God is, what God has to say, who you are, and what the character of others is. A Christian will be led to honor the word and will of God, according to the path of Christ. However, the most critical realization of a believer will be found in the ability to deny one's self in Christ, understand the word of God, follow Christ and stay committed to growing in Christ. The Christian's ability to move beyond one's personal perceptions of God, self, and others and understand and follow God's principles will assist them in developing an appropriate understanding of salvation and an appropriate understanding of a partnership with God. This is a partnership with God that is Spiritual and unites the spirit of a person with God according to the teachings of Christ through God's word and the help of Holy Spirit and not according to one's personal perceptions.

Although it may appear a bit obscure, these discussions about self-perception, salvation, associations, communications, and the operations of the Holy Spirit are important. These topics are important when it comes to understanding the concept of personal responsibility and the personal transformation needed to have an appropriate partnership with God and others in Christ. The understanding of these elements will help a person formulate an appropriate understanding of being a Christian. These elements help Christians define and identify the characteristics that partners should possess and display as Christians consider partners in business, friendship and marriage? Studying these concepts offer the mankind insight and understanding about the nature of God, the nature of who mankind is in God, and the nature of the supernatural warfare that exists in our world.

What defines Us?

When choosing whom one should partner themselves with, the most telling element about the individual that should be examined is seen in the nature of an individual. The nature of a person is synonymous with the character of a person. The character of a person is a good predictor of behavior. The character of an individual will help define decisions he or she will make, who that person will associate with, and the type of communication or relationships the individual will develop or are capable of developing with others. A person is first evaluated by overt/visible behavior displayed, but the best definition of an individual is found in his or her heart and spirit. The Holy Spirit is a gift from God that is imparted into and dwells within the spirit of a Christian who is committed to submitting to the authority of God (obeying God) **(Acts 5:32)**. Salvation starts in the heart and spirit of a person. However, the manifestation of one's heart filled commitment to God is seen in one's behavior. **Romans Chapter 6** tries to convey to the reader that it is the Christian's responsibility to pursue the ways of the Lord and press to continue this pursuit on a daily basis.

The spirit of a person will temper one's heart and the heart of a person will define the fundamental direction of one's actions. **Mark 7:18-23** informs us that the heart of a person can play a major role in one's behavior. The ability to temper one's spirit and heart is found in one's spirit. The Christian who is best equipped for Christian partnership is one who is empowered with the Holy Spirit. This is because the Holy Spirit, is able to affect one's heart in a way that gears it toward embracing the things of God, resting the inclination to be selfish and with an empowered ability to resist evil. This is a disposition that will help guide the actions of a person and will be the guiding force that helps mankind formulate and define mankind's most important partnership. This is the partnership between God and a committed Christian who is filled with the Holy Spirit. The Holy Spirit is also the defining factor that will serve to unite the body of Christ and will establish all Christian partnerships when a Christian submits to the guidance of the Holy Spirit.

To summarize, if a Christian partners with an unbeliever, they will compromise and jeopardize their partnership with God. An act such as this could lead to eternal damnation for the Christian. But, possible damnation is just a tip of the iceberg, when it comes to the fallout that can and will occur when a Christian partners with an unbeliever. Such a partnership is a recipe for conflict between the Christian and the unbeliever. The Christian's commitment to God will conflict with the unbeliever's desire to make choices outside of the word of God. Remember, the "I" concept diminishes in the life of a

Christian. Because of the guidance of the Holy Spirit, these individuals should seek to live a God enriched lifestyle that is void of one's flawed personal perceptions. Christians should be working toward allowing God to increase in their lives. The uncommitted Christian and the unbeliever will find it difficult to understand and accept the need to move away from one's personal opinions. They will also find it difficult to understand and accept the committed Spirit-filled Christian's devotion to the things of God **(Romans 8:4-14)**. This lack of understanding and unwillingness to commit to the word of God on behalf of the unbeliever or uncommitted, can and most likely will lead to all out disaster between them and the Christian, whether it is for business, friendship, or marriage.

Therefore, the fundamental approach to establishing appropriate Christian partnerships starts with a Christian conforming to a focus that seeks to understand, accept, and follow how God would have a Christian partner with others according to the written word of God through the power of the Holy Spirit. This is an individual and personal adaptation that must be adhered to by each Christian partner. It is this understanding that opens the door and leads to appropriate partnerships in the lives of God's people.

The Christian's perception of partnership is established with an acute understanding of God and an awareness of the fact that God has a plan for everyone and one's life partners. God's plan for Christian partnerships encompasses one's partners in business, friendship, and marriage. This perception is grounded and rooted in the understanding found in **II Corinthians 6:17-18; II Thessalonians 3:6 & 14,** that there are **NO** valid partnerships for Christians outside of the arch of God through His Son Jesus Christ. This is because a person who is not committed to the authority of God and does not embrace Christ and His teachings is not filled with the Holy Spirit. Therefore, their heart is not tempered by the guidance of the Holy Spirit. This is a disposition, which causes an unsaved person to be less sensitive or insensitive to the things of God. A disposition that will eventually cause an unbeliever to be at odds with the Christian. This is because a committed Christian is naturally inclined and sensitive to the things of God.

Facing the reality of what it means to be a Christian and the meaning of Christian partnership is difficult for many. The foundation of the Christian's perception of partnerships is built upon the principle; the Christian lifestyle should acknowledge and honor God and God's approach to how we should live our lives in **EVERYTHING** we do. However, the lifestyle and perception of many Christians appear to be grounded in the acknowledgement of God, but they do not embrace the notion that they should honor God and God's approach as to how they should live their lives. Many will conclude, **"Noooooo, I cannot do all that or one does not have to do all that to be a Christian!"** This perception compromises the commitment of those striving to walk appropriately in Christ. This perception will compromise the Christian's commitment to live an appropriate Christian lifestyle. These Christians do not feel that they should have to go out of their pleasure or comfort zone to honor God and may explain why many Christians find it difficult to accept the word of God found in **II Corinthian 6:17-18; II Thessalonians 3: 6 & 14**. These types of individuals cannot walk in the fullness of Christ, nor can they receive the fullness of what God has for them, no matter what their lives currently look like or how many people support them.

A simple example of how many Christians fail to understand what it means to be a follower of Christ is found in the following example: It is the norm for many Christians to say that they love God, confess to accepting God as the only living God and Jesus Christ as the Son of God and Savior sent by God; however, when they read in the word of God that they should not engage in fornication, they do not honor nor do many Christians want to honor this commandment and established principle of God in their lifestyle.

Failing to live by God's commands and/or principles is a failure to honor God. A failure to honor God is an act of disobedience and defiance. An act of defiance places one in the position of being separated from God. And when one is separated from God, one is at the mercy of the enemy. **The enemy, Satan, has no mercy!** He comes to steal, kill, and destroy **(John 10:10).** Many Christians and unbeliever do not want to hear the whole truth of the matter, when it comes to understanding what it is to be a Christian. Also, when discussing the definition of sin and the negative consequences of being in opposition or in conflict with God, many Christians and others, will say that this is an act of beating them down!

Some may even say that this is an act of "judging" them and their actions. Conclusions such as these, in most cases, may be unfounded because the reality is that the laws of God and nature of God have already judged sinful behaviors. **Proverbs Chapter 1** reminds us of the importance of adhering to instruction. To remind and inform someone of the established judgments of God is not an act of judging, beating one down, nor is it an act of hatred.

When accusations such as these are made, they could be more of a conscious or subconscious attempt to shun and/or stop the truth of God's word from going forth. It may also be an act of rejecting God and the truth of God as it is presented in the Scriptures of the Holy Bible. Sad to say, many people do not really want to know how God perceives their thoughts, perceptions, and behaviors. It appears that these people cherish the notion that those who do not know God's truths (i.e., remaining ignorant), will be excused from the consequences associated with engaging in behaviors that are in conflict with God's truths; however, this is not the case.

The word of God in **Proverbs 4:7,** exhorts and encourages all Christians and non-Christians to prioritize the act of seeking an understanding of all things. It is hoped that one is driven to gain an understanding of a person or situation prior to making a conclusion about the person or thing in question. We see this in all professional fields. As explained, having an understanding of a person or entity before partnering with them should be a priority for everyone. The act of applying the principle of having an understanding of all things, in question, while making decisions will improve one's ability to make good decisions. This principle is powerful and effective and it will aid in the efforts of anyone trying to live a successful Christian lifestyle or become a success in anything.

The principle of having an understanding is also the primary way in which God expects Christians to define issues, resolve issues, and develop relationships and/or partnerships. It is the knowledge of being acutely aware of the fact that God would have Christians apply this principle while making decisions, which improves a Christian's ability to perform their role in Christ. It is also the Christian's willingness to implement this principle during the decision-making process, which improves their ability to make good decisions. It is safe to say, whether it is in business, friendship or marriage, a person who has a history of embracing the principle of seeking an appropriate understanding and making good decisions is an asset to any partnership, whether they are in Christ or not.

CHAPTER SIX
Examining One's State of Mind

The perception that a person is beating one down or judging while offering advice or correcting others, unknown to most, is a byproduct of a state of mind/mindset (way of thinking) that is unrealistic, negative and oppositional. A mindset such as this reflects a strong resistance to a willingness to listen and consider the opinions of others. **Proverbs 1:5** tells us to listen, is to learn. A person who is unwilling to listen to the things of God cannot be taught the things of God. How can one learn to follow God, if he or she cannot be taught or refuses to listen?

This leads to another question: How can someone be a good candidate for Christian partnership, if he or she is unwilling to listen to appropriate feedback form others and is unwilling to learn of the things of God? This is a **Red Flag! Matthew 11:29-30** invites us to learn of God. This brings about one of the first conflicts between a Christian and such a person. Such a person's resistance to learning the ways of the Lord will eventually lead to anger, hostility, and may even incite rage in a partner such as this. However, a partnership with such a person will not fare well with the Christian's ability to be at peace with their partner(s) and grow in God.

It is one's ability to have personal peace with self and others and grow in God that prefects their press to live a Christian lifestyle. The intellectual and moral growth of an individual is rooted in the social nature of being human. Most sociologists and psychologists will agree that humans are social beings and much of how humans learn to function intellectually, socially, and morally in a society is accomplished through the encouragement and instructions of others. There is a learning curve in perfecting any skill or job. No one can take on a new job and think that they know it all, if they want to keep their job. There is a diagnostic disorder found in the Diagnostic and Statistical Manual of Mental Disorders 5 (DSM 5) for people who think that they know it all; it is called **NARCISSISM (Narcissistic Personality Disorder 301; 81)**.

Without the learning and encouragement that comes from others, living a constructive and well-rounded lifestyle would be very difficult for most. In the same breath, without learning and encouragement from other Christians, living an appropriate Christian lifestyle will be unnecessarily difficult, if not impossible. Even Moses' willingness to listen to his father-in-law's advice about how to address the needs of the tribes of Israel was proven prosperous for Moses and for the people of God **(Exodus 18:24)**. To give legitimacy to the notion that input and/or correction from another is a beat-down, an act of judgment or an act of hate is to endorse the idea that mankind's learning experience is an island unto itself. **Not!**

To believe that a man or woman is defined only by his or her own self-determination or makings is not realistic and is antisocial, anti-Christian, and anti-God. To partner with someone who has an aversion to listening to the advice of others and rejects correction is to bind yourself to a person who also has difficulty listening to the needs of others. This type of person is self-centered and has an inflated opinion of personal beliefs.

What another person or the word of God has to say about a topic does not compare to what such a person thinks. This type of person will rationalize and argue about a matter until they get their way. These types of people most likely will put their opinions first and foremost and leave his or her partners standing out in the cold on many decisions. **Proverbs 1:7** informs us that a fool despises wisdom and instruction. Now, **who would be willing to partner themselves to a fool?** A good Christian partner can listen and is more than willing to research, listen, and learn how he or she should function within the will of God in a given partnership or situation. It has been often said that God gave mankind two ears and one mouth, because He intended for mankind to listen more than talk **(James 1:19)**.

Some may beg to differ, and say, America is a free country and there is nothing oppositional about believing that people should mind their own business and leave others alone! However, as previously discussed, one's ability to listen and consider the correction and advice of others is very important in defining the character of and predicting the potential of the individual. Before concluding on the subject of the importance of partnering one's self with a person who is willing to listen to others and conform to the word of God, let us examine some of the various mindsets, which may lead one to reject advice and/or correction from others.

Why would one feel beaten down, judged, or hated when questioned, advised or corrected about their behavior or perceptions, when it is evident that instruction and advice from others are a natural part of the learning and socialization process of mankind? If we value the word of God, which states, "As a man thinks, so is he," one would have to accept

170

the following premise to answer this question: **A person who does not think that he or she should have to answer to others for his or her actions, will not answer or listen to others for his or her actions (Proverbs 23:7)**. Therefore, could the answer to this question be, individuals with this perception do not want to answer to anyone for their behavior. These individuals would like to say and do whatever pleases them without considering the ramification of their actions. In many cases, these individuals will indorse statements like, "To each his or her own!" In this case, it is safe to conclude that a person who believes that he or she does not have to consider the opinions of others will display many behaviors and perceptions that are inconsiderate of others. This is not a quality that is Christ driven and is a quality that defines a person who is not a good fit for partnership.

Romans 12: 2-3 informs us to change by the renewing of our minds. According to this Scripture, the hallmark ability that defines a successful Christian lifestyle is one's ability to readjust one's way of thinking through a relationship with Christ. Successful Christian living is the ability to renew one's frame of mind from that which focuses on self (personal perceptions) to that which focuses on God (God's Perception). Paul confirmed this mental transformation in **I Corinthians 15:31** when he wrote, "I die daily." Paul is saying that being a Christian extends beyond just believing that the answers and purpose for life is found in God through the teachings of Christ.

Here, Paul indicates that being a Christian requires a mental transformation that leads to a lifestyle transformation. In other words, Christian living is working to renew one's thinking (mindset) from valuing personal formulations and perceptions as the fundamental framework of reality to becoming God conscious and Christ-driven in one's thinking and actions. This also tells us that one's mindset, Christian or not, is a very important predictor of the way a person will perceive and process information, behave, and address others. As a result, it can be concluded that one of the most telling predictors of human behavior is defined by the person's state of mind.

With this understanding, it is safe to conclude that a person who is to be considered for partnership must be examined, observed, and studied to gain an understanding of that person's mindset. Potential Christian partners should have mindsets that value listening, learning, and growing and are God focused in a way that produces Christ driven behavior in their actions. To evaluate an individual for Christian partnership, the evaluator must first have a God centered mindset and a Christ driven disposition that, include having the ability to listen and a willingness to submit to the word and authority of God. For example, one cannot evaluate a partner for marriage and function or operate outside of the will of God with the person in question for partnership. This is because, if a Christian is engaging in behavior with another that is outside of the will of God, such as fornication, that Christian's ability to listen to Godly instruction and make Godly decisions about one's self and that partner is flawed. The act of engaging in sinful behavior has a way of obstructing one's ability to listen to the word and Spirit of God and one's ability to adhere to God's fundamental truths.

Sexual Ties and Mindset

The Christian's decision-making process, when operating in a sexually compromised situation is disrupted for two major reasons: 1). The Christian is engaging in sin and God cannot have anything to do with sin. Sinful actions will muffle or stifle the voice of the Holy Spirit. As the individual insists on continuing his/her participation in sinful behavior, the voice of the Holy Spirit will become more and more distant. The act of engaging in sexual iniquity, like fornication, will separate the Christian from the Spirit of God (**Isaiah Chapter 59)**. Don't be confused; God still loves you, but He will not have anything to do with your sinful behavior or lifestyle. As a result, the Christian is no longer fully empowered with the ability to rightly divide the truth from a lie, which comes with an appropriate partnership with God and the guidance of the Holy Spirit. **In other words, the Christian is operating in a lawless backslidden state... a state that interrupts the Holy Spirit's ability to order the Christian's steps.** The Christian now has unclean hands and dirty hands cannot produce clean results; 2). The physical and emotional pulls of sexual iniquity and many other sinful behaviors are strong and very disruptive. The physical and emotional pulls associated with these behaviors will distort the Christian's ability to focus and/or stay focused on the things of God, no matter what one may believe. One need only to reference the lives of Solomon, David, and Samson to understand the distracting role engaging in sex outside of the will of God played in the lives of these men of God.

Individual Mindsets and Broader Societal Partnership Objectives

If a Christian is considering partnering in business with another, when the Christian has received perks prior to establishing the partnership or during the partnership, his or her mindset can be adversely affected by these gifts. These perks can hinder the Christian's ability to stay focused on how this partnership will help him or her maintain his or her salvation and grow in God. Under these circumstances, a person is not to be considered for partnership if the following are not evident: (1) The individual or group's personal history does not indicate that they are committed to the word and nature of God; and (2) The individual's mindset is not one that is willing to conform to the things of God and help you maintain your salvation and grow in God. This is why **Proverbs 29:4-5** advises us to be aware of those bearing gifts.

The promotion of the perception that a person is trying to beat one down or judge another when offering advice or insight as to various behaviors and concepts has crippled the cohesiveness of our society. As individuals become more committed to creating rules and laws, which prohibit questioning their actions, society's need to address the reality of how many of these nonconforming actions and perceptions affect the social structure and weakens the basic fiber of our society. This "do what you want to do," mentality of those with their own personal agendas fosters confusion and splinters the cohesiveness and stability of America and other societies. Partnering with such a person or organization destroys the body of Christ. The Christian lifestyle and livelihood thrives within a unified body of Christians operating according to God's word with the guidance of the Holy Spirit in Christ. **Matthew 12: 22-28 and Mark 3:25-27** remind us that a house/body divided cannot stand.

Most will agree that the fabric, strength, and survival of any group or society are grounded in the ability of its members to perceive that they have more commonalities than differences. These commonalities are found in a group or a society's ability to share information and grow together. Getting group members to focus more on their differences than on their commonalities and common interests is an age-old method of compromising the strength and cohesiveness of any group. The principle of "divide and conquer," applied in military practice, is relevant here. Central to this principle is the understanding that the more segmented a group is, the weaker the group becomes relative to the enemy. Members of a group, society or partnership who are unwilling to learn how to embrace the commonalities of their existence are a weak link in the unit and strengthens an enemy's ability and position to weaken and/or destroy the unit.

When the majority of the members of a group or a society do not perceive that they have to consider each other or have irrevocable core commonalities or interests, these members will experience difficulty maintaining cohesiveness. As a result, groups and members of a society or partnership have difficulty coming to a meeting of the minds. When partners or the majority of members of a group or society cannot have a meeting of the minds, they experience divisiveness that will most likely hinder their ability to function as a unit. When the majority of a group or society's membership are unable to function cohesively, that entity experiences frustration and anxiety which, if prolonged, will most likely hinder growth and ultimately lead to its demise. The laws, commandments, and principles of God's indisputable and irrevocable status provide stability, put a bridle on chaos, and grounds all who are willing to abide in them. These are characteristics that enable any partnership or entity to function as a unit.

The nature of God and His truths are indisputable and irrevocable. They secure the livelihood of mankind and when adhered to, will maintain cohesiveness in any partnership, group or society. God's laws are life and work to unify mankind. God is life and living by his word is life and anything contrary to His word (sin) and selfishness leads unto death **(Romans 6:23)**. Adam and Eve were able to work together and live in peace and did not experience any form of death until they disobeyed God's command. This was a command that was in place for their stability, peace, safety, protection and prosperity. *From the beginning, we see that mankind's stability, peace, safety, and prosperity are about adhering to God's plan for mankind and His fundamental truths. This is why God's word and truths will never change and this is why it is important for mankind to become familiar with God's truths. As mankind positions themselves in God's truths, according to the leadership of Christ, the unity and strength of any nation, society, group or partnership will grow and prosper in God and in its' ability to establish appropriate partnerships for business friendship and marriage. God's truth/word is the tree that is good for the living of the nation.

However, the extreme promotion of self-expression, as seen in today's society, is an incubator for children of perdition. Such individuals show little regard or are indifferent to the impact that their perceptions and behaviors have on the survival, strength, safety, and longevity of themselves, others or society. The mentalities of these individuals are fixed on how their style of thinking and behaving will situate them and give them pleasure and prosperity. They are lovers of self and self-perceptions, money, and pleasure!

The word of God does not condone one pursuing a self-indulgent lifestyle **(Matthew 16:24-25; Luke 9:23; Timothy 6:10)**. The narrow view of those who are fixed on keeping the focus of social behavior and perceptions on personal feelings and personal happiness can offer little consideration for the constructive long-term survival unity, safety and peace for themselves and others. People who live for self-pleasure tend not to be concerned with the socialization process that governs and maintains a society, group or partnership. They simply do not want to be socialized. Instead, these individuals would like to be allowed to pursue their personal agendas (i.e., self-pleasure) with very little concern for the consequences or the effect their behavior may have on others.

If they are concerned with the socialization process, their concerns tend to focus on ensuring that societal norms and laws and interpersonal interactions allow them to be self-centered. Many will not address how unstructured self-centered behaviors may possibly be destructive for the future of them or others. The motto of these individuals appears to be, "Every person for him or herself." Most of these individuals refuse to accept that the survival and longevity of any partnership, group or society is grounded in the united efforts of all of its members having an attitude of accountability for self and others.

In general, unless unity supports their concerns and personal agendas, these individuals will also reject the notion of a society or partnership working together towards maintaining a healthy state of unity and cohesiveness. **Therefore, they welcome chaos when cohesiveness and unity impedes their ability to have their selfish desires met**. A self-centered individual's perception of life is in direct opposition to God's perception of what God has for the body of Christ and others. One cannot be in Christ and be self-centered and show little or no desire or action to move away from things that contradict

God's will for them and mankind. Due to the destructive nature of one who is self-centered, God will not have His people partner with a self-centered person **(Matthew 16:24).**

A self-centered individual is blinded by a strong desire to continue doing whatever he or she pleases. He or she has little concern for what pleases God and his or her partner's needs are not a primary issue. To be forced to consider that his or her position on various topics is in opposition with another, especially with God, will most likely create feelings of negativity. These negative feelings may make the individual misconstrue any confrontation as an act of passing judgment. This perception may lead to hostility and negative feelings toward the person who questions them, which can lead to the individual spitefully striking out towards those whom have questioned their opinions or behavior. This type of person will be in constant conflict with those in Christ and with those who value opinions other than their opinion.

So, is the act of questioning or calling someone out on behavior or thinking that is in opposition with the word of God or societal values really an act of beating the individual down, hatred or passing judgment? Not necessarily. It may be an act of encouraging the individual to question the logic, sensibility, morality or legality of the perceptions or behaviors condoned. However, as mentioned earlier, a self-centered disposition tends to evoke negative thoughts when questioned about his or her behavior/s. Many of these individuals simply do not like having to question the logic, sensibility, legitimacy, normality, practicality or even the morality of thought patterns and behaviors they value. Many have a negative or an indifferent disposition toward opinion's that are in conflict with their own opinion.

Giving and Receiving Behavioral Advice

Keeping in mind, that social and environmental constructs are important and are a natural part of the learning process, it is safe to conclude that much of one's thinking and behavior is a reflection of learning and environmental reinforcements. Therefore, **the Christian philosophy embraces the belief that Christians are teachable or should be teachable to the things of God**. They are teachable in all things that work to the good of mankind in Christ, and the people they partner with must also be teachable in the things of God, according to Christ.

Therefore, the act of one encouraging another to reexamine the appropriateness of one's behavior should not be offensive to a Christian and should not be offensive to a Christian partner. From a biblical perspective, for an individual to conclude that someone hates them, is trying to beat them down or execute judgment upon them when they are being informed that they are in opposition with the word God, is to display a poor understanding of the word of God. This type of reaction from an individual also suggests that the accuser has a poor understanding of God and has a compromised perception of what God expects of Christians and those who claim to love Him. Let us not forget the words of the Apostle Paul in **Romans 2:2**, where he explained that **the judgment of God is truth**. To speak the truth is not an act of judging, but it is a statement of God's judgment, an expression of faith, an act of love, and a show of commitment to the obedience to the word of God and a statement of fact.

Matthew 10:26-33 tells the Christian that the salvation of the Lord should not be kept secret. The truth is, one will never understand the meaning of salvation, if one does not consider the important role that God's truths has on one's state of mind, behavior, and conduct play. Therefore, according to the principle of understanding, the secret of salvation is effectively shared when the messenger addresses all of its elements, including the element of how one should behave as a person of God. **Mark 16:15** tells the people of God to proclaim/share the truth of God's word throughout the world and **Psalms 119:125** helps us to understand that the people of God seek His teaching, guidance, instruction and understanding of His word. **Jeremiah 26:4-6** reminds us that if we do not listen to the word of God's servants and His prophets, who He has sent to share His word, it will be a curse to us. Meaning, to commit one's self to a person who cannot listen to instructions is to commit one's self to a person who is cursed.

Many individuals may claim that Christ commanded His followers to proclaim or share the word of Christ in the context or confines of the church (a physical building) only; however, this could not be further from the truth. Christ gave the example for the Christians to follow. In His example, He shared the truth of God with everyone He came in contact with. The Apostle Paul also spent the latter years of his life teaching and instructing others, the saved and the unsaved, everywhere he went. Others may say that one should share the good news of God's salvation and the word of God by focusing on the joy found in the salvation of the Lord and not by discussing the judgments of God. A response to that conclusion is that the truth of God is the truth of God, and although one should always be led by the Spirit of God, one should never limit, compromise or stifle the truth of God.

The truth is, one cannot share the truth of God's word without including the whole word of God, which includes God's principles, commandments, and judgments. To limit the sharing of God's truth would cheat God out of the ministry He is trying to perfect in the lives of Christians. The primary ministry of all Christians is to love God first, love one another in Christ according to the nature of God and to proclaim the truth of God through the teachings of Jesus Christ throughout the world (**Mathew 28:16-20 & Mark 16:15**). In **II Corinthians 7:9-11,** Paul discussed that sharing the truth of God might bring about sorrow to some who hear it, for whatever reason. However, the truth of all of what God has to say brings joy and life to the lives of all who receive His word and gift of salvation.

To bring attention to the fact that one's actions are not in line with God is a Godly act. When Christ mandated Christians to share the truth of God, they were mandated to help others gain insight as to the detriment of inappropriate behaviors or thoughts and the sinful nature of such actions or thinking, as well as to bring attention to the joy of living in Jesus, void of such behaviors. Although correction may make one feel bad for a period of time, the hope is that the individual will at some point reconsider their actions and thoughts and repent. It is also hoped that the individual will not only gain insight and repent, but eventually rejoice in knowing the truth of God and how that truth works for their good.

God's truths are seeds which have the ability to produce growth. The seeds of God will embed within the physical, psychological, and spiritual make-up of all who are exposed to them, saved or not. These are seeds of truth that never die and God can give increase to them at any point. **These seeds** of truth breed and breathe life and hope into the lives of men and women, right up to the brink of death. **This simply means when someone has been exposed to the truth of God, this seed breathes hope and opportunity for redemption, salvation and deliverance right up to the last minute of life.** Satan is aware of this and this is why he fights so vigorously against the truth of God going forth. Satan does not want a person who has behaved badly to know that there is hope for them, and through the redemption of Christ, their life and destiny can forever change for the good.

Therefore, **reproof that is in line with the word of God, is reproof founded in helping an individual experience the joy of knowing and living in the truth of the Lord.** This is a form of correction that is done unto the glory of God with the intent to direct individuals toward a Godly path that will lead them to Christ. If the correction was done to help the individual come into the knowledge that he or she needs to repent and draw closer to God, it was well done. Correction or confrontation in this context, plants a Godly seed and is a good thing and God is well pleased. Addressing inappropriate behavior(s) is not just a command to help your fellow man, it is also a Christian's responsibility. **(Ezekiel 3:18). Isaiah 58:1** instructs us to "Cry loud, spare not, and lift up our voice like a trumpet, and show (by sharing the word of God and your behavior) my people their transgression, and the house of Jacob their sins." Remember, although this is a sensitive and difficult process at times, this is not a spiteful or negative process.

Therefore, if one questions or advises another about behaving in ways that are in conflict with the word of God, it should be known that God may have already judged the behavior in question as being unacceptable. One will discover many of these judgments in the books of **Leviticus, Numbers, Deuteronomy and Romans** and throughout the Bible. As a result, an individual cannot judge what God has already established as being acceptable or unacceptable. From this, it can be concluded that when an individual is sharing with another the appropriateness of a given issue or behavior in God, the person is simply relaying the message of God's judgment/s concerning the matter. To share the truth of God's word is not an act of implementing one's personal judgments and personal opinions. This behavior is the act of following the commands of God that state: Christians should share the good news and the secrets of salvation and proclaim the whole truth of God's word throughout the world.

To say that you do not appreciate a person educating others about what God has judged to be inappropriate is one thing; however, to say that this individual is passing judgment or hating is not necessarily true. Also, if one has a complaint about God's judgments, the argument is with God and not the messenger. Don't kill the messenger. The fact that one perceives an individual as being hated or beat down, when others offer correction, may suggest that the perceiver has a rebellious oppositional disposition toward God and the things of God. The accuser is most likely engaging in behaviors that he or she does not want others to question. As a result, the person takes the position that everyone should mind his or her own business. Christians cannot afford to allow anyone but God through the truth of His word and the nature of His creations, according to Christ's example to direct their behavior in Christ.

Also, it is wise for all to know what is acceptable and what is not acceptable in God. In order to gain a better understanding of what is acceptable or unacceptable behavior in God, start with reading the Bible. Be careful, not to be misled by one of those modern translations of the Bible that water-down the truth of God's word. Then, with the knowledge gained from reading, rather than becoming angry with a person for questioning another's unacceptable behavior in God, you may want to spend time in constructive introspection. Incorporate the facts learned about the issue in question to help develop a healthy resolution about why another may feel it is appropriate to call someone out about a given behavior.

As a result of reading the word of God, one may choose to conclude what God has to say about the matter is not relevant to them. Reading what God has to say about the behavior in question may even strengthen a person's hostility concerning the concept of others giving or offering input about the behavior of another. No one can say what another may think about God's opposition of a given concept or behavior, but reading the word of God, prior to making decisions is recommend for the wise. This is because reading the word of God will empower an individual in his or her ability to make an informed decision, Christian or not.

Salvation is a Spiritual Calling

The reading of God's word is important. However, encouraging one to read the word of God should not be met with the expectation that one who reads the word of God will submit to the authority of God or convert to Christ. The act of reading the Bible alone will not necessarily lead to salvation. It is not the reading of the Bible that saves; it is the living Spirit

184

of God and an individual's willingness to answer the spiritual call of Christ unto repentance and submit to the authority of God that saves.

God is a Spirit and we must worship Him in spirit and in Truth **(John 4:24)**. Within the knowledge and understanding of the Spiritual nature of God, one must learn to acknowledge, respect, and accept the Spiritual nature of God to be a believer. In other words, it is God, Himself, who saves, not the reading the Bible or going to church or a person's ministry **(I Corinthians 3:6-14)**. We know this because the word of God in **John 6:44** states: How could one come to Christ/God unless God draws him or her? This scripture is an indication that salvation is a Spiritual process that is connected to God's efforts and not defined in the efforts of mankind alone. Although, many of mankind's actions are ordered by God, this scripture highlights the spiritual nature of salvation and the personal spiritual nature of the partnership that must exist between an individual and God. **Salvation is a Spiritual calling and an act of spiritual submission on behalf of mankind**.

One should know, a spiritual relationship was established between an individual and God when God created that individual. When God breathe His Spirit of life into mankind, the connection between mankind and God was fixed. Mankind is tied to God just by the nature of God being the Creator **(Acts 17: 28-29)**. This relationship is enhanced and perfected through the individual's willingness to submit to God's authority, accept the salvation God offers to mankind through Christ, and the willingness to partner with God to fulfill God's plan of salvation for them. Therefore, mankind are "God's being"; beings that are connected to God although they could never be God, they are an extension of the nature of God (a portion of God in the flesh). Just as our children are an extension of us, though they can never and will never be the parent **(Act 17:27-29)**. Children have biological features and characteristics of their parents, but they are not their parents. They are independent of their parents and they can separate themselves from their parents at any point.

Satan hates God and he is well aware of the genetic and innate connection mankind has with God, making Satan a natural enemy of mankind. As a result, mankind can never be a friend of Satan. So, do not be fooled that a connection that occurs though sorcery, black magic, satanic worship or witchcraft will somehow work on behalf of an individual or others. It will not! Also, individuals who use their God-given spiritual gifts (gifts unrelated to receiving the gift of the Holy Spirit) to engage familiar spirits or operate outside of the will of God render themselves vulnerable to Satan's strongholds and attempts of destruction toward them and others. These spiritual gifts are for the wellbeing and operations of the body of Christ. When used outside of the will of God, the operation of these spiritual gifts make room for Satan's antics.

Individuals who use their spiritual gifts outside of the workings of the Holy Spirit are powerless in Christ and are tapping into the spiritual world without and appropriate understanding of their gift and what it means to use their gifts in this manner. These individuals do not have the authority of God when dealing with the spiritual world. This is an act that will make them vulnerable to the manipulations of demonic spirits and Satan. An individual who is attempting to operate in the spiritual world without Christ is dealing with something that is beyond his or her control and something that will allow spiritual strongholds that thrive in this world to impose upon their lives and attach themselves to all who are involved with this process. Without the power of God, a person cannot stand down or up to anything in the supernatural world. This is why God forbid His people from seeking out people who use their spiritual gifts outside of the will and command of God **Leviticus Chapters 19 and 20, Galatians 5:19-21, Deuteronomy 18:10-13, Exodus 22:8, Micah, and many others.**

Christians must respect God's warnings concerning the spiritual nature of mankind's existence. Due to the Spiritual nature of mankind and the nature of salvation, a person can preach or teach at a person from the word of God all day, but unless the individual on the receiving end of the teaching and preaching submits to the Spiritual calling of God, salvation and redemption will not occur. This is why all teachers and preachers of the word of God need to be filled with the Holy Spirit. The calling of God is on the lives of all mankind **(I Timothy 2: 2-4)**. However, many, maybe even most, will not accept this calling. Many may commit to attending church services and listening to or reading the word of God through the urging of others. But, unless the individual is convicted by the Holy Spirit and acknowledges the Spirit of God and is willing to answer the call of the Holy Spirit with repentance in Christ and submit to this calling, the impact of one's teaching, preaching, hearing, and reading of God's word is limited and will not lead unto salvation. **It takes a willingness to acknowledge and submit to the calling and authority of God for the effectiveness of salvation to operate in the life of an individual (Matthew 23:37).** This understanding reminds us, and if adhered to, will help us stay focused on the fact that salvation and redemption is not about what a ministry does, but it is about God. It will also help us to be mindful that a ministry must not only share the word of God, but also be empowered by the Holy Spirit to be the ministry God is calling for.

The Word of God, the Holy Spirit and Salvation

An effective ministry also accepts and understands it is the power of the Holy Spirit in partnership with mankind that will help them address the needs of the people. It is also the Holy Spirit that empowers any ministry or individual in their ability to work through and triumph over issues that haunt the ministry and the lives of their parishioners. Therefore, a ministry that is about salvation will focus on allowing the word of God, freedom of personal choice, and the Holy Spirit to rest, rule, and abide in the operations of their ministry **(II Corinthians 3:17)**. Too many Christians partner themselves with individuals because the individual reports that he or she reads the Bible and/or attends church frequently. To do so is a grave mistake. A true Christian displays the fruit of the Holy Spirit found in **Galatians 5:22**. Furthermore, a Christian who is worthy of partnership is one who not only reads the word of God, but one who also applies the word of God and the word of God operates in his or her life.

When the word of God states in **Romans 10:14, "How can one hear without a preacher?"** The word is speaking of an anointed person who has submitted to the authority of God and is operating under the authority of God (according to God's word, the history of His creations and His nature) who is filled with the Holy Spirit and the power of the Holy Spirit (Spirit of God) **(Romans 10:15)**. God's Holy Spirit will commission a righteous person to preach and minister the word of God. This Holy Spirit-filled preacher/teacher/person (male or female) is an instrument of God operating in partnership with God **through their submission to God**. It is the Spirit of God at work here and not the person alone, as Jesus explained in **I Corinthians 3:6**.

This is not to say that the Spirit of God will not use the reading of the written word to draw individuals to Christ. No one knows the mystery of how God will choose to show Himself to a given person. **I Timothy 2:4 and II Peter 3:9** report that God would have everyone accept His salvation. However, the self-centered and/or stiff-necked person may not adhere to the Spirit of God, even when the Spirit of God is clearly convicting the heart and life of that person, for whatever reason, no one knows. Once again, it is one's submission to the Spiritual call of God that allows and individual to adhere to the word of God and receive and stay committed to the salvation of the Lord.

No matter one's state of salvation, the Christian should encourage others to read God's word: First, as an act of obedience to the command of God, which instructs us to proclaim the word of God throughout the world; and secondly, as an act of encouraging individuals to become knowledgeable about God, the things of God, and the love, freedoms and liberty given to all mankind by God through Christ **(II Corinthian 3:17)**. The Christian ministry has great trust in the ability of God's word to convey to others who God is, what God stands for, and the fact that mankind has only two true choices in this earthy life. **Mankind has the choice to conform to the will of God or the choice to oppose the will of God**.

You're either with God or against Him **(Matthew 12:30)**. The word of God and the teachings of Christ are in place to truly inform and instruct all, of the judgments and commandments of God and one's God-given freedom to choose to return to God or not. The word of God also informs mankind that the judgments and commandments of God are designed to work in their favor. It is not in God's plan for mankind to make a person submit to the authority of God **(John 12:46-48)**. Submission is a personal choice of accepting and following the will of God. **Salvation is personal and it is a choice**.

The Freedom of Personal Choice

Although God's teachings can be quite persistent when it comes to encouraging individuals not to oppose God's commandments, God condones the freedom of personal choice. As previously discussed, God will not force an individual to live a godly lifestyle. Freedom to choose God's way or not is a liberty that was given to men and women by God. This is what makes mankind unique and different from all of God's other earthly creations **(Joshua 24:14-15)**. Mind you, the freedom of choice does not change the way God perceives things or addresses issues. Therefore, it is advised that a person read the whole word of God, understand the liberty given to them, and walk thoughtfully within this freedom.

Not only should one read the word of God, but it is important that one becomes familiar with the established mandated consequences associated with choosing to oppose God's word. However, let it be known, no one can judge another's choice to oppose the will of God. God has already judged that; it is a person's right to oppose Him. But, the reading of God's word provides all who do so the comfort of knowing that they, unlike Jerusalem in **Lamentations 1:8-9,** have made their choice from an informed position that considers one's future and destiny. A position that truly allows an individual to choose with the understanding of what kind of choice he or she has made, and what he or she will be brought into judgment for by God on earth and on the day of judgment **(Ecclesiastes 11:9-10, 12:13-14).**

A profound understanding of why a person should not think poorly of those who attempt to inform others of what God expects of them is made clear in **Ezekiel 3:18-21**. These Scriptures show that the people of God are obligated to inform those who are operating outside of the will of God's word, they are in a state of trespass against God. These Scriptures also remind the people of God and others that they are held accountable, if they see another in a fault and fail to inform them of their fault. Whether one believes it or not, God's word informs us, we are our brother and sister's keeper. God wants all of us to be saved and know the truth **(I Timothy 2:3-6)**. But, salvation is about accepting the fact that we must recognize God, Jesus as the Son of God, repent of our sins (sins of omission and commission), and submit to God's authority. Therefore, God uses every righteous avenue possible to encourage all of us to walk in the necessary path that helps us accept that Jesus is His Son, our Intercessor, and a relationship with Him is a partnership that is established through personal repentance and personal submission under grace. He also uses every righteous avenue possible to encourage mankind to receive His desires for us on earth that we may join Him in heaven.

The Partnership Role of Redemption

The most powerful method used by God to accomplish His desires for mankind to live within His will is seen in the first social structure designed by God; the union of Adam and Eve. This was a union of two independent beings, capable of functioning independently, but were instructed by God to work together as partners. The couple's union and role was that of being partners within the will of God. The depiction of this partnership is never seen clearer than in God's disciplinary approach when the forbidden rule was broken. Both partners were held accountable and their disobedient behavior caused a shift in the manifestation of God's plan for them both.

Adam and Eve's partnership was beholden to God and worked within the commands of God for their livelihood, success, and lifestyle. Although the couple's acts of defiance had severe consequences, their behavior did not change the fact that God would like to continue in partnership with mankind. Also, their behavior did not end God's hope to fulfill His desires for them on earth. God's offer of redemption for mankind was not about God moving away from His love for mankind or original plan for men and women on earth. The vow of salvation offered by Christ is a righteous effort on God's part to encourage men and women to return to God's original plan for mankind. To return to living a loving lifestyle in partnership that complements each other (the qualities of each make a whole) and operates within the will of God.

When questioned about why one should acknowledge God and accept the vow of salvation, the response of many will focus on the concept of an individual being able to go to heaven. The closer a person draws to Christ, the more profound their understanding becomes that the totality of God's offer of redemption is not just about having mankind join Him in a utopia or after life. It was not until after the sins of Adam and Eve, in the Garden of Eden, was the concepts of hell and heaven for mankind mentioned. Prior to sin, God's plan for mankind was all about the life that God designed for Adam and his partner (Eve) on earth. Life for this couple was about partnership and teamwork, and their united efforts to live the life that God planned for them on earth. This tells us that a big part of God's salvation for mankind is about life on earth!

God's offer of salvation to mankind is about extending an offer for them to recommit to the will of God on earth! It is also about an offer of restoration for mankind on earth! The restoration of mankind is also about restoring mankind to a former state in God that existed prior to Adam and Eve's transgression. Therefore, salvation is first about God giving mankind the opportunity to commit and commune with Him and one another in partnership as mankind did prior to the interruption of sin. The disposition of Satan and mankind's fleshly weaknesses has destroyed mankind's chances of living the unblemished life that God originally had for mankind on earth. However, God's commitment to mankind through Christ Jesus and the grace Christ brings to the table through the power of the Holy Spirit, has empowered men and women with the ability to once again honor God and God's desires for His people on earth. We know this because without living a lifestyle on earth that is acceptable to God in Christ under grace, there is no heaven for mankind. **Therefore, let Christians be about living God's original plan of**

partnership for them on earth, as they embrace God's promise of eternal life.

Christians who are prepared for partnership understand the significance of helping others walk in the necessary path that leads to success in God on earth. The Christian who is prepared for partnership has a lifestyle and history that reflects a disposition, which is disciplined in Christ. These individuals also, embrace their roles to share God's word and is committed to living a Christian lifestyle on earth and helping and working with others to do the same. Therefore, Christians do not oppose partnership. **"Red Flag!"** They also do not oppose being corrected in God and they do not oppose others being corrected in God. Now ask yourself, are you partnered with someone who respects the will of God for mankind and the partnership role of salvation that allow God to encourage you and others to live a godly lifestyle? Better yet, does your partner/s encourage you to live a Christian lifestyle and encourage you to encourage others in the things of God? If not, the ministry of Christ is not working in your partnership(s) as it should. Also, the partnership is most likely working against you fulfilling your destiny in Christ with ease. One's ability and willingness to partner with God and others, through their submission to God for His will for mankind on earth unto the coming of Christ, is what Christ's redemption is all about.

CHAPTER SEVEN

The Nature of God and Salvation and their Relationship to Partnerships

Although God desires to have a relationship with all of us, it is not a need for Him. God's existence and state of being does not depend on the existence, wellbeing or His relationship with mankind. Who man is or what mankind does will not take away from or add one thing to who God is or to His greatness. God existed just fine, forever, before He created mankind. Obeying God enhances the survival and livelihood of mankind, but mankind's disobedience and lack of respect toward God will not diminish who God is, nor will it affect God's course of existence. Remember, God intended to wipe out mankind with the flood of Noah. If mankind's existence was vital to who and what God is and what God needed to exist, God would not have considered such an act. Unlike many, God does not jeopardize who He is or His status for the love or dislike of others or the love or dislike of things.

Therefore, we must understand that the salvation of mankind is about more than vowing to acknowledge Jesus and following godly principles and it surely is not about obeying God for God's sake. God does not need mankind to obey Him for His benefit. To put it plainly, mankind's obedience to God is not a benefit to God. It is the other way around, the benefits of mankind's obedience to God, mankind's faith/trust in God, and mankind's acknowledgement of God is to the glory of men and women. Mankind should walk in the ways of God unto the glory of God, but one's obedience to God is to the benefit of him or her. Mankind's faith in God and godly behavior improves the life and wellbeing of mankind, not God.

Although God enjoys hearing the praises of men and women, those praises do not lift God up. God is lifted and nothing and no one can bring Him down. God's status does not rise or fall according to the willingness of mankind to obey or praise Him. If that were the case, God would have bottomed out a long time ago. Man's willingness or unwillingness to obey and praise God will not add one thing to God or take anything away from God's awesomeness. If mankind never obeys or praises God, the awesomeness of God does not diminish.

God is awesome all by Himself! Once again, what mankind does in God is for the good of mankind. You may not like this, but the good that a person does or what one may justify as righteousness in his or her own eyes is not necessarily justified by God **(Isaiah 64:6)**. No one can define righteousness but God, because **righteousness is defined by God through the grace offered by Christ, according to the individual's personal commitment to God in spirit and truth (Romans 10:3; Romans 9:31-32)**. Therefore, many individuals need to stop working themselves up when it comes to justifying what they do for God and defining the righteousness of themselves and others. However, God is moved and seeks to sanctify mankind and will count all mankind's committed efforts in Christ as righteousness and glorify mankind's sincere commitment and obedience to His word and ways (Holy conduct).

Jesus' actions and lifestyle were a reflection of the Word and Spirit of God living in Jesus. Mankind's sincere acknowledgement of God will also give way for the Word and Spirit of God to live in them. This is why Jesus said, "When you see me, you see my Father" **(John 14:9).** Jesus' sincere effort to obey the word of God and faithful Spirit caused God to account all of Jesus' actions on earth as righteousness and glorified Jesus on earth and in heaven **(Philippians 2:8-12).** Jesus sits at the right hand of God because of Jesus' commitment and obedience to God and the will of God. God will also glorify those who choose to follow in the footsteps of Christ. God will bind in heaven what a righteous man or woman bind on earth **(Matthew 18:18; Matthew 16:19).** This means that a man and woman's commitment and obedience to God motivates God to make room for them and their wellbeing and their desires on earth and in heaven. Living a Christ-driven lifestyle in God on earth will cause God to honor an individual on earth and in heaven, as He does Jesus.

Submissive behavior toward the will of God also allows God to draw closer to an individual, allowing God to share wisdom, knowledge, and understanding as God communes with those who respect His authority. The closer one gets to God, the more the glory of God is transferred to that person on earth and in heaven, not the other way around. This was never more prevalent than in the book of **Exodus 34:29-35** with the physical transformation of the face of Moses after his continual communion with God. The closer a person is to God, the greater spiritual and physical transformation will be seen in that individual. This transformation will cause the individual to become more and more favorable toward the things of God. Also, the more others, the angels in heaven and on earth, and Satan will have to acknowledge that God is with that person and will see the need to address that person accordingly **(Acts 19:13-16; Philippians 2: 8-12).** All will have to recognize that God is with those who have an authentic and vested relationship/partnership with God. This is seen in the lives of Abraham, Sarah, Isaac, Moses, Joshua, Ruth, Ester, Joseph, Mary, Paul, and all the great men and women of God. We also see the ultimate fall of those who are distracted or were somehow duped into walking away from the authority of God. Note: Just because others can see the glory of God in you, does not necessarily mean that they will acknowledge and respect the God in you. Many may rebel against you even more because of it.

Salvation is Not Only a Partnership, It is a Contract

The offer of redemption is about a humble, righteous, just, responsible, and merciful God's decision to extend an offer of forgiveness and redemption to His free-willed creation (mankind). However, there is an "If" in this offer. The "If" is found in the individual's willingness to respect and follow necessary boundaries, as it was with Adam and Eve. Therefore, the salvation of mankind is about forgiveness, healing, and restoring mankind's relationship and partnership with God and others through his or her willingness to submit to God's will. As a result, through the vow of salvation, one is agreeing to receive God's plan for him or her on earth and in heaven. This agreement embodies a contract between God and all who accept His gift of redemption. This is a contract for all who are willing to pick up their cross and follow Christ.

This contract defines how both God and the individual will work together to maintain the individual's commitment (vow) lifelong, as it was with Jesus. This is a commitment that vows one to put forth his or her best efforts to develop and maintain an appropriate relationship and partnership with God and others, according to Christ's example. This relationship and partnership operates within the statues of grace and is designed to educate and prepare the individual for a successful Christian lifestyle on earth and for Christ's return. This education defines conduct according to **Holiness, a state that considers the needs of God and the transformation needed for mankind to operate within the word of God and be ready for the coming of Christ**.

Many may not perceive their salvation as a contract between them and God. This is because many have an underdeveloped perception of salvation and may view salvation as a fixed state of being. Many view the fullness of salvation as sealed through their repentance of past sins and the acceptance of Jesus Christ as the redeemer, and not as a living contract between them and God that can be made void by a person whether through neglecting the vow of salvation or being defiant toward God's word. They have no clue of what it means to work out one's salvation in fear and trembling (**Philippians 2:12**). To believe one's salvation cannot be made void would ignore the word of God found in **Ezekiel 33: 11-16**, which explains God's position on sin and those who turn from righteousness to sin. This also excludes the word of God seen in **John 14:15- 24**, which informs us that to love God is to obey God. **Joshua 24:15,** commands us to choose this day whom you will serve. In **Matthew 16:24 & Luke 9:23-25** Jesus instructs his disciples to pick up their cross daily and follow Him. **Matthew 24:13** also reports only those who endure unto the end, the same shall be saved, and **I Timothy 4:1-3** informs us that many will turn from the faith, which means many who are in the faith (saved) will abandon their salvation.

These Scriptures suggest that there is more to salvation than repentance and the acceptance that Christ is the Son of God, alone. These Scriptures suggest one's redeeming relationship with God also requires submission and obedience to God through a self-willed commitment to obey God beyond the act of coming to the cross. **In other words, there is a life beyond meeting Jesus at the cross when it comes to being a Christian.** One does not just step to Jesus, one must submit to the authority of God by embracing a daily lifestyle that follows Jesus' example of submission and commitment to the authority of God. One must pick up **his or her own** cross (God's will for them personally) and work toward committing to obeying the will and word of God in Christ, daily!

Philippians 2:12-13 reports, individuals are required to work out their own soul salvation. To work is to imply a state of motion toward a goal. Why would one have to work out one's salvation, if his or her salvation was a fixed state that occurred during one's original conviction and submission to God through Jesus Christ? **James 4:7** instructs Christians to submit to the authority of God and resist Satan and his antics and Satan will flee from you. This implies that "true" Christians have the power and must work on willing/disciplining themselves to resist and not to submit to things that are not of God. It also tells us, one's legitimate state of salvation does not make void the free will of an individual to choose to commit to the things of God. A person could have met God at the cross of Jesus and **choose** to move away from God at any time.

Note: In **Galatians 2:16-21** when discussing the fact that mankind is not justified by the works of the law, but by faith in Christ, it does not suggest that our faith in Christ does not produce works/actions. This scripture is not informing us that living in God is not about His people working in His name, according to His laws. Nor is this scripture suggesting that the laws of God are made void in the life of mankind when they chose to follow Christ. On the contrary, it is informing us that operating in the laws of God and the works of a Christian are now subject to the grace offered by Christ. This is a grace that is gifted through one's faith in Christ and will cover a multitude of faults. These are faults and circumstances associated with issues that hinder or cripple an individual's ability to fulfill every aspect of the law of God. This is also a grace that justifies an individual when he/she seeks to and is committed to operating within the will and laws of God to the best of one's ability. Grace picks up the slack, for whatever reason, in the sincere efforts of a Christian to commit to the will and laws of God. **Grace deals with intent and circumstantial evidence**. Therefore, the law must bow/bend the knee to the promises of God offered to mankind through Christ. This is because the promise of eternal life is not found in the law, but in Christ through grace **(Galatians 3: 22-23)**.

The Permanency of Salvation is Defined by Commitment

God is all about commitment. His commitment is to His word, first and foremost. Note: God's laws are found in His word and the Word of God is God **(John 1: 1)**. Therefore, one cannot exclude the laws of God and be considerate of Him. God's commitment is then to those who are willing to respect and accept His word and His design for mankind. **Therefore, the perception of salvation should not be interpreted as a proclamation only, but as a work in Christ through grace (James 2:26)**. A work in Christ that contracts mankind through his or her vow of salvation to work towards committing and staying committed to and submitting to obeying the will of God, more perfectly. Not perfectly, but more perfectly. Therefore, salvation defines how God and an individual will relate to one another through one's commitment to God under the principles of grace, to achieve and maintain that individual's redemption until death or until the coming of Christ. These Scriptures not only indicate one's salvation is a contract with God, but they also denote that **salvation is a partnership** between the individual and God for redemption until death or Christ's return. The question of salvation then is: Are you committed to the word of God and the design that God has for mankind? Salvation is about commitment.

More clearly stated, through the vow of salvation, God commits Himself to not only being the God and defender of the individual in question, but He is committed to helping the individual workout his/her soul salvation in Christ. This commitment is established through the ordinance of grace and the power of the Holy Spirit **under the authority of the individual's willingness** to commit and submit to the authority of God and obey the will of God.

Unlike the mercy of God, the power of grace and the favor of God is defined and activated through an individual's willingness to surrender to the authority of God through Christ, to the best of their ability. The history of the Old Testament shows us how to work on obeying God and be in a relationship with God primarily through the written laws of God and His prophets' teaching and intercessory on behalf of those who believed in the God of Abraham. This was done in combination with personal willpower, personal strengths and abilities. Prior to Christ, the perfection of living in God was not about an inner power living within an individual, but about the power of the Holy Spirit falling upon and walking with those who loved God and chose to operate within the laws of God. The individual either followed precisely the commands of God or repented for every possible mistake through ritual sacrifice or failed to meet the mark and received the judgment(s) thereof.

Although the covenant of the Old Testament embodied a need for sincere personal responsibility through repentance and a willingness to sin no more, the weaknesses of the flesh and Satan's antics has caused many of God's people to lose focus of this fact. Due to fleshly weaknesses and Satan, the Old Testament's covenant, expectations of a self-willed individual to perfect their walk of obedience in God was not an effective approach for most. This approach of trying to walk with God or obey the will of God solely by personal effort did not do enough to take into consideration the weaknesses, limitations or selfish fleshly nature of mankind on an individual level. This is why after living in the flesh, Jesus asked God to send mankind a helper (Holy Spirit) that will empower them from within **(John 14:16-17)**.

The Ordinance of Grace

In combination with the gift of the Holy Spirit, the ordinance of grace is in place to help mankind answer the call of God and to justify mankind's best efforts to live within the will of God. Grace addresses the flaws and weakness of mankind. Meaning, **grace is in place for mankind's imperfections and the Holy Spirit is in place for mankind's empowerment**. Grace is also in place to help mankind have an interpersonal relationship and partnership with God. Grace allows God to blot out an individual's sins and imperfections. This is because sin and the imperfections of mankind can limit their ability to communicate and commune with God. Grace is also in place

203

to help mankind understand that God is not focused on their ability to understand everything about Him, nor their ability to understand the call of God on their life or their ability to conform to His authority perfectly.

The salvation offered by Christ's life, death, and resurrection has helped God make plain the statutes that constitute the ordinance, which embodies the definition of God's grace. Through Christ, we begin to gain insight as to the depth, width, and breathe of God's commitment to the redemption/salvation of mankind and His grace. By allowing Christ's redemption to be bonded or attached to the ordinance of grace, **God wanted to convey to everyone that the ordinance of grace will work to the advantage of all who accept and submit to the authority of God, to the best on one's ability in Christ**. The blood of Jesus Christ not only clarify the definition of grace, but also empowers God's ability to justify an individual's lifestyle as Holy. **The ordinance of grace work to increase the legitimacy of one's heartfelt sincere best efforts (what one's does with all one's heart, mind and soul and strength)** to question and understand their own humanity, to love God and others and walk according to Christ's example and God's expectations of them.

Note: Grace and mercy are two different things. Grace operates within the framework of God's desire to redeem mankind from a state of sin or fallen state. God's grace is in place for the people of God who desire to please God and has shown sincere commitment to acknowledge God in all their ways but cannot live up to the commands of God according to the letter of the law. In other words, grace is in place for the imperfections of those who seek to know the truth and for those who are trying to live according to the will of God.

Note: When a person is questioning one's own reality, what is the meaning of life or one's meaning for being in the world and wondering about the world and the truths of God. Knowingly or not, one is really reaching out to God. This is because only God can answer these questions. In order for God to address such a person, He must make that person presentable (clean that person up) in order to present them Holy that they may commune with a Holy God. Grace allows God to answer to the call of wonder. This may explain why many acknowledge experiencing a spiritual awakening during times of wonder.

When a person is in proximity of the King, they must be presentable. God uses grace to blot out the sin and imperfections of an individual so that they may be presentable when addressing Him, the King, or communing with Him. Grace is in place for those who want to address God, commune with God, and return with Jesus when He returns for His people. Grace allows God to reach out to mankind on an interpersonal level. Grace allows God to reveal Himself to all that seek Him or His truths. In His reveal to an individual, God will beckon the individual unto Him. Some may call this act of beckoning, God convicting an individual's spirit. This is because when someone is in the presence of God, God's presence will have a supernatural effect on them that summons them to draw close to Him and beckons them to His call of redemption.

In the midst of an individual's desire to understand the truths of life, God will present Himself to that individual with the help of the power of grace. This presentation will embody an opportunity for that individual to accept God's gift of salvation. The possibility that a person may have an encounter with God, when truly searching their soul, may explain why Satan does not want to give mankind the time to think or truly ponder about who they are and the meaning of life. Satan is bent on trying to get mankind to either avoid God or fall from grace. Therefore, he is always trying to keep mankind in a frantic state, emotionally unbalanced, and moving at a fast pace. **Don't think, just do, is the spirit of the devil**. To not know where you are going, but you are going fast, is also indicative of a satanic influence. **I don't know where I'm going, but I'm going fast**, is not a logical state of existences. The spirit of thrill seeking, drugs and alcohol, sex and Satan's minions are prize tools used by Satan to push mankind down a fast road of illogical and thoughtless travels, in the hope that they will not take the time to think and ponder, and possibly meet God on their life journey. It is Satan's hope that mankind move as quickly as possible, pass go, to join him in eternal damnation.

God's grace is never more highlighted than in the age of Jesus through God's offer of redemption in Christ **(Ephesians 2: 7-8)**. God's intent for grace has always been to address mankind's desire to understand Him and commit to His authority. Once again, God's grace is an extension of outreach to those who are interested in knowing the truth of their existence and to those who love Him. In other words, grace is the tool God uses to extend Himself to the unsaved as He offers them His gift of salvation, and grace is also the tool He uses to justify those who are committed to Him in Christ. God's commitment to making grace a principle part of one's ability to acknowledge His truth and be committed to Him is best highlighted when He encoded the operations of grace within the need for personal repentance in Christ and one's desire and willingness to commit and stay committed to His authority as the requirements for the salvation of Christ.

Therefore, those who are unwilling to repent of their sinful state of existence and commit to the authority of God in Christ, cannot operate under the statutes of grace. These individuals cannot commune or partner with God. In Christ, grace is for those who repent, receive the salvation of the Lord, and are willing to commit and stay committed to this vow. Committed Christians operate under grace. The favor of God is also a byproduct of one's willingness to commit to God and discipline one's self to operate in God. On the other hand, the mercy, blessings, and love of God abounds for all mankind **(Romans 9:16-18)**. Meaning, you don't have to be saved to receive the mercy, blessings, and love from God.

Therefore, one can live a very pleasing and comfortable life on earth, by way of God's love, mercy, and blessings and be hell bound, because the grace of God is not operating in their lives. The lifestyle of these individuals, although some may have proclaimed the salvation of the Lord or submitted to God's authority at some point in the past, they do not have a desire to respect the word of the Lord or the truth of God consistently and/or are not committed to submitting to the authority of God. Remember: The statues of grace operate according to one's intent/desire and one's committed press/effort to submit to the authority of God and do His will. Therefore, their sins are not blotted out and their lifestyle cannot be justified under the blood of Jesus as Holy. This may explain why many of those who chose to engage in sinful lifestyles are able to do so for long periods of time. These individuals, groups, and organizations are living off of God's love towards mankind, God's willingness to bless them, for whatever reason, and God's mercy, but they do not have the grace of God operating in their lives. They also do not have the favor of God and cannot return with Christ when He returns (Psalm 5:12; Matthew 24:13; Matthew 7:21-27; & I John 2:6).

Christ came to confirm that we all need the salvation offered by Him to experience an appropriate relationship with God and to return with Him when He comes back. He did not come telling us that those who do not receive the salvation of the Lord will live an impoverished lifestyles on earth. The salvation of the Lord is about one's relationship with God and others and preparing for the coming of Christ. Although prosperity is a good thing and God is about blessing His people, prosperity and blessings are not the be all and end all in God. Christ's lifestyle and redemption was about helping mankind accept the transformation needed to be what God is calling for mankind to be and not about prosperity or worldly goods.

The grace offered through the redemption of Christ, came to enact a more personal and individual approach as to how God will consider dealing with a being that was born in sin, shaped in inequity, and is bound by the limitations and selfish nature of the flesh. The salvation offered through Christ did not come to change the fact that one's relationship with God requires personal effort. **Grace addresses and highlights one's efforts and intent more than one's ability to perfect a religious lifestyle or ritual in God**. Grace is designed to affirm God's original intent for mankind to put forth his or her best efforts to submit to His authority and commune with Him. This is an expectation which was, in many cases, lost or distorted prior to Christ' redemption, as a result of Satan's craftiness and the influences of sin and iniquity and the weaknesses of mankind's fleshly disposition. Christ's redemption allows God to help mankind through the ordinance of grace and partnership with Him and others, fulfill the expectations of God. However, Christ's redemption and the ordinance of grace were not put in place to change who or what God is or what God expects of mankind. Once again, **Malachi 3:6** informs us God changes not. Therefore, nor was Christ's sacrifice or the ordinance of grace put in place to dismiss or minimize the nature, character of any of God's commandments, judgments or His expectation of mankind to do his or her personal best to obey His word and follow His plan for them and others **(Romans Chapter 5 & 6)**.

Some may call grace a type of affirmative action. Romans 5:16-21 reports, where there is sin or imperfections found in a Christian who is trying to love God with all his or her mind, soul and heart, grace abounds much more than sin. In other words, there is no sin, past or present, except for blasphemy against the Holy Spirit, found in mankind that overrides God's grace when an individual is putting forth his or her best efforts to fulfill his or her partnership obligation to God in Christ. Once again, grace is in place to override, address and consider mankind's imperfections **(Romans Chapter 6). Grace is not in place to overlook or justify a person's desire to continue in sin**. Nor is grace in place for those who are unwilling to accept God's will for them and others. As noted, grace is for those who respect God and is in search of the truth and for those who believer in Christ. This means, although Christians are not perfect in their efforts to submit to the word and authority of God, when the Christian puts forth his or her best do so (to do what they know is right in God and to seek the truth in God), the grace offered by Christ will justify/affirm such a lifestyle as Holy. The committed and dutiful Christian is covered under the blood of Jesus.

Grace allows God to partner with mankind one-on-one through the power of the Holy Spirit, without the distractions of rituals, traditions, doctrines, and others. Grace allows individuals to live lifestyles that fulfill God's will for mankind and commands the favor of God with the help of the gift of the power of the Holy Spirit living within those who put forth their best efforts in Christ. According to **Genesis 15:6 and Romans 4:3-5,** righteous **favor is accounted to those that are committed to living a lifestyle that is pleasing to God**. A lifestyle that is pleasing to God is just what it says: An individual's behavior and disposition is committed to a lifestyle that aligns with how God would have that person honor Him (God!) and fulfill His plan for mankind unto His glory, through grace. This means, an individual living a life in God, to the best of their ability, has their righteousness affirmed by the blood of Jesus under grace. **God will meet you in the middle of your best efforts of trying to fulfill His will for your life and the lives of others**, as He did with Jesus when physically carrying the cross of crucifixion was standing in Jesus' way of fulfilling God's destiny for Jesus and mankind.

God the Father met Jesus the Son at Jesus' best efforts, when the limitations of the flesh challenged Jesus in the garden and at the cross. God did not call Jesus' fleshly weaknesses and limitations failures. God honored Jesus' commitment, best efforts and submission to God as Jesus partnered with God. God did this through others and by strengthening Jesus' faith and Spirit and Jesus' commitment to His partnership with God's will for Jesus and mankind. This partnership with God carried Jesus through and all Jesus did in His life was accounted to Him by God as righteousness.

God was not punitive toward Jesus because His flesh was too weak to physically carry the cross or because Jesus grieved the idea of Him having to endure suffering in the flesh. God recognized the position Jesus was in (a being in the flesh) and, as He will you, God acknowledged Jesus' best efforts to fulfill God's plan for Jesus and mankind. Here, God shows mankind that one's best efforts may not be enough for others but as your partner in Christ, your best efforts are enough for God and will cause God to move on your behalf. A Christian's committed best efforts are enough to command God's favor, allow God to assist him or her, allow God to account his or her actions as righteousness and move the Christian to the next level of his or her destiny in Him.

Christians, Jesus did not come to show mankind how to be perfect in the flesh because the flesh cannot be perfect. **Perfection in the flesh "is not" a commandment of God**. God commands mankind to love Him and others in Spirit and in truth and to obey His word. Note: This love is found in the truth of who God shows you who a person is and as presented in one's actions. This is also an expression of love that is defined in how God reveals how you should walk with a person **(Isiah 48:17: Psalm 32:8; & Psalm 73:24)**. Jesus came to call mankind to repentance and to **show mankind how to be perfected**, by the power of God and His grace, in the flesh through one's best efforts of trying/pressing to fulfill the will and word of God for one's self and others **(II Corinthians 12:9; Hebrews 2:10; Hebrews 10:14)**.

In His moments of weakness, Jesus exemplified how mankind would succeed and receive favor in God through

prayer and God's grace. This favor accounts one's best efforts in God as righteousness. One's best efforts not only command the favor of God, these efforts also define a lifestyle of Holiness in the sight of God. And **Holiness, "is" something that God is asking of mankind (I Peter 1:16, Leviticus 20:26).** Therefore, the primary purpose and concern God had when offering redemption to mankind, was to allow men and women to reconnect with God and each other in partnership through Christ under grace on earth! Such grace acknowledges and operates within the limitations and weaknesses of mankind. These operations go forth as God prepares Christians through the power of the Holy Spirit and their best efforts of submission, obedience and partnership for the coming of Christ.

Mankind's redemption by God through Christ takes into account the limitations of a fleshly being. This is why informed Christians know to consult God on all things (i.e., "What Did Jesus Do?"). Informed Christians are highly aware of and acknowledge the limitations and weakness of the flesh. These Christians are also aware of the fact that the success of their redemption is found in knowing that their weaknesses and limitations can only be overcome through the power and direction of God's Word through the Holy Spirit under Christ's grace. They also acknowledge that their deliverance will manifest under the authority of God, and in their ability to put forth their best efforts to love God and obey the will God, throughout their lives. In other words, Christians are well aware of the limitations of the flesh to accomplish the things of God without the guidance of God's word and the power of the Holy Spirit. Christians also seek to learn and accept and understand the nature and strength of the flesh and that there is no victory in the flesh without the discipline and the power found in God through His word and Holy Spirit. **The Christian also understands that God's task(s) for him or her and his or her partners in all things should work in conjunction with the desire to please God and live in Christ, according to God's plan of redemption for them on earth and in heaven.**

A partnership with God is one that must be acknowledge

God has obligated Himself through partnership to keep the attention of His Christian partner focused on Him and the Christian partner's preparations for Christ' return **(Mark 13:32-33; Matthew 24:35-38)**. However, the Christian's obligation in the partnership with God lies in the press to submit to God's guidance and will for them and others through the word of God and the teachings of Christ. This act of submission is accomplished through their best efforts, according to the example(s) given by Christ. Therefore, a Christian's role is to acknowledge that they have a partnership role in their relationship with God. They must also acknowledge that they need to study to show themselves knowledgeable in what is appropriate for one who is in partnership with God, obedience, and what is not appropriate for those in partnership with God as they stay the course in their commitment to God. This knowledge and preparation is done to help the Christian put forth their best efforts when choosing to submit to the authority of God according to the teachings of Christ.

God is the guiding force in the partnership between mankind and Himself. This is because God knows how to prepare for the coming of Christ. God is also the only one who knows when Christ will return **(Mark 13:32)**. Therefore, God is constantly reaching out to His Christian partners, in the Spirit of guidance, in a way that encourages His partners to move more toward living in a state of Holiness. He is encouraging His people to live in a state that allows God to have a connection with them and moves God to attribute/account the product of their lifestyle as righteousness. **God encourages His partners in Christ to put forth their best efforts to love, honor, obey and worship Him in Sprit and in Truth, not for His personal ego**. God is doing this in order to relay to His partners that living in such a state is the true expression of Holiness (a state of existence needed to commune with Him) and the definition of the righteousness that secures one's redemption unto the coming of Christ.

Understanding the meaning of salvation is critical because the meaning of true partnership is scripted within the definition of salvation. Many Christians have a poor understanding of partnership because many of them have a poor understanding of salvation. Many Christians truly do not understand or accept that **salvation is defined within the context of an explicit (clearly-defined) contract and partnership agreement between an individual and God through Christ**. They also have a poor understanding of the fact that the sanctity (quality or condition of something considered Holy) and validity (truth or realness of) of their salvation is defined within the context of their partnership with God and within this partnership they have a role to fulfill. *The Christian's ability to fulfill their role in this partnership is also what secures the Christian's salvation. **Meaning, the quality, condition, Holiness of and assurance of one's salvation is established and defined within their partnership role with God**. In order to fulfill this role, an individual must acknowledge their sinful state, repent and vow to submit to and obey the authority of

God. Their obedience is according to His word and His history under the acknowledgement of Christ's blood sacrifice. This is an act of submission that demonstrates a willingness to follow the teachings of Christ throughout the individual's lifespan.

Because many Christians truly do not understand or refuse to accept that their salvation is a partnership with God, their perception of God, salvation, relationship with God, and partnerships with others is flawed. As a result, their template for partnership is not appropriately in place for them to follow. This underdeveloped understanding of salvation and their partnership role in their salvation with God will cause many to perceive their relationship with God one-sided. These individuals are more likely to view salvation as a God effort and not as a team effort between them and God and others. This perception works against understanding how to love God, love others and establish appropriate relationships and partnerships in Christ. This poor understanding also hinders an ability to accomplish Christian goals and understand the true meaning of teamwork.

Therefore, many proclaimed Christians' focus is on expecting God to do everything to ensure the fulfillment of the promises attached to the vow of salvation. These Christians give little attention to what is expected of them, as one who vows to honor God. As a result, these individuals never learn the true meaning of accountability and teamwork. Their poor understanding of salvation and partnership with God limits their understanding of what it means to be accountable and a team player with God and others when addressing their salvation and ensuring the fulfillment of God's promises for them and those in Christ. As a result, their role in their salvation is overlooked and the conditional nature of the promises attached to the vow of salvation is not accounted for. These individuals do not know how to work on behalf of their own salvation in God, and their ability to work on behalf of or with others for salvation is flawed and limited.

This underdeveloped understanding of God, salvation, and partnership prevents many individuals from working with others to accomplish Godly goals in Christ effectively; neither can these individuals help another effectively define who they are in Christ. Many of the problems of the Church/body of Christ may be due to the fact that the house/s of God is filled with many who do not understand what it means to be a Christian. As a result, many proclaimed Christians are existing in a gray zone (state of jeopardy) or in a backslidden state of existence and are not aware of this fact. The word of God in **Hosea 4:6** reports, "My people are destroyed for a lack of knowledge." Satan is destroying mankind and the body of Christ because many of them have a poor understanding of God and their partnership role in their salvation.

We Must Live Within Necessary Boundaries

Many do not understand or accept the fact that they have an active role in securing their own salvation, beyond the act of making a proclamation of salvation. They ignore the word of God when it reports, one must work out his or her own salvation **(Philippians 2:12)**. These individuals also do not understand or accept that the definition as to how they should work out their own salvation in Christ is defined by God's word. They also do not understand that **God's word introduces mankind to and encourage everyone to live by necessary, soul-saving, boundaries. Meaning, the word of**

God has set forth boundaries; not adhering to these boundaries can lead to unnecessary life issues and/or eternal damnation, even for those who have accepted the vow of salvation.

Due to the free will of mankind, the nature of salvation, Satan's crafty nature and the weaknesses and limitations of the flesh, God must impose clearly defined boundaries for the behavior and disposition of everyone. These boundaries not only define a Christian's lifestyle, they also define how to establish relationships and partnerships. It is mankind's role to trust in God's guidelines to understand how relationships and partnerships are established, by submitting to these boundaries. These boundaries and standards are designed to help give the Christian and others a clear mindset in all things, encourage a godly lifestyle and to keep them focused on God and the coming of Christ.

Keeping a Christian focused on God is the primary role of God in His partnership with mankind. This is because, once again, the promises of God and one's readiness for the coming of Christ are manifested through one's ability to stay focused on Him (the guiding light). Some of God's boundaries and guidelines may seem drastic, but when much is at stake (your peace of mind and your soul), drastic measures are called for.

As noted, humans exist within the midst of supernatural warfare between God and Satan. This war, led by Satan, is about separating mankind from God and the values of God **(Ephesians 6:12-15)**. Satan is focused on this separation, because he knows when a person is separated from God, he can be assured of them accompanying him in hell. To be prepared for the coming of the Lord, one can let nothing separate him or her from the love of God and His light of guidance. Therefore, Christians and all who would like to return with Christ must continually ask themselves: do I show myself to love God through my actions and do I respect the guidance of God? Also, am I focused on the things of God, as reflected in my actions? They must also remind themselves not to allow their mates, sex, children, organizations, money or material things to distract them from their vow to God and His gift of salvation. This type of self-discipline anchors the Christian. Understanding God's expectation of those vowing to honor Him will help all to have a clearer understanding of God and of who and what one should partner themselves with in their life's journey.

A focused Christian will come to understand that their partners should embody characteristics similar to those of God. This means Christian partners are focused on helping their partners in business, friendship, and marriage live lives that understand and embrace the need for necessary boundaries which keep them focused on God and the return of Christ. Amen! Therefore, when another in Christ corrects a Christian, one should not be quick to conclude that the act of correction is an act of judgment or condemnation. One should consider the notion that the individual correcting them is reminding them that their actions are in conflict with God and their commitment to Christ's return. Also, know that such a reminder is done in the hope of helping them make an informed decision to repent and respect the established commands of God. However, the informing Christian should respect the choice of the individual to reject the reminder. The informing Christian should not become angry and feel a need to lash out against the rebellious Christian or unbeliever's rejection of the truth of God. God said, "... If you find one in a fault, tell them…" **(Galatians 6:1)**. This is not a command to make another do anything. Remember, **this is not your battle**, but the Lord's battle. However, everyone should **be advised to move at supernatural speed** to distance themselves from those who cannot accept or chose to oppose appropriate correction and teaching in Christ.

When gaining an understanding of what God expects of mankind, most will quickly grasp an understanding of the promises and blessings that God has in store for those who chose to adhere to His word. However, it must be said once again, when looking at those promises, one should not overlook the consequences of ignoring or opposing the governing of God, as expressed in the Bible. In doing so, one will overlook the totality of who God is and be unaware of the curses and snares that befall even the do-gooder's ability to prosper. God's word is explicit and clear about God's expectations of us, because He would have all of us make an informed and logical decision when choosing to comply or reject His will for us **(Ephesians 5:6-15)**. This is because to know God is to know God's word and decisions **(Romans 1:20)**. Also, it is important to know that God is commanded by His word, a word that will not change.

God's decisions are His fruit, **and the more an individual feeds on the fruit of God, the better he or she is able to make decisions that conform to the will of God (Galatians 5:16-26)**. Also, the more a Christian understands about God and His word, the more aware the Christian becomes of what one should expect of God and his or her partnership role with God and with others and the importance of necessary boundaries that strengthens these partnerships. The clearer one's understanding of the importance of necessary boundaries and the partnership role he or she has with God, the more complete the individual's understanding will be about the dangers of a Christian partnering with those who reject God or behave in ways that oppose God. This is because the Christian who has a partnership with God, studies the word of God, and understands the need for boundaries will show him or herself approved in the understanding, people who oppose God and/or behave in ways that are in conflict with God, may be scarred with curses. These are curses, which hinder their growth and prosperity and the growth and prosperity of those involved with them. **Note: Growth and prosperity is not limited to financial growth and prosperity.**

The Sins of Your Partner Can Affect You

There are many examples in the Bible detailing tragedies that consumed people who were associated or partnered with those who disobeyed, opposed, or trespassed against the will of God. Two prime examples of such tragedies befalling the innocent, as a result of being associated or partnered with a person who trespassed God are: (1) The details of the killing of all the members of an Achan's family as a result of his trespass against the will of God found in the book of **Joshua, Chapter 7,** and (2) found in the book of **Jonah,** when the writer details the mishaps that befell the men aboard the ship with Jonah.

There are also many examples in the Bible that detail how individuals were blessed by their association with persons who honored the commands of God. Rahab the harlot's association and partnership with the spies sent by Joshua to Jericho is a prime example **(Joshua 6:25).** The blessing of a safe voyage by the men on the ship with Paul as he was being taken to Rome to stand trial is another example of being blessed by association **(Acts Chapter 27)**. Also, being cursed by association may explain why many Christians lack growth and blessings in their lives, regardless of their diligent efforts to live according to the commandments of God. These Christians may be in association with individuals, groups or organizations that are in opposition with God and what He has for His people. As a result, they are experiencing the negative fallout of these associations.

Examining the Totality of Who a Peron is in Christ

One's associations and partners are very important and this is why God lays it all on the table concerning what it takes to have a relationship and partnership with Him. God is truly a believer in one's ability to choose. God will not make anyone conform to His way of viewing things and He does not want an individual to enter into a partnership with Him with his or her eyes closed. His example of partnership is all about the knowing. God shuns the idea of being passive, simple minded and or prone to maintaining secrets, when it comes to choosing a partner. God's perception and explanation of someone or anything is comprehensive and not partial to itching ears (what a person would like to hear). The word of God clearly conveys to its readers that it is in the full knowledge and logical understanding of God and the ways of God that God recommend one make a decision concerning Him. Therefore, all Christ centered decisions and assessments of others should also apply this principle of acknowledging the totality of who or what a person or entity is.

Also, God values one's ability to process information in a logical way. The complexity of the human brain is an example of how important one's ability to process information in a constructive manner is to God. As a result, logical thinking is another fundamental principle of living a Christian lifestyle. The Christian perception of the principle of logical thinking, as it relates to decision-making and choices, is about considering facts and then examining how those facts align with the commandments, principles, and nature of God. The logical conclusion concerning the matter of choosing to commit, associate with or partner with a subject in question will rest in how well the facts about the subject in question line up with what God expects of the subject, according to the word of God and the nature/history of what God has created. There is no speculating in this process and there is no excusing one from opposing the word and will of God because others have done so. Christians must learn to stay focused on the facts of who or what a person is in Christ, as evidenced by the decisions a person has made and his or her history, which is found in his or her creations (outcomes in life).

For example: if an individual or organization has a history of making decisions based on partial facts and lies and has a history of functioning in a web of lies, no matter how things may look at the present time, Christians should not partner with such an entity. Logical thinking and decision making in Christ is vital for the long-term growth and prosperity of a Christian. This type of thinking is one of the primary elements of a Christian's vow of partnership with God. The thinking that everything must align with the word, commandments, and history of God, according to who God has shown Himself to be through His creations, is the philosophy of the Christian lifestyle.

A Christian lifestyle is grounded in an individual's ability to accept that the ability to understand and address life issues, experience constructive psychological, emotional and sexual growth, and prosperity are found in God and His principles. These individuals also understand and accept that their ability to embrace and grow in the principles of God is solidified and made clear through the lifestyle, sacrifice, resurrection, and teachings of Jesus Christ. This is why **Romans 12:2-3** reports that living for Christ requires a renewing of one's mind. **Christians must learn to apply the principle of logical thinking in Christ and renew their minds unto the principles and thinking of God.**

One's ability to apply the principle of logical thinking in the context of God through the teaching of Jesus Christ has a defining quality of a candidate for Christian partnership. This is because if a Christian truly believes in the all-knowing God of Abraham, they must trust His word found in **Romans 8:28-32**. This Scripture tells us that God works all things out for the good of His people. Christians must then also believe that the commandments and decisions of God are in place for the good and safety of mankind and this universe. Embracing this perception should not be difficult for most, if considered closely. This is because many of the consequences associated with positive (not in conflict with will of God) or negative (in conflict with God/sinful) behaviors are self-evident.

A Clear Example

For example: **I Corinthians 6:19-20** reports that the body is the temple of the Holy Spirit and men and woman should not participate in anything that is harmful to the body. Therefore, let us examine the simple and popular act of smoking a cigarette or marijuana. The negative consequences of smoking become quite clear to most from their first puff. This is because most people choke or begin coughing when they first inhale a puff from a cigarette or marijuana. The coughing appears to be the bodies attempt to discourage the individual from continuing to engage in an act that is offensive and harmful to the body.

If examined closely, the lips of a smoker become discolored soon after they begin smoking cigarettes. The discoloration of the lips occurs when the cigarette or marijuana releases heat and chemicals during the smoking process. The heat and chemicals released from smoking will cause damage to the skin. The discoloration of the smokers' lips is the visual indication of the damage being done. This discoloration generally manifests in fair or light skinned individuals as red or as a dark ruby red lip color and in darker skinned individuals in the form of black lips.

The harmful effects of smoking leave a mark on the participant and serves as a constant reminder to the individual and others that he or she has participated in an act that is harmful to their body. It also serves as a reminder that the individual has or may continue engaging in an act that has stripped them of the beauty of their natural God-given lip color. This discoloration can also serve as a reminder of the broken instructions from God to do no harm to one's body.

By now, most are familiar with many of the dramatic long-term negative consequences associated with smoking cigarettes and marijuana.

Jesus came to offer/gift mankind the opportunity to choose to re-establish their relationship with God. Once again, the salvation offered by Jesus Christ will not take away mankind's free will to choose, to make choices, whether these choices are for or against the things of God **(John 12:47-48)**. God decided to give mankind a free will and His word will not be made void. Therefore, Jesus can and will do almost anything for an individual except make them submit to the authority of God. Also, Jesus' submission to the cross will not take the place of an individuals' willingness/free will to choose to accept God's gift of salvation, to love God and obey God. Jesus did not come to stand in for one's willingness to love God, accept God's gift of salvation, submit to the authority of God or retain God's gift of salvation once he or she has accepted it. Jesus came to offer mankind the redemption of God by calling mankind to repentance, and to fulfill what God had already established in His laws **(Matthew 5:17-19)**. Mankind's commitment to God and His laws is about personal choice and not about "making" mankind submit to Him. Therefore, Jesus did not come to make anyone submit to God.

God is not about making mankind do anything or having His people impose His will on others or kill for His sake. Due to mankind's selfish disposition and Satan's manipulative ways, there will be wars and Christians and others will have to fight mentally, emotionally, physically, and spiritually. This is not the will of God and the taking of another's free will or life is not a noble act from God's perspective. **Deuteronomy 32:29** reports God saying, "He (God) kills and makes alive." God does not need anyone's help to defend Him or implement His vengeance **(Hebrews 10:30; Deuteronomy 32:35; Romans 12:19)**.

Depriving others of free will and the killing of others are a byproduct of selfishness and sin. Where there is selfishness and sin, the door for war is opened. Psychological, physical, and spiritual warfare and chaos is rooted in the workings of selfishness and sin. When selfishness and sin is present, lies, oppression, death, and destruction flourish. Therefore, Jesus came to perfect mankind's ability (free will) to choose not to engage in selfishness and sin (to resist sin) and to do what God would have them do (deny self). In this choice, God is also asking mankind not only to submit to the authority of God/accept God's gift of salvation, but to also stay committed to this choice. Jesus came to empower mankind to choose to accept God's desire for them to repent, love God, submit to His authority, love others, and stay committed to the authority of God and not to impose, oppress, take away or kill another's free will to choose God's will for mankind.

Jesus can and will teach you why and how to choose God. He can show you the way to God, and He can empower an individual's ability through the Holy Spirit to perfect this choice. Through the power of the Holy Spirit, Jesus will even manipulate the environment for which an individual is operating in to help an individual understand his or her need to submit and stay submitted to the will of God. Neither Jesus, nor the salvation offered by God through Jesus Christ, will make an individual obey the will of God or submit to, or stay submitted to the authority of God. This is neither the will of God, the role of Christ nor the role of the Holy Spirit. **Mark 8:34 states**, "Whosoever "will" come after me…"

The security of one's salvation is found in one's willingness to love, embrace, commit and submit to the will of God (Matthew 23:37; Revelation 22:17). The fulfillment of these elements in the life journey of a Christian is the work of the righteous and will produce good and righteous fruit in the life of that Christian. Yes, Jesus can do all things, but Jesus will not take on an individual's personal need to love God and submit to the authority of God. Once again, this is not the calling of Christ. This, an individual must do for him or herself. To make a person love God, submit and stay submitted to the will of God is not in the design of God for mankind. Jesus came to fulfill the will of God for mankind, not add to it or take away from it **(Deuteronomy 4:2; Matthew 5:17-19)**.

Jesus' life also serves as an example of the fact that a relationship with God is a partnership that requires anointed (ordained by God) teamwork, which is driven by the Holy Spirit. Jesus' life/earthly role and His relationship/partnership with God were about loving God and submitting to God's will for Himself and for mankind **(Philippians 2: 4-8)**. Now, God's role in His partnership with Jesus during Jesus' life journey was conditionally based on Jesus' ability to fulfill His (Jesus) role in the partnership to the best of His ability in the flesh. The two were working hand in hand with the power of the Holy Spirit to accomplish the same goal, redemption for mankind and Jesus' crown of glory (both God's will). The trinity of partnership was at work for our redemption then, as it is today.

Embedded in God's role of His partnership with Jesus, a characteristic of all appropriate partners, is God's willingness to acknowledge and address the totality of what it took for

Jesus to fulfill His mission as a fleshly being on earth. This included acknowledging and addressing the challenges of the weaknesses of the flesh Jesus experienced on earth. God also acknowledged how these weaknesses affected and could possibly cripple an individual who is trying to accomplish a Godly mission. As noted, God addressed these weaknesses in how He structured the principles and statutes of His grace. God's principles and statutes of grace did not change God's expectations of mankind or excuse mankind from his/her partnership role with God in Christ. However, they were designed to affirm an individual's **best efforts** to submit, obey, and love Him and others in Christ.

CHAPTER EIGHT

The Conditional Nature of Salvation

Jesus came to save all who are willing to pick up their cross, follow Him and choose to obey God, as Jesus did, until the end **(Matthew 16:24-26; Luke 9:23; Philippians 2:8; Ezekiel 33:10-33)**. As noted, the gift of salvation embodies not only a partnership between an individual and God, but also an explicit contract between them. This is a contract between each individual and God with the expectation that the individual and God will fulfill their part.

Leviticus Chapter 26, Exodus 19:5, Ezekiel Chapter 33, Jeremiah 7: 23 all depict the nature of God when it comes to being in a relationship with mankind. In these scriptures, God vows/contracts Himself conditionally to be the God of individuals who vow/contract themselves to obey His will. Please, focus! Therefore, following the understanding that the nature of who and what God is and how God operate does not change, one can logically conclude that a relationship with God, as in the history of who He is, **the vow of salvation is contractual and comes with a set of conditions**.

Remember, redemption through Jesus was not offered by God to change the nature of God or God's expectations of mankind. There is no wrong to be found in God or in what He expects out of His creation. The redemption of God for mankind grew out of God's love and mercy toward mankind. God's redemption was offered to mankind as an opportunity, through grace, to those who are willing to accept God's established conditions, as Adam and Eve did prior to sin, of how one must behave in order to have an appropriate relationship with and be beholden (bound by obligation) by a Holy and Just God.

God's redemption is about giving mankind another opportunity to experience a loving and nurturing interpersonal relationship with their Creator and others in the Spirit of God and in the Spirit of God's truth that must be acknowledged and adhered to for the good of the individual and God. This is a truth that cannot be one sided or idealistic, nor can it be about just feelings. Is this not what true relationships are all about, two or more beings learning to communicate, share, and love one another within the context of each other's truth and needs?

Operating in Holiness

The truth of God is, He cannot and will not function outside of Holiness. Therefore, mankind must understand, acknowledge and accept, that to have a relationship with God he or she must learn how to operate within the context of Holiness. This is why God requested of mankind in **I Peter 1:16, Leviticus 20:26, Leviticus 11:44-45** to be Holy because He is Holy. **I Peter 1:14-15** reports that God is calling Christians to move away from former lust and ignorance and do their best to be Holy in all their conduct. This means, in order to have an appropriate relationship with God, mankind must learn to discipline themselves to function and operate within a lifestyle that has boundaries, laws, and judgments that are Holy and are obligated to God and their safety and protection.

Therefore, God would like mankind to know through Jesus' life, teaching, death, resurrection and the history of God's judgments, commands and actions: He (God) is bound. **God is** bound in Holiness and contracted and obligated to those who are also bound and obligated to Him in Holiness. Holiness is attributed to those who are faithful unto God through grace. Understanding the characteristics of God and how God operates is important. Also, the knowledge that God can and does function on more than one level of existence is important. He operates in the heavenly plain and the earthly plain of existences and who and what He is does not change on either plain. He is Holy, and what is required of Him and how others must relate to him to experience a favorable relationship with Him will not change from one plain to another.

Mankind must begin to understand their redemption is highlighted by their ability to stay focused on living a lifestyle through grace that allows them to bond with God through the reality of God's Holiness. Christians must live Holy to have an appropriate relationship with God. This means the reality of an appropriate and true relationship with God is found in Holiness. God is Holy by nature and cannot change. Therefore, a relationship between mankind and God is found in the transformation of an individual's ability to move further and further away from a state of being carnal/fleshly and self-centered, to an entity which is God-centered, within the context of Holiness. **This transformation is made possible by Jesus' sacrifice which evokes the statutes of God's grace when an individual puts forth his/her best efforts in Christ. Holiness is accomplished through one's best effort to acknowledge, love, and consider the truth of God, and to consider the truth of who and what God truly is, as reflected in His actions and the creations He has made (His judgments and His commands).**

Mankind's ability to operate in Holiness is found in the ability to commit to living a lifestyle that displays, in spirit and in truth, one's best efforts to operate within the laws, judgments, and boundaries of God's existences through grace. Meaning, the nature of this transformation is considerate of the needs of the Christian's most valuable partner (God). The authenticity of a person's willingness to commit to this transformation will also define the genuineness and soundness of a relationship between God and everyone that is willing to accept the gift of salvation, as they vow to partner with God for their redemption in Christ.

If a person chooses not to commit to a lifestyle of Holiness, it is his or her choice. However, it must be understood, the standard of Holiness that must exist within a relationship between God and mankind will not change and is a requirement for all of God's relationships on earth and in heaven. To walk in Holiness, one must learn how to operate within the statutes of grace. Operating in grace requires an individual to exist in a state of prayer that embody a desire to submit to the will of God and Godly guidance through the Holy Spirit. This is why the word of God, in **Thessalonians 5:17** states, "… mankind should pray without ceasing." Prayer will help keep an individual in a more receptive and humble state toward the will of God. Also one's daily walk in grace, requires a willingness to acknowledge and repent of one's daily acts and/or behavior that work against the word of God and the teachings of Christ. This is because behaviors that work against the word of God will hinder one's ability to allow Christ to increase in them. These behaviors hinder one's ability to grow in one's understanding of the things of God and live in the truth of Christ.

Christians must transform from operating from one's personal perspective to a perspective that is more inclusive and God centered. Most do not acknowledge a need for change in their lives or anything, if he or she does not believe, cannot comprehend or understand that there is a possible need for change. When one acknowledges and understand the need for them to change a given behavior in Christ, one maybe more prone/inclined to move away from engaging in a given behavior. One is also more likely to work effectively at repenting of various sinful behavior when one understands how destructive these behaviors are toward them and others. This is why God is invested in mankind gaining an understanding of all things.

Prayer and a willingness to repent will beckon/cause/commissions the Holy Spirit to help an individual gain the understanding needed to help him/her move away from being self-willed. The Holy Spirit will also strengthen one's ability to resist operating in behaviors that are unacceptable in Christ and do not consider their primary partner, God. This state of repentance also activates the statutes of grace, which ushers an individual into a state of Holiness. Holiness is a state that mankind must exist in to commune with God. Holiness is the permanent state of God's existence. So, if an individual cannot commune with God in Holiness on earth or does not see the necessity to seek and press to operate in Holiness on earth, this individual must accept that he/she cannot reside with God in heaven, because one must operate in Holiness in heaven as well.

To Continue in Sin is not a Reflection of One Who is Operating in Holiness

Although God's grace is highlighted in His willingness to acknowledge and accept mankind's repentance of sins within the context of salvation, or when it comes to a person's willingness to keep his or her vow of salvation, continually repenting for sinful behavior without any intent and/or effort to change (a desire to move away from sin) is not pleasing to God **(Romans 6:1-4)**. One's desire or willingness to continue in sin is a reflection of someone who is not in a covenant with God according to Christ and are not covered under the statutes of grace. This is also someone who is not operating within a state of Holiness. These individuals are operating in the world. They are in a state of sin and are in a backslidden state. A backslidden state exist when a saved person turns his/her back on his/her relationship with God and have chosen to live their life in their own way. These individuals have chosen to forge his/her own path by embracing his/her own personal desires and perceptions, embracing the ways of the world and/or embracing sinful ways, behaviors, and relationships. Worldly things and ways of the world have priority in their lives. These are also individuals who will distort and twist the word of God to fit their personal perspective as to how one should operate in Christ. They will not take into account the whole word of the Lord but pick and choose portions of God's word that they can try to use to falsify the meaning of the word of God to fit their agenda. Therefore, the Spirit of God is not in a person who operates in this way, nor can it be **(John 14:17)**. These individuals conduct themselves in a way that is not indicative of one who would like to be in an appropriate and healthy relationship with a Holy and righteous God.

One's desire to continue in sin and is unwilling to receive and accept the truth of God's word, although they may have a willingness to repent of sin, is not one who is conducting him/herself according to God's plan for His partner(s) in Christ. This type of commitment is similar to the commitment of a spouse who asks his or her spouse to forgive them for infidelity after each act of infidelity. The spouse continues in infidelity and shows no intent to be faithful but goes through the motions of trying to appease the spouse when he/she is caught engaging in this behavior or this behavior causes a problem for the cheater. Also, God is not pleased with the perception that it is okay for one to continue in sin, as long as he or she repents. If this was so, God would not have commanded His people to abstain from every form of evil in **I Thessalonians 5:22**. The word of God, His judgments, commandments, actions and the history of who God is, clearly depict God as one who would have all who are willing to accept His gift of salvation; love God and stay committed to God and His will for mankind lifelong.

However, In **Jeremiah 3:12-14 and Luke 9:62,** although expressed a little differently, these scriptures clearly address the idea that a relationship with God depicts having an understanding between an individual and God that require the individual to continue in God and honor God as the authority in their life, forever. These scriptures address how God perceives His interpersonal relationships with mankind. They attempt to help all who read them understand, those who would like to have a relationship with God are expected to accept the authority of God throughout their relationship with Him, lifelong.

Luke 9:62 also addresses the kingdom of God and the fact that one who walks away from the salvation offered by Christ is not worthy of the kingdom of God. **I Corinthians 6:9-10** reports, "… the unrighteous will not inherit the kingdom of God." Both books, **Jeremiah and Luke,** clearly convey to the reader, an individual can choose to reject the authority of God at any point, even after having a meaningful relationship with God. Also, according to these scriptures, distractions and a change in one's commitment to their relationship with God and/or commitment to the will of God will cause friction and/or disconnect between them and God. In **Luke 9:57-62** Christ reports that this disconnect can jeopardize an individual's ability to join Him in the kingdom of God. So, if you can't join God in His kingdom (the afterlife) one must ask: "Where will you be?"

The aforementioned scriptures in **Jeremiah and Luke** should help Christians understand that an established relationship and/or state of salvation, in most cases, is not the be-all and end-all when it comes to being prepared for the return of Christ. Here comes the eye-opener! These scriptures also address the fact that once God's offer of salvation has been accepted and embraced by an individual and the individual is in a relationship/partnership with God, at any point, the individual can renege or pull away from this commitment by omission or commission.

This act of reneging will show itself through indifference toward and/or a continuous display of having a rebellious and defiant disposition against the commandments and authority of God (sin). Even if a person continuously repents of their sinful behavior, living a Christ-driven lifestyle is about choosing to discipline one's self to submit and stay submitted to the things of God. At some point, one must resist the desire to operate outside of the will of God and make every effort to abide within His will for mankind. At some point, to be with God, one must choose to show himself or herself as one who loves God as an act of commitment and devotion. This is why the word of God in **John 14:15** reports, if you love me, obey me, and **John 14:23** reports to love Jesus is to obey His teaching. **This love that God has for and expects from mankind toward Him and others is an expression of commitment and faithfulness in action**.

To have a meaningful relationship with God, at some point, Christians must resist the desire to throw God under the bus when they have an impulse or itch for self-gratification that leads to sin. At some point, mankind must learn to endure temptation that they may be approved to receive the crown of life, which the Lord has promised to those who love Him **(James 1: 12-15)**. Don't forget, it was the sin (their unwillingness to obey God) of Adam and Eve (God's people), His first creation, two who God had a long history with, that separated them from God.

God was so pleased with His creation of Adam and Eve that Heed proclaim, their creation was "very good" **(Genesis 1:31).** It was the sin of God's very good creation, which hampered their relationship with God and opened the door for eternal damnation to be an option for mankind. Now, you don't think you are better than Adam and Eve, do you? Therefore, history of who God is and how He operates makes it evident, that sin (unwillingness to obey God)/rebellion against the commands and authority of God can damage and can destroy one's relationship and connection with God unto damnation. Many Christians don't want to consider the fact that sin and one's continuation in sin, the unsaved and those who have accepted Christ's redemption, can end up in hell. This is why God said in **Isaiah 5:14**, "… **hell has enlarged herself that he/she who rejects the will of God, shall descend into it.**" II Peter 2:4-22 reminds us, if God did not spare the angels when they sinned, but He cast them in to hell and committed them into chains of darkness. How much more will He do to those who forsake the right way and go astray to follow the way of unrighteousness? **II Peter Chapter 2 and 3**, clearly convey God's position on the backslider and one's willingness to continue in sin.

The salvation of Christ gives mankind the ability to reconnect and offers a better opportunity through grace (through helping mankind in their ability to stay the course in God) to maintain a physical and Spiritual relationship with God, which was broken when Adam and Eve sinned. Christ's redemption does not nullify God's word found in **Hebrews 12:14**, "… those who are not Holy (who are not operating under grace to conform to the will of God to the best of one's ability) will not see the Lord." Also, **Matthew 24:13** reports, "He that endures to the end, shall be saved", and **Romans 2:12** reports that the "… doers of the laws of God shall be justified."

Salvation is also an established partnership between an individual and God through God's grace. But, the free will of mankind to choose to maintain or continue in a relationship/partnership with God through Christ is not nullified through the salvation of Christ. Human beings are free agents **(Revelation 22:17). However, it is a state of submission and obedience which allows God to order the individual's steps to fulfill the plan that God has for him or** her on earth and in heaven. II Corinthians 10:18 states, "For not he who commends himself is approved, but whom the Lord commends." Submission and obedience also builds character and the style of discipline needed for Christians to allow God to fulfill His plan for their life, the life of others, and in the lives of the people they partner with.

A Christian's inability to receive the fullness of the salvation of the Lord is similar to a parent having a plan to bless their beloved child but discovers that the child has a disposition that is oppositional and/or the child is engaging in behaviors that should not be rewarded. Therefore, the child's disposition and/or unacceptable behavior has tied the hands of a just and responsible parent in their willingness and ability to reward and bless the child (Jeremiah 5:25). The child's disposition and behavior has tied the hands of parents who are working to help their children think and operate in ways that will help ensure the child's safety and wellbeing.

Christians must begin to understand that when they participate in sin, they bind the hands of a righteous and just God who is bound by His word in Holiness. Also, one's continuation in sin will bind the hands of a Holy and just God's ability to help them avoid eternal damnation. This is why God's word in I Timothy 2:4 reports that God's desire is for all mankind to be saved. However, God's desire requires cooperation from a free will human being; a being that is empowered with the ability to submit to the God's desires for them or not. Additionally, God's word reports, the unrighteous will not enter the Kingdom of Heaven (Revelation 22:15; I Corinthians 6:9-10). The unrighteous are those who refuse to be bound (by omission or commission) to a lifestyle of Holiness under the ordinance of grace. This is an ordinance that is in place to help an individual live a lifestyle in holiness. How much more plainly written can the word of God be in these scriptures? One must press to move away from sin and to embrace the word of God and the teachings of Christ to be saved and ready for the coming of Christ.

Christians must also accept that salvation is much more than heartfelt feelings of love about Jesus and Him being the Son of God. Feelings of love and acknowledgement may be the beginning and end all of salvation, if the individual in question die, like the thief on the cross, at the point of receiving salvation or establishing their vow/contract with God. However, when salvation is granted, a vow/contract is entered into between the individual and God. A vow/contract is all about the expectation that one will fulfill the terms and intent of the vow/contract, if possible. This is why **Ecclesiastes 5:5** reports, "It is better not to make a vow than to make one and not fulfill it." **Ecclesiastes 5:4** reports, God expects the individual, as He will, to make every effort to fulfill his/her part of the commitment (researching the nature of what it means to have an appropriate partnership with God and to allow God to govern their lives accordingly).

The fulfillment of one's contract of salvation requires work, action, and the production of fruit. We know this because the Scriptures found in **James 2:17-26** reports that faith without works is dead. **Matthew 7:13-20** reports that by their fruits you shall know them and **Philippians 2: 12-13** Paul instructs the saints to work out their own salvation with fear and trembling. Also, let us not forget, **Revelation 2:26,** which addresses God's people as being **overcomers in the works of God until the end**. These Scriptures are clearly trying to convey to the people of God that having a relationship with

Him duties them to partner with Him in fulfilling the plan He has for their lives and the lives of others.

These Scriptures not only help us to understand that salvation is a byproduct of a partnership and contract but continuing in God is a maintenance process that is not stagnant and requires work. Why is it that most Christians do not have a problem understanding that one should keep their houses orderly and clean, but find it difficult to accept that one should also keep their lives orderly and clean? Many will invite any old thing into their lives, but when it comes to their houses, they are all about keeping the filth out. The aforementioned biblical principles and scriptures are in place to help Christians understand that salvation requires one to press toward living a clean lifestyle in Christ, to the best of one's ability, and to produce Godly fruit. This means, the lifestyle and fruit of a Christian should reflect the values and principles of God, as seen in Christ. Meaning, the very same values and principles and fruit that were embodied and produced by the earthly life of Jesus Christ should be seen in a Christian's lifestyle. The fruit of a tree is the byproduct of the life and health of the tree. If you are a Christian, you will press to produce Christ-like fruit/works and behavior.

Also, the quality of the fruit produced will reflect the state/health of the tree/one's salvation. If one's fruit is limited to believing in Jesus and having heartfelt feelings of love about Jesus, one should conclude that this person needs more of Jesus to produce a better quality of Godly fruit. These types of people need a better understanding of Jesus and His obedient Godly mission. They need an understanding that helps them move beyond just having loving feelings about Jesus. Their understanding should embody the word of God in **Matthew 16:24**. In this scripture, Christ commands His follows to follow His example. This is an example that asks all to submit to the authority of God in obedience, as He does. The love of Jesus is not just in your heart or your feelings; it is in your **walk/lifestyle, choices** and the **fruit** you bear!

The Fruit You Bear

A well-rounded, devoted Christian will produce quality Christ-like fruit that is empowered with the word of God and can stand the test of time. A weak neglectful Christian and/ or backslider will produce malformed fruit and/or attempt to fake godly fruit. Malformed Christian fruit may sometimes have qualities that resemble the fruit produced by a devoted Christian, but when examined closely, one will find their fruit cannot stand up to the word of God in the way that it should. Malformed Christian fruit will lack the strength and power to resist the workings of evil and survive the test of time. Also, this type of fruit will lack the appropriate level of impartial love toward all mankind, especially those in the body of Christ. **Fake fruit will shatter under pressure and under the word of God**. Fake fruit cannot be supported by the word of God. Meaning, fake fruit is not biblically sound. Fake fruit is used and incorporated into Satan's schemes to get others to rationalize why it is okay to break or twist the laws of God and continue in sin.

The Christian's ability to apply the word of God to his or her actions, environment, and actions of others is noteworthy. It is this ability that will help them avoid pitfalls, frustration, and losses in Christ. It will also help them avoid engaging in inappropriate partnerships. Note: Babes in Christ, those who have a poor foundation in Christ, and those who are working through interpersonal issues in Christ may produce fruit that may look malformed. However, as long as these individuals are putting forth their best efforts in Christ as they press to grow in Christ, their fruit will present as well defined in the sight of God and will be counted to them as righteousness by God **(Mark 12:41-44)**. However, a telling characteristic that distinguishes these individuals from the uncommitted is seen when these individuals find themselves in error. These individuals will not display rebellion against the word of God and will seek to conform to God's word, unlike those who do not honor God.

Jesus' Example

Therefore, Christians do not view salvation as a one-time commitment and they know that the blood of Jesus is not about covering the sins of individuals who want to continue in sin. The blood of Jesus is about all that Jesus came into the world to do as mandated by God. Jesus' bloodshed is about all that Jesus endured for mankind as a result of God's will for Him and mankind's redemption, including His crucifixion. Jesus' redeeming blood offers grace for those who contract themselves to and express a lifelong commitment to the guidance of God.

Compounded with having a clear understanding of what salvation is and the fact that Jesus' mission for God required His devotion, commitment and partnership, Christians must also accept that Jesus' mission on earth serves as their example. Also, they should know, Jesus' example is God's expectation of the Christian. Although a man could never die for anyone's sins as Jesus did, God does expect believers to partner with Him and others in their best efforts to follow the same example of acknowledgement, love, submission, commitment, devotion, obedience, discipline and personal sacrifice as displayed by Jesus.

Jesus' example defines how a Christian should strive to partner and walk with God. Accepting the fact of who Jesus is, what He did, how He did it, why He did what He did and the fact that He is the example a Christian should follow is an important growth factor for everyone. This understanding will help mankind know they can appeal to the favor of God, a favor that will adorn the Christian on earth and in heaven, as it does Jesus. This understanding will also help Christians accept that Jesus' relationship with God is embedded in a loving partnership that establishes and embraces a set of conditions. These conditions contracted Jesus to fulfill all that God expected of Him in the flesh, the joyful aspects of living in the flesh (His relationships with family and friends and the joy He had when sharing the word of God) and the painful (rejection, homelessness, physical pain, suffering and crucifixion).

As a partner with God for the redemption of mankind, Jesus also needed to inform and confront others about the detriment of sin. Jesus' ministry was not only required to share the good news of His sacrifice and God's offer of redemption. Jesus was also obligated, as we are, to share with mankind the negative consequences of engaging in sin. He was obligated to inform mankind of how engaging in concepts, ideologies, behaviors and partnerships that are contrary to the will of God pains and hurts God and will cheat them out of God's plan of redemption. Paul depicts this in **Galatians 2:11-21** when Paul had to address Peter and the leaders of the Jewish congregation about their hypocrisy. Jesus was contracted, as we are, to bring to mankind the full gospel (the promises, blessing, commandments, judgments and consequences) of what God has for mankind and expect of mankind. A ministry in Christ that does not share with mankind the full gospel of God would have caused Jesus, as it will all Christians, to fail in His ability to fulfill the plan God has for Him and mankind.

A Relationship with God and the Favor of God is Conditional

Jesus was committed to God and contracted and devoted to partnering with God. We also see God address His connection with mankind in the context of a contract in the Scriptures found in **II Chronicles 7:12-22 and Leviticus Chapter 26 and in Jeremiah Chapter 4** when God informed the children of Israel of His relationship and expectations of them through His word: "**IF.**" This **"IF"** clearly implies that God's acknowledgement and continual recognition belong to those that love and honor Him according to His laws, commands, and His will (His conditions). God's favor is a byproduct of a lifestyle that adheres to Godly conditions in the context of appropriate love and partnership toward the needs of God and others in Christ. We also see the conditional nature of having a relationship with God in **Romans Chapter 2,** where the word of God defines the true meaning of who will be considered just in the sight of God. Here, the word of God clearly reports that **it is the doers of God's word/law**; those that conduct themselves within the laws and commands of God, **who will be justified by God. Now, don't think you are going to enter the kingdom of God without being justified**.

This **"IF"** also implies that although God has a general unconditional love for all mankind, His deep love and acknowledgement belongs to those who love, honor, obey, and respect Him and His needs and His will for them and others. It belongs to those who partner with Him to love others and work toward helping Him fulfill His will for mankind within the context of His word and His will. Here, God shows us that a relationship with Him is conditional and involves having a partnership with Him that requires effort, discipline and duty on behalf of all who choose to accept His gift of redemption.

God's favor and relationship with mankind has always been conditional. We see this in the garden when God clearly expressed to Adam and Eve, life in the garden was defined by their willingness to choose to obey His command, not to eat fruit from the forbidden tree. God cannot lie, so He will keep His end of the partnership and contract. Jesus is in partnership with God. Jesus' partnership with God produces workings which are in accordance with the command of God. The salvation Jesus offers is about obeying God's command for Him and extending Himself to people who are willing to repent and respect God's state of Holiness and are willing to partner with and be governed by God **(Revelation 22:17)**.

God's will is the way. This is why when Jesus was in the Garden of Gethsemane **(Luke 22:39-46),** struggling with having to endure the physical crucifixion of the cross He said, "Not my will, but Your (God's) will be done." This Christian understanding of what it means to truly be in Christ and be a partner with God will help shape the Christ driven Christian's template of what it means to be a true partner in business, friendships, and marriage. These Christians learn from God, their root relationship/partnership builder, that **when one enters into an agreement, one is expected to consider and respect the individual they are agreeing with and the**

conditions of the agreement. They also understand that all partners should be vested/committed to fulfilling the expectation of the agreement, to the best of each partner's ability.

Christian partners learn from God that it takes work and it is important to work at maintain a partnership. They learn that it is also important to work at producing quality godly fruit as individuals and as a team when faced with any task. They learn from Jesus' example, not to give up during difficult times. Christians understand and follow God's word found in **Ecclesiastes 5:5**, which informs us, "It is better not to make a vow than to make a vow and break the vow." These Christians also know that the fulfillment of a vow/contract is the byproduct of the combined efforts of all partners involved (you, your partner(s), and God through God's grace). The Christian partner's template is, "I have a constructive role in all of my partnerships." As a result, these partners are more than willing to fulfill their role of actively participating in the success of any partnership, may it be for business, friendship or marriage.

Individuals who view information about the expectations of God as a beat down also do not appear to grasp the fact that one cannot maintain a partnership with God while operating outside of God's will. Operating outside of the will of God is the act of existing in a state of sin. God can have "nothing" to do with sin. Once again, being a partner with sin or partnering with one that openly or secretly continually engages in sinful behavior is not an option for God. To engage or not to engage in sin is a choice for mankind, not God! For God is righteous and Holy and He expects those He partners with to be Holy (striving to put forth one's best efforts to operate within the will of God through grace) **(I Peter 1:15-16)**.

Not Perfect, but Committed

One cannot go any further without addressing the following questions: Is a person who is committed to salvation perfect and will do no wrong? The answer is, No! Does this mean a committed Christian will always walk within the will of God? The answer to this question is also, No! However, a true Christian person will do everything in his or her power to show God he or she loves Him and is willing to maintain his or her commitment of submission and obedience to the will of God. Also, once a Christian who is functioning outside of God's will comes into the knowledge of, or one might say, comes to his or her right mind; as David did in **II Samuel Chapter 12** when the prophet Nathan informed David of his sinful behaviors, that their behavior opposes the will of God, he or she will repent. These individuals will not get defensive and say, "Don't judge me: all have fallen short." These individuals will also pray and seek God's strength through the power of the Holy Spirit, to resubmit to God's will and make every effort to sin no more.   **However, these individuals will not try to justify or rationalize their sinful behavior as Saul did in the Old Testament, nor will they seek to continue in sin! God forbid Romans 6:1-2.**

A person who responds to being called out for misbehavior with repentance and makes every effort to resist continuing in that sin, qualifies for Jesus' covering of grace. God's grace is filled with His consideration and mercy. A Christian who values his or her relationship with God is not marked by a spirit of rebellion, but is quick to adhere to God's will for him

248

or her to the best of his or her ability. These people value their partnership with God and do not want to intentionally or unintentionally jeopardize their relationship or harm their partnership with God. These individuals are well versed in the scripture found in **Proverbs 14:12** that reminds us there is a way that seems right to a man, but that way is not right, because it is not the will of God. These individuals will accept that they need to work on improving their walk in Christ and not try to justify their bad behavior.

Note: There are many who are working through issues of abuse, and emotional, psychological, and developmental issues which make it difficult for them to turn from dysfunctional and/or sinful behavior patterns with ease. Cases such as these should be addressed with personal prayer and united prayer with Christians who are called and anointed to address and help others with these issues. These are individuals who are empowered by the name of Jesus, due to their calling and commitment to Christ, to rebuke and help others work through psychological, emotional, and demonic strongholds.

Note: Christians who are called to address those with issues such as these do not deal with this task by minimizing God's word as to the sin of the individual's behavior(s). The goal of these missionaries are focused on helping individuals work through their issues within the context of God's word, within the Spirit of God and within the truth of the situation and God's will for the situation. This is a focus that seeks to help these individuals understand God's position concerning their behavior(s) or thought patterns and the destructive nature of engaging in such behavior(s) or thought patterns for them, others and the body of Christ.

Through their relationship with God, devoted believers have developed a partnership with God that inspires growth in their ability to love God and others and in their willingness to receive God's will for them and others. A diligent walk with God has taught them that psychological, emotional, and demonic strongholds exist and a person can operate and live in a state of dysfunction and sin and feel comfortable doing so. **This is an insight that will help them resist the notion that one's feelings or comfort level justify or legitimizes a behavior or ideology. These individuals have learned and are highly aware of the fact, [sin] can feel real good to the flesh.**

However, Christians must understand that salvation and being in a relationship/partnership with God is not just a feeling, but a choice and is a lifelong commitment that is not defined by one's comfort zone, but by doing the right thing in God. Christians should at least do what they know is right in God and be willing to learn how to improve one's relationship with God and others. **Salvation is a conscious experience of faith, love and knowledge of God that brings about a committed endurance and growth toward the things of God (the focus of a Christian's affection).** This is so, even if the individual is not comfortable with a given position or does not always understand God's reasoning for a given position. One's ability to gain such wisdom from a relationship/partnership with God is needed and will work for the good and longevity for them, others, and for any partnership.

Note: Sinful behavior is not always about behaviors many may perceive as negative, but sinful behavior has everything to do with not obeying God through His word, God's will and the precedents set through the history of who God is and what

He has made. Many behaviors, whether they seem negative or positive, can be defined as sinful when an individual is operating in these behaviors outside of God's plan for them. Therefore, Christians must seek to be in tune with God and His word on a personal and spiritual level.

For example, if a person is extending him or herself to a group of people and God did not command him or her to do so, the person may be operating outside of the will of God (sinning). In the book of **Numbers Chapter 20,** God instructed Moses to speak to the rock and Moses struck the rock, God accounted his behavior as an act that failed to follow God's instructions, (i.e., sin) and punished Moses accordingly. Although Moses' act of striking the rock would appear okay or even appropriate to most, Moses disobeyed God and his act of striking the rock and not speaking to it was not in the plan that God had for His people; a plan that was designed to address various needs and doubts of the people. Therefore, this was sin in the sight of God. Yes, the people of God make mistakes and are known to sin when they lose sight of their Christian goal or are distracted, for whatever reason, from the commands of God. Therefore, Christians must think, consider, and consult God before they act to ensure that their acts will not cause them and others to falter. This expectation maybe difficult for many, but it is God's way. Therefore, it is the appropriate Christian way and it does not require perfection. Once again, living for God is not about perfection, but about commitment, focus and discipline.

Now, to better empower the Christian in their efforts to partner with appropriate Christian partners, there must be a clear understanding of a person who accepts the vow of salvation and decide to operate outside of the will of God.

Within this understanding of a person proclaiming salvation but operating outside of the will of God, Christians must never forget **Deuteronomy 7:9**. This Scripture reports: **God keeps covenant with those that keep covenant with Him**. The backslider and their lifestyles are marked by sin and the rejection of the fullness of Christ/covenant of God and/or display an ambiguous disposition toward Christ/word of God. They have a lot of doubt and half-hearted behavior toward God and the things of God. These individuals may also be in full rebellion against the things of God. In other words, a backslider has shown him/herself not to keep covenant with God, as displayed by their neglectful and/or rebellious disposition toward God and His word.

The Backslider

There is a difference between a Christian that makes every effort to please God but has periods of not being at their best in God and a backslider. Some individuals may be in a slump, experiencing difficulty accepting God's truth/growth periods, and are going through family or relationship issues, but these individuals are not in a rebellious state and although troubled, have not abandoned their commitment to their vow of salvation. They also do not make excuses as to why it is okay to reject elements of God's word. However, a backslider is in full disconnect with God and is in a rebellious mode against the things of God. Their state of neglect or rebellion may be aggressive, passive or passive-aggressive, and is always seen in their actions and the decisions they make. However, the backslider is forever chained to God because of the individual's past relationship with God. This is why God reports in **Jeremiah 3:12-14 that,** He is married to the backslider.

252

The connection that exists between God and a backslider is all about the backslider's past encounter with God and God's desire to honor the backslider's original vow of commitment. It is not about permanency. Meaning, it is not about the backsliders currently existing in a state of salvation. By definition, the backslider is in a fallen state. He/she has turned his/her back on God and God's will for him/her, like Satan did in heaven. Now, we know what happened to Satan when he turned his back on God. The backslider has broken his or her vow and has nullified or made void the vow/contract between him or her and God through omission or commission. It is also made clear in **Daniel 9:4** that **God will keep His covenant and mercy with those who love Him, and with those who keep His commandments**. A backslider is not committed to keeping covenant with God or the commandments of God and this lack of commitment is seen in many of his/her actions, disposition, and the people they partner and associate with.

However, God's desire, unlike with Satan, for the individual to be saved will forever stand. God is waiting for the individual to recommit and God longs for the commitment and/or partnership that He and the backslider once had. It is the backslider's insistence on following his or her on path that blotted out his/her name from the book of life. I am convinced, the place where the backslider's name once existed in the book of life will remain open, in hope for their return to God as the father of the prodigal son did not forget his son, nor did he stop hoping for the return of his child. The father of the prodigal son never forgot his son and did not close his heart or door to his wayward son.

But, the prodigal son's father did not follow after his son and he respected his son's right to choose to follow his own path. He also did not change his standards or redesign his lifestyle or the order of his village for his son. As the father of the prodigal son (an individual who insisted on defining his own path) hoped for and waited for the return of his son, who could have died in a pig pin and never returned; so is our heavenly Father (God) hoping for and waiting for those who have chosen to walk away from Him to return. However, as with the father of the prodigal son, God will not change and God is hoping for and waiting for the backslider to humble himself/herself as the prodigal son did and return and submit to God, the Father's established plan and lifestyle for the backslider. However, if the backslidden Christian die in his/her desire to follow his/her own path, he/she will be lost unto eternal damnation.

God's hope and desire for the return of the backslider is so strong, He will even commission other Christians to beckon the individual back to Him. However, God's willingness to accept and maintain a relationship with a free-will person does not seal the deal of salvation because the seal of salvation is grounded in repentance, personal choice, personal commitment, and partnership with God. God has always wanted to be in a close relationship with all of mankind **(I Timothy 2:3-4)**. This is why God commissioned Jesus to live and die for the redemption of mankind. However, **salvation is a relationship with God that is grounded in a person's free will to choose to love and submit to God and stay committed to that choice in partnership.**

When **John 10:28** reports, nothing can pluck a repented Christian out of the hand of God, this word is not made void when one turns from God. This is because one can chose to leave the protection of God's mighty hand and move away from God at any point. Choosing to leave God, is not the result of the action of another but the free will of the individual in question. This is why the word of God, concerning this matter, is clarified even further in **Romans 8: 39** when the word of God informs that, no other created/creation shall be able to separate us from the love of God. Note: The key word here is "other". In other words, the power of one being separated from God lies within the will of an individual. This is why Satan tries so hard to break the will of an individual toward the things of God. He knows, salvation is about one's personal relationship and will power to commit to God's authority that is a game changer for him. Salvation is about you and God and when your will is in God, Satan does not have a chance. He cannot bring you down or move your position in God. Concluding, the acceptance of salvation is a personal act and the rejection of salvation is a personal act that is defined by one's will to commit to the will of God. The question then becomes, do you have the will power to discipline yourself to commit to the authority of God? This is an authority that is good for your safety and wellbeing and for the constructive survival of mankind.

An individual has the right and power to choose to remove him/herself from the hands of God. This is why the word of God report, "No one will pluck/snatch them out of My hand." It does not say the Christian cannot climb out of His hand or walk right out of His hand. This is because a Christian is a free will individual who choose to commit and stay committed to the authority of God and can work him/herself or allow another to dupe/trick them into walking away or working his/her way out of the hand of God. This is what Satan did in heaven. He chose to rebel against God, an act that separated him from God. If one can separate one's self from God in heaven, how much more can an earthly being do the same? This is why in **Joshua 24:15** God told "His people" to, "Choose this day whom you will serve." This scripture fully informs us that God's people have a right to choose not to serve God or stay with Him.

One's choice to choose or reject God is expressed through one's desires and actions. These are desires and actions that are expressed in ones' ability to respect and submit to the word and the authority of God. However, to submit to the authority of God is a choice and to continue in this state of submission is a choice, Christian or not! Let us not forget the word of God in **Romans Chapter 11**, giving attention to verses **20-23**, where it discusses not only the goodness of God, but also the severity of God. Here, Paul addresses one's ability to be separated from God, due to an inability to continue in the faith. Note: where there is faith, there is "action". Examples: Abraham's faith produced "action". Jesus' faith in God's will for Him and mankind produced "action". **Faith is not stagnant and faith without works is dead**.

When a Christian is focused on and committed to God, God will embrace the Christian. God will not allow anything to separate the Christian from Him. God can and will stand down any and all forces that come against the Christian and His relationship. However many fail to understand, when God proclaims His defense for the Christian and His relationship **Romans 8: 38-39**, God is addressing external forces that seek to destroy the relationship between Him and the Christian. This proclamation does not address denying the Christian of his/her free-will to take the position, that serving the Lord is not what they would like to continue to do, for whatever reason **(Joshua 24:14-15)**.

Note: Once again, a verse in **Romans 8: 38** reports "...**nor any other creature** shall be able to separate us from the love of God". This reference clearly is in place in this proclamation to sum up the conclusion of the proclamation and to help all understand that God is addressing forces that operate outside of the Christian and God's relationship. God is trying to convey that He is not addressing the will and desires of the Christian. However, when the Christian neglects their responsibility to stay committed to loving God and keeping covenant with God and disciplining themselves to adhering to necessary boundaries that protect them and their relationship with God (the faith), the Christian, not other forces, can cause a separation between the Christian and God. **Romans 8: 38-39** does not make void God's gift of choice and free-will of mankind. Mankind is empowered with the freedom to choose who he/she will submit to or serve throughout life, saved or not.

When a mankind understands the true meaning of God's gift of choice, one will begin to understand the true meaning of the definition of salvation and the definition of being a backslider and how to develop an appropriate partnership with God and others. And the Christian will know not to partner themselves with those who have not shown themselves in the past and present to be committed to God. Christians should pray as Daniel did for mankind to turn from their iniquities and understand God's truth of who He is and what He expects from mankind **(Daniel 9:13)**.

At some point, a backslider chose to commit to God's offer of salvation (take the vow). In this process, he or she has invoked a God-given choice, which follows him or her unto death, a gift that allows him or her to opt out of or into any vow **(Romans 11: 22-23)**. Therefore, a backslider has chosen, or may have been duped into walking away from his or her vow or partnership with God and the reality and knowledge of God experienced during their time together. However, what the backslider experienced in his or her past relationship/partnership with God will never leave God or the heart and mind of the backslider.

Because of an authentic Spiritual relationship and/or partnership that once existed between God and the backslider, neither God nor the backslider can ever deny the reality of their past relationship. The backslider can never deny the reality of God and His Son Jesus. This is the meaning of God's statement mentioned earlier: "I am married to the backslider." Although the backslider knows the reality of God and Jesus and acknowledge and accept this reality, he or she has chosen to allow or has been seduced into allowing personal perceptions, material things, ungodly fleshly desires, greed, power, money and/or doctrines and traditions of men or whatever to fog that reality. This is why you will hear many backsliders say, "I know God is real, 'But.'" The **"But"** is the excuse Satan has seduced the backslider into believing why he or she had to abandon his or her vow of salvation. Satan assigns seven devils to every person that turns/backslides from God to make sure that "But" stands firm **(Matthew 12:45, Luke 11:26)**. The phrase "But" is the hallmark of the backslider. Appropriate Christian partners do not "But" about the things of God.

Satan's goal is, through the assignment of demons, to keep the backslider from reminiscing and thinking on the reality, love, truth, and beauty of his or her past relationship with God. Satan knows that if he allows a person the time to think on or remember their experiences of love, trust, peace, and freedom found in their relationship and/ or partnership with God, the person may repent and return to God. Therefore, Satan is taking no chances. Satan's imps and minions are busy encouraging those not governed by God to keep the backslider focused on things that pleasure the flesh (selfish things) and things of the world like the following: money, women, men, power, racial issues, status issues, drugs, alcohol, sex and sexual issues, division, social issues, opinions, and feelings of those in opposition with God or anything and everything but the love of God. People who have partnered with a backslider will not only have to deal with the personal and sinful issues of the backslider, but the seven or more imps assigned to him or her by Satan.

Also, Satan knows that there is a personal reference of the backslider with God, a reference that also reminds God of the relationship He had with the backslider. Satan is also very much aware of the fact that a backslider is no longer a child of God in Christ nor can God abide with the backslider as long as that person is in an un-repenting rebellious state of sin. This is because God cannot and will not connect Himself to sin or those who continue to engage in sin **(I Corinthian 3:16-17)**. However, God is waiting, some may say calling, for the backslider's return to a true state of repentance, commitment and partnership with Him.

Therefore, unbeknownst to some, Satan is on high alert when it comes to the backslider. Satan knows that there is no "once saved always saved in God" for those who continue in sin and show themselves to be in opposition with the word and will of God **(Hebrews 10:26-29)**. However, Satan is pleased with the idea that an individual perceives that his or her lifestyle has little or nothing to do with their salvation. Satan and his imps are more than pleased to "But" the backslider and all who are willing to attach him or herself to the backslider right to hell. Even if the backslider returns to God or repents on his or her deathbed, the backslider's display of sin and rebellion against God will be used by Satan to pain God and lure others into his web of destruction against God and mankind. Meaning, a backslider's rebellious disposition plays into Satan's plan to pain God and to rob, kill, and destroy mankind.

The backslider's relationship with God is something like a couple that truly loved one another at one time, but one of the partners later chose to go their separate way. The love that this couple shared has branded the heart of each and neither of them can ever truly deny the reality of what they shared. In the backslider's case, the backslider is the one who chose to abandon the relationship with God.

Although, the couple once shared a deep love and possibly a partnership, the love they shared in their past does not mean that they are currently united in their thoughts and feeling about one another; that they will always have a relationship; that they will support one another through partnership; nor does it mean that they will one day return to each other. It just means they have a true knowledge of and a past relationship with each other.

There is no current relationship or partnership between the two. A relationship and/or partnership requires agreement, commitment, cooperation, and teamwork between the two which do not currently exist. However, they will always have a sense of one another. Also, there is a stronger chance than with most that the love the two once shared could reconcile them. Only if both of them could come into agreement and commit to working together to resolve the issues that separated them and stay committed to these resolutions. God's perception of the backslider clearly corresponds with this depiction in **Jeremiah Chapter 3 and Chapter 4: 1-2** when He equates His relationship with a backslider to that of a divorce. Divorce by any definition means, both parties are free to go their separate way.

Note: Satan knows who God is and accepts that Jesus is the Son of God sent for the redemption of mankind. However, Satan has chosen to oppose God's will. This oppositional behavior by Satan has completely severed Satan's relationship with God and condemned him forever. Christ's redemption is not about God allowing mankind to continue in sin. God forbid! (**Romans 6:1-2**) The word of God in **Matthew 7:21-23** reports: **He who does the will of My Father in heaven (God) shall enter into heaven. In other words, he who shows in his/her "sprit" and "actions" that they are committed to the will of God, shall enter into heaven.**

Also noted: there are many who identify themselves as Christians because they acknowledge and accept the fact that Jesus is the Son of God who came to die for the sins of mankind. However, just as Satan refused to be governed by God, it must be understood: Being in a state of acknowledgement and acceptance, does not classify one as Christian. The process of becoming and remaining a Christian is primarily about the willing choice to repent and submit to being governed by God spiritually and physically according to the sacrifices He (God) made through the life, death, and resurrection of His Son Jesus. This is why **John 15:4-8** report **those who abide in His word abide in Him**. These Scriptures also ask Christians to try the spirit of one claiming to have the Spirit of God in them. These Christians are to try the proclamations of others, according to the word of God, His creations, and the history of His actions. This is the nature of God that is seen in the Spirit of God and should be seen in one's proclamation of salvation.

A misunderstanding or underdeveloped perception of what it means to be a Christian may explain why some say a Christian can be possessed by an evil spirit. An individual who is willing to be corrected in God and has a committed partnership with God through Christ, cannot be possessed by an evil spirit. However, these individuals can be troubled and/or hindered by such evil spirits **(Thessalonians 2:18)**. But, those who classify themselves as Christian, but are not committed to being governed or corrected by God through Christ, are not empowered with the Holy Spirit to effectively resist the powers and antics of Satan. These individuals can be possessed or overcome by evil.

Due to disobedience toward God, many proclaimed Christians are unacknowledged backsliders and, like King Saul in his backslidden state, do not have the power of God working on their behalf when it comes to addressing evil and overcoming challenges **(I Chronicles 10:3-6)**. These are individuals who, due to their poor understanding of salvation and their partnership role in their salvation, have backslidden and are not in the full knowledge of this fact **(Romans 1:21-32)**. Yes, one can be in a backslidden state and not realize that they are, due to their unwillingness to obey God and/or poor or inappropriate teaching in Christ. This is why most of all God would have all have an appropriate understanding and instructions of His word and the true meaning of salvation.

Therefore, the understanding of what it means to be in a committed relationship/partnership with God is to know that when others share the truth of God, this is not an act of beating someone down. This is an act that will strengthen and enlighten and empower anyone on how to build and maintain an appropriate and good quality Christ-driven lifestyle, relationship and partnership with God and others. So, sharing the understanding of what offends and pains God and the consequences thereof with someone, is truly an act of love. To know God is to know the whole truth of God through His revelations to mankind, found in His word. Yes, God is about forgiveness, goodness, joy, love, and prosperity, but the truth of the matter is, there is no true forgiveness, goodness, joy, love, or prosperity when one refuses to align their lifestyle with the plan that God has for him or her.

To silence the truth of God's word will not change who God is, nor will it change His position concerning any situation. But, to know the truth of God's word gives an individual the opportunity to make an informed decision/choice, an act Satan hates. For one to choose to reject God's will and commandments without knowing these commands/judgments or having an understanding of the negative ramifications of this act of rejection, is sad and regretful and very pleasing to Satan. Mankind's rebellion and ignorance are doorways of opportunity for Satan and can cause mankind to fail in their ability to live in the fullness of Christ. On the other hand, learning the truth of God, as found in His word, will give hope to all that hear it (**Romans 15:4**). This is a hope that will strengthen everyone in a world of discord. **The truth of God grounds all who are willing to abide in it and provides a solid foundation for victory in all things**.

Making choices without appropriate insight works to the advantage of Satan in every way. Satan would have men/women live their lives oblivious to the effect that their life choices have on God, themselves, and/or others. Satan would have men and women live their lives as **John Lennon** once wrote asking his listeners to, "...imagine there is no heaven or hell." Such an approach is not acceptable in God. It is also something Satan longs for mankind to do, because to do this, men and women would have to reject the truth of God that states: There is a heaven and there is a hell.

This type of thinking would also encourage men and women to live lifestyles that are outside of the will of God and hell bound. What better way to manipulate mankind into not staying focus on the things of God, but by encouraging them to embrace an unrealistic perception of life and the reality of God's truth with beautiful sounding words. To embrace a lie! Getting individuals to buy into a lie is Satan's number one mind game. **Where there are lies, you can bet, Satan is in the midst working his crafty destruction**.

Being a Christian and developing partnerships are about knowing, understanding, and disciplining oneself to make appropriate informed choices. One should seek to know about one's self, God and one's self as it relates to God. Knowing also means being informed about Satan and how Satan operates. This is because Satan has great faith in his ability to dupe men and women who make life choices, from the standpoint of ignorance, out of their earthly and divine inheritance.

Satan's supernatural attacks on men and women work best when these individuals operate in the realm of ignorance or in a lie. It is a person's knowledge and understanding of who God is and how Satan operates that helps to maneuver around hurdles and over pitfalls presented by Satan. This is why the word of God in **Hosea 4:6** reports, "God's people are destroyed for a lack of knowledge" and the word of God in **Proverbs 4:7** commands us, "In all of one's getting, get understanding." **Knowledge and understanding is best accomplished through God's word and appropriate partnerships**. This is why God sent those operating in God's word forth by twos **(Luke 10:1)**. God sent forth partners in Christ to do His will, further laying the foundation that the will of God is found in Christian partnership.

Strength improves with numbers. However, **numbers that are ignorant to the truth and are not unified, are less than the strength of one knowledgeable focused individual**. Therefore, one's love, knowledge, understanding, commitment, devotion, and strength will improve when partnered with knowledgeable like-minded people. An individual's willingness to accept this philosophy will improve his or her chances of developing appropriate partnerships in Christ. The salvation offered by God through Jesus, embraces the reality of the conditional nature of salvation and partnering with other Christ-driven individuals **(I Corinthians 5:11-13)**.

CHAPTER NINE

Satan's Opposition: "Imperial Narcissism" and Protecting the Mind of Your Child through Appropriate Partnership

A lifestyle patterned after Christ also serves as protection from the wrath of God imposed on all who work against the will of God. Satan opposes the fact, God has provided a way through Jesus' life and death sacrifice for mankind to receive God's grace and favor and has given mankind an escape from God's wrath of eternal damnation. Therefore, Satan's desire is to keep individuals unaware of their need to seek the covering offered by God's grace and mercy through Christ's love, obedience, submission and appropriate partnerships. Satan also desires to weaken Christians in their united efforts to live a Christ-driven lifestyle

Satan understands that there is no grace and mercy for him and the wrath of God is upon him. Satan has lost his relationship with God forever. Satan is angry and miserable and he is jealous of the fact that God has offered mankind a way to salvage and restore their relationship/partnership with God. In other words, God has given mankind another chance for love and partnership with Him and others. Satan knows that there is no redemption for him and he does not want to face the consequences of his sinful actions alone, eternal damnation.

As the old saying goes, "Misery loves company." Therefore, until Jesus returns and completes God's plan for mankind, an act that will silence Satan and his antics forever, Satan will continue in his efforts to blind men and women to the truth of God and fight against Christian partnerships which strengthen mankind and their ability to receive the redemption offered by Jesus. This is Satan's last-ditch effort to pain God and recruit or dupe others into joining him in his fate of eternal damnation. The question then becomes: Will you give Satan his most treasured desire?

Although Satan would like to fulfil his take down of mankind in one blow, it is not within his power to do so; however, his best chance of taking mankind down is by promoting a lifestyle that is in conflict with the word of God in Christ. A lifestyle that is in conflict with God, in many cases, promotes a mindset that justifies and/or condones a lack of appreciation for the truth of God's word. One may say this type of lifestyle fosters a disposition that is intolerant of God's truth found in His word. These people may find themselves rationalizing and looking for ways to minimize or discredit the truth of God's word. Their beliefs and value systems may become more and more grounded in their personal opinions and/or in the opinions of those that support their way of thinking. The word of God speaks of this in **II Timothy 4:3-4** when referring to those who have itching ears. Most would describe this type of thinking as self-centered.

Self-centered thinking is at odds with God and His plan to have mankind live and prosper in unity without partiality. This type of thinking works against the concept of teamwork and partnership. When one is focused on one's personal perceptions of how the world should function or how God should address issues, it does not allow that person to be an objective thinker and it does not leave room for the truth of a situation to be seen in a clear light. Self-centered thinking and behaving and the act of limiting one's self to acknowledging concepts which support one's own emotional and psychological comfort level. It separates mankind from God and gives way to an evolutionary mental state. This mental state can be defined as a psychological condition that embodies having a very high opinion of one's self, one's personal views of social and governmental issues, and having an obsessive desire to impose his or her personal and worldview on others.

Let us call this psychological condition "**Imperial Narcissism (having an excessively high opinion of one's self and one's perception combined with a God-like mentality to control situations, outcomes and impose one's views on others).**" This type of narcissist shares many of the characteristics seen in the general definition of narcissism. However, this type of narcissist is not satisfied with just being obsessed with personal image and one's personal perceptions, but is also obsessed with having others view the world from his or her narcissistic perspective. These individuals will promote the need to change social norms and comfort levels from that of the norm, to that of his or her perception of what it means to be comfortable/normal and/or acceptable. In other words, they will push for a break in the norm/acceptable, to push their agenda of personal and social normality as they push for their worldview to be the norm.

An Imperial Narcissist will go out of his/her way to develop and follow through with his/her personal agenda(s) that impose his or her views on others. They are very calculating and crafty in their press to impose their agenda and worldview on others. This type of mentality is best seen when an Imperial Narcissist is wealthy or has a position of authority in a group or society (members with the financial or political power to make change). These individuals will first focus on pushing for their self-centered behavior and thinking to be received by others on an individual level. They do this by appealing to the personal needs and fleshly desires of a number of members in a partnership, group or society. Once the Imperial Narcissist and his or her minions have created discord in the partnership, group or society by appealing to the selfish nature of mankind, they will push for this transformation to become the norm by pushing for changes in rules and laws which govern social and governing bodies. If examined closely, their explanation for such a change will be vague and carnally/fleshly driven and will not address the long-term ramifications of a partnership, group, society or world functioning in a continual state of self-gratification.

Such individuals have the power, and will promote and surround himself or herself with concepts, behavioral patterns, and people who make them feel emotionally, psychologically, as well as physically comfortable with their style of thinking. They will also aggressively seek out the support of others that support his or her way of thinking and/or behavior. An Imperial Narcissist and his/her support system will gradually, and in some cases, systematically shun and/or avoid behaviors and or ideas that do not allow them to feel comfortable about their way of thinking and behaving. In extreme cases these individuals will plan and attack on those who oppose their way of thinking through bullying, financial and political undermining, and even physical attacks. They will use their power and make every effort to diminish or demonize the perceptions and opinions of those who differ from them.

The approach of those who prioritize their personal sense of emotional and psychological comfort will inevitably reject the idea to turn to the established rule of law or the word of God for insight and guidance. This is because the origination of many laws and God's Word and His worldview for mankind is not driven by one's comfort level; nor are they driven by personal feelings. However, the aim of an Imperial Narcissist is to recruit and convert others to their personal worldview and to get others to personalize this worldview.

For these individuals, personal feelings and how **"I"** perceive things and what **"I"** think is their fundamental approach to behaving and resolving issues. The word **"I"** is their hallmark. The individual will seek out and attach him or herself to others and social support systems that water down, rationalize, overlook, and/or could flat-out reject using the laws of the land and the word of God and other materials that do not support their way of thinking. For an Imperial Narcissist, the process of excluding God's word and the views of others will become an ongoing process. This is because, from their pathological perspective, everyone should think like they think. Therefore, they feel it is their duty to press toward this goal of being in control of what others think. Controlling the thoughts and social norms of others is an obsession for them. Also, because getting others to conform to their way of thinking consist of many facets about a person, which defines how they think and behave. Changing one's ability to feel comfortable about thinking and behaving in ways that are not widely acceptable or that may not be their own requires time and effort from a number of forces. The Imperial Narcissist will continually work toward trying to harvest the necessary resources that will allow them to manipulate and push for his or her agenda to transform the thinking of others to their own.

Imperial Narcissist Push for Change

To get others to participate in defiant forms of social and/or religious behavior and thinking can be time consuming. It will also most likely require manipulation and an evolutionary process, which involves the collaboration of those with the same agenda. The breaking down of behavioral and social norms can take months or even years to manifest in the typical person's thinking and behavior. The level of God consciousness a person has for a value, the level of commitment one has to a value, how well rooted one is in a value system, and the tangible gratification one receives from a given element will all play major roles in how quickly one is able to abandon one's personal and social values and/or God's values. However, most people are not operating in a mindset that considers the fact that there are others who are not satisfied with tolerating existing societal or religious values, but are working to or maybe even plotting to get others to embrace values that are all about their personal worldview. The naiveté of most people, about the selfish and controlling disposition of some, will give the Imperial Narcissist an advantage.

Satan is very much aware of the evolutionary process of embracing concepts, thinking, and behaviors that are in conflict with God and its' effect on established God-centered value systems. He is also aware of the collaboration and manipulation needed to cause a defiant social framework to evolve. Satan is in tune with the role this process plays in moving men and women in a direction that rejects God and

God's will for mankind. Satan has become a master at manipulating many of those who are sold-out to the idea that one's personal perceptions and comfort should be the driving force behind conduct and behavior into making it their mission to encourage others to do the same. This is because Satan is well aware of the negative affect a movement such as this has on God's plan for mankind.

Satan is also conscious of the social support and brotherhood and sisterhood needed to live a Christ-driven lifestyle with ease. Therefore, it is more than necessary that Christians understand the evolutionary process of self-centered thinking and the partnering element of this thinking. This understanding will help the Christian know that partnering with those who are not empowered with the ability to resist the calling of (that promotes selfishness and personal comfort) and those who cater to the flesh, will gradually encroach/intrude upon a Christian's ability to live for God in Christ.

Protecting the Mind of Your Child

Understanding the evolutionary process of Imperial Narcissism also highlights the important role of appropriate Christian marital partnership and its role in **parenting children**. This is because while Satan is committed to getting all of us to buy into the idea of self-gratification, he targets the youth first and foremost. Children are in the early stages of their development and Satan can attack them on all fronts physically, spiritually, psychologically, and sexually. The underdeveloped psychological, physical, and sexual state of children and young people weakens their ability to resist Satan's lure and manipulations. This is why Christian training and discipline in a Child's early stages of development is important **(Proverbs 13:24: Proverbs 22:6)**.

Satan also has a sound understanding of the word of God where it informs parents in **Proverbs 22:6, to raise up a child in the way he or she should go and the child will not stray far from their teaching when the child is older. These Scriptures address all of the child's developmental processes and the child's need for instruction, guidance, and discipline. These Scriptures also inform parents, the parenting process is a conditioning process that has a lasting effect in the lives of their children and it is the parent's responsibility to take on the leadership role in the child's learning experience, not the child.

Christian parents can find solace and assurance in their parenting through God's partnership with them. This is because God has a vested interest in the Christian parent and their role to raise their children in the things of God. As a result, He seals their Christ-driven parenting approach with a promise. This promise assures the parents that their parenting efforts in Christ will not be in vain, and God will embed the parent's values into the hearts of their children. This promise offers Christian parents peace of mind that surpasses the understanding of most during times of adolescent growth and development and throughout the child's life.

Satan is also aware of God's promises and the fact that they will not return void **(Isaiah 55:11)**. Not only that, but he is also acutely aware of the fact that sin and iniquity can embed itself in the flesh of mankind. Therefore, Satan seeks to work God's promises associated with appropriate parenting/teaching/ conditioning of a child to his advantage. He does this by attacking the child's developmental training, conditioning, sexual development, and disciplinary process. His goal is to defile the child's training, conditioning, and developmental process, in an effort to embed dysfunctional behaviors and thinking and anti-Christian values in the heart of the child. One way of doing this is to prompt Imperial Narcissists (with their god-like mentality) and their recruits to target the youth and the youth's training, conditioning and developmental process through inappropriate and anti-Christian parenting, teaching, training and social structures.

It is Satan's goal to work God's irrevocable promise and operations of the flesh/body and mind to his advantage by exposing a child to parenting, teaching, training, and discipline that is poor, selfish, dysfunctional, malformed and/or sinful. Therefore, just as a child will find it difficult to move away from appropriate Christian training, the child who has received dysfunctional malformed, sinful training and conditioning will also experience difficulty moving away from such training. Yes, Satan is crafty! Therefore, appropriate marital partnership and a parent's associations are vital in the developmental process of children.

As a result of God's promises associated with a child's training and one's ability to understand Satan's crafty ways, Christian parents and guardians should take child rearing very seriously and be extremely leery of those they invite into their village. This is because Christian parenting is not only a partnership between a parent and God; it is a communal process and a commitment between them and the people they partner with. The primary goal of Christian parenting should be found in the parent's willingness to maintain a partnership with God and in their ability to partner themselves with others who understand the dynamics of appropriate Christian parenting, whether these partners are for business, friendship or marriage.

The Christian parents' partnership with God requires them to adhere to God's will for them to raise and instruct their children in all the things of God. These parents acknowledges and accepts, they are raising the future body of Christ and the future of our country. Their relationship with God has given them the insight that rearing a child is not about them, but about the needs of the child's future survival in this world and in Christ. They embrace the understanding that Christ-driven instruction starts before birth and continues throughout adulthood addressing all personal, worldly, and Christian issues.

These parents have partnered with God to instruct their children in matters of manhood, womanhood, love, kindness, social issues, friendships, business, partnerships, and sexual behavior in God. Christian parents should have addressed these issues in God on a personal level and as partners and are united in their ability to communicate God's position on these issues to their children. They understand that discussions and training addressing these issues are not done in one or two discussions but is a lifelong learning process for the child. These parents also realize that it is their responsibility to take these issues to their children and will not wait for their children to bring these topics to them.

Partnerships with individuals in marriage, friendship or business who are not Christ-driven and are not committed to the Christian approach to the development and training of children, will allow Satan to manipulate a child's training process. To allow this could be very costly for the child throughout his or her life and in the child's ability to accept Christ and grow in Christ. Inappropriate partnerships by Christian parents and poor or mixed messages about who and what the parent's values about God are, may explain why many children and adults, raised in Christian homes, are unstable or may not find comfort in their ability to commit to God and live a Christian lifestyle. This is because one's ability to commit is strongly associated with ones perceived understanding, comfort and/or trust level with that to which he/she is considering committing to.

Some Common Issues When Positioning Yourself In Christ

Some people actively move toward creating social systems that alienate God's will for mankind. In the minds and hearts of most, moving away from the things of God may have less to do with the concept of good or evil, but more to do with the fact that most organisms tend to shy away from or avoid stimuli that they don't understand or perceive as a threat. An individual who engages in sinful pleasure-seeking behaviors and does not understand God's position concerning such behavior, could become anxious and perceive God's rejection of this behavior as a threat to their lifestyle or existence.

Therefore, for the individual's personal sense of wellbeing, they may seek to justify reasons why they should design their lifestyle in a way that rejects or diminishes the truth of God's word. This may especially be the case when the will of God conflicts with what the individual perceives as a sense of identity, family structure, or culture. In order to avoid many of these conflicts, it is important that a person does not develop a relationship with or ties to, and/or sympathies for something God has defined as unacceptable. As a result, one will not have to wrestle with the possible emotional, psychological, and/or pleasure or distress that the forbidden behavior(s) or relationships may evoke in you, when faced with trying to obey God's word. Therefore, do not fall for Satan's mind game that challenges mankind to try engaging in, exploring (experiment with) or testing sinful or questionable thought patterns, behaviors or relationships. This is the same mind game Satan manipulated Adam and Eve with in the garden when he challenged them to taste the forbidden fruit.

"Try it, you might like it" or "don't judge" is an age old strategic move Satan has used to lure mankind into breaking the laws of God and engaging in self-destructive behaviors. Satan is acutely aware of the nature of mankind and of sin's ability to embed itself in the mind, flesh, and spirit of mankind. Therefore, his goal is to get mankind to submit to sin, that the virus of sin may have the opportunity to invade the operations of mankind and develop strongholds in an individual's life. It is his hope that the virus of sin will grow to command natural operations of mankind's desires, urges, and impulses in a way that causes mankind to behave and conduct one's self in ways that are in conflict with God's design for them. Christians must become alert to who they are in Christ and how mankind was designed to operate in Christ and to the games and strategies of Satan **(II Corinthians 2: 11)**.

In the Garden of Eden, Satan challenged the couple to move beyond God's established boundaries. The word of God does not report that the couple experienced any physical ills as a result of eating the forbidden fruit. However, the consequence of their actions was devastating for them and others. This is why **Christ's example does not focus on His ability to feel comfortable, but on His ability to stay committed to the will of God**. Christians and others must remember that life is not always about feeling comfortable with self or others for a period of time or all the time. Nor is Christian living about liking something or feeling good, but about loving God and others, doing the right thing and staying committed to the authority of God.

In other words, mankind should not expect to feel good about everything God expects of them, but they can expect that submission to the will of God will always work for the good of mankind **(Romans 8:28)**. Jesus's flesh did not want to drink of the bitter cup of being crucified, but His discomfort worked for His good and for the good of mankind **(Luke 22:42-44, John 12:27)**. Also, sin will not always make one feel bad, but sin will always have a negative effect on one's life and wellbeing. This is because the nature of the operations of sin is designed to bring an individual down and strip an individual of their God given characteristics and gifts, as it weakens them for Satan's plan for their demise/destruction. For example: Sex can feel real good when engaging in the act, for a saved individual or unsaved individual. However, the ramifications of engaging in sexual behavior outside of the will of God can be devastating far beyond the pleasurable act emotionally, physically, socially, and spiritually. This is why one must learn to **think beyond the moment before engaging in anything. Impulse control and discipline people!**

The pleasure or comfort a Christian or an unbeliever may receive from participating in behavior denounced by God will evoke feelings of anxiety, in most. The level of anxiety associated with knowingly participating in behavior that is not acceptable will most likely drive the individual to determine whether or not to continue the behavior. Now, the choice to embrace or reject a given lifestyle choice may not manifest clearly in the person's actions. This choice can sometimes present as acts of avoidance, hostility or ambiguity. This is because the individual may have an issue with having to make the choice in general. The individual's style of expressing the choice will most likely reflect the individual's level of commitment to the entity that condemns the behavior. For example, one who has a strong commitment to God's word or to one's parent's opinions concerning the issue will behave significantly differently, when troubled by a given ordinance, from those who do not value God's word or their parent's opinions.

If the individual has a lukewarm level of commitment toward the entity that condemns their behavior, he or she may come across as wishy-washy when addressing the issue. This type of person's position on the matter and ability to follow through with engaging in or withdrawing from the behavior will most likely be determined by his/her social support system. However, once the decision to engage or not is made, the person will most likely make attempts to position themselves to live within their choice. If the person chooses to reject the ruling, the person will consciously or subconsciously alienate the source that condemns their behavior of choice.

Their attempts to remove themselves from the forces that condemn their choices will most likely lead to the individual fostering an attitude and social environment that rejects the condemning force and supports their choice. The individual will most likely associate more with others who embrace their choice and move away from those who do not. If the force that condemns the individual's behavior is the word of God, the individual's social environment will most likely become diluted or void of the things of God. This disposition will most likely cause them to become combative with, or avoidant of, individuals who disagree with their choice to continue in the questionable behavior. This highlights the need to give attention to the choices a person makes and the company they keep.

Children who are raised in ambiguous environments by Christian parents who do not display their commitment to God and explicitly convey, through their lifestyle and partnerships, the strengths and beauty of living a Christian lifestyle are at risk. They are at risk of experiencing ambiguous perceptions and marginal comfort levels about God and living a Christian lifestyle. Such children are also at risk for partnering themselves with others who are ambiguous about the things of God or oppositional when it comes to the things of God. Such mindsets and partnerships will further diminish the child's ability to accept the calling of God and grow in the teachings of Christ.

A partnership between a Christian and a person who refuses to hear and accept God's truth is toxic for the Christian and their children. This is because this type of partner will most likely resist even fight against the Christian's efforts to stand firm in the word of God and many of the things of God, in their life and in the lives of their children. The Christian with a partner such as this, may find himself or herself wrestling with this partner while attempting to accomplish or teach their children even the simplest things in God.

This type of partnership will be stressful for all parties involved, to say the least. The stress generated in the partnership could cause the Christian to lose his or her focus on Christ and hamper or even cause failure in the Christian's ability to accomplish their walk in God. The children of such parents will be ill equipped in their ability to grow in God and in their ability to understand and accept even the fundamental principles of God, crippling each child's ability to answer the call of God. This is Satan's goal for mankind in general. It assures Satan that he will not be alone in the place of eternal damnation that God has prepared for him; therefore, **Satan embraces the thought of a Christian partnering with one who is not Christ-driven with a smile**.

The Support a Christian Needs

An appropriate Christian partner is one who "always" does his or best to encourage their partner to honor God and the word of God.   These partners are chosen by God and introduced into the life of a given Christian with the expectation of God that he or she will press forward in their own personal walk of faith. This includes an expectation by God that the partner(s) will do everything in their power to help their partner do the same. An individual's willingness to honor God in all things is a clear indication that the given individual most likely has a Spiritual partnership with God.

People who do not have a Spiritual relationship/partnership with God that is reflected in their willingness to make every effort to conform to the will of God are not partners with God, and the Holy Spirit of God does not dwell in them **(Romans 8:1-14)**. Nor does the grace of God abide with them. This is because the grace of God is in place for those that accept, honor, and submit to the authority of God and put forth their best effort to do the will of God. Be warned all; to honor is to exalt and embrace. When one embraces something, they respect and consider it and draw close to it. Closeness is about sharing and oneness and not about disrespect, defiance and separation. To think that one can love something and continually behave in a disrespectful, inconsiderate and defiant manner toward the object of affection is an expression of immaturity, confusion, or ignorance. **A continual lack of consideration, continual disrespect or defiance toward an individual in the context of business, friendship or marriage is not a depiction of love or honor**.

This does not mean a person of God will not have issues that may cause them to wrestle with submitting to His authority. This also does not mean that loved ones or partners of a Christian will not have issues or questions that must be addressed or resolved in their partnerships. However, the Christian's core/foundation will always show respect for God and who and what their partner is as a person and as a person of God. These partners will make every attempt to learn of God and help their partner/s work through their unique differences and momentary misunderstandings in their relationships and life within the word of God. The partners' combined faith in God and commitment to the truth of God and God's commandments will keep them on a path of working together to achieve oneness. This is because the harmony of a Christian partnership is derived from the commitment that each partner has toward achieving the things of God and following the teachings of Christ.

Each partner's commitment to achieving the things of God is the primary element that anchors and unites them. It is also each partner's commitment to God's will that brings about feelings of peace and favor toward each other. Each partner experiences feelings of goodness and safety when observing the love and commitment that the other partner(s) has toward them and the things of God. This is because each partner knows that their love toward one another and each partner's commitment to God will strengthen their union and ensures a prosperous future for them all. The fact that a partner is committed to living a Godly lifestyle that evokes the favor of God **(Proverbs 3:1-4);** a favor that extends to all that he or she does, brings about feelings of peace, admiration, and favor towards partners. These feelings of peace and the disposition of favor that Christian partners will have toward each other is also a by-product of the unifying nature of the Holy Spirit that dwells within each partner's soul.

The Spirit of God bears witness to all Christians that they belong to Christ and they are connected to the body of Christ in partnership **(Romans 8:14-17)**. The evidence of this Spiritual connection is manifested in the ability of each partner to allow open expressions of their love and commitment toward God and each other. It is also seen in each partner's ability to encourage other partners to improve their individual relationship/partnership with God and others through Christ. Each partner's ability to openly express their love for God and each other strengthens the partnership. It also strengthens each partner's ability to love the other partner and encourages agreement between all partners. The agreement between the partners will always start with their agreement to submit to God and the things of God, first.

Let it be known, the question of agreement between two or more Christian partners will always start and end with: "What will God have us to do in this situation?" or "What will God have us to do about this situation?" The partners' agreement to submit to God first allows the Holy Spirit of God to freely operate in their partnership. Once the Holy Spirit is able to freely operate in the partnership, the Holy Spirit will encourage and formulate the interactions and the actions of the partners in a way that strengthens the partnership and produce the appropriate answer or solution to any problem, whether it is for business, friendship, or marriage. It will also move the partners toward accomplishing their goals together and help keep the partners focused on accomplishing their goals in accordance with the word and will of God.

The partners' collaborative commitment to God has put God in control and paved a successful path for any solution. This is why the word of God in **Amos 3:3** states, "How can two walk together unless they agree?" In other words, unless they are committed to the same things, the ability for two or more to come to an agreement is flawed, whether it is for business, friendship, or marriage. This Scripture reminds us that commitment is a driving force in one's ability to be a good partner. Commitment helps define behavior. It also tells us that the ability for two or more to work together is found in the spirit of each individual and in the things that each individual partner is committed to. The questions then become: 1) What are you committed to, and 2) Are you and your partner's commitments in agreement?

To answer these two questions, let us go back to the discussion of the concepts of love and honor. When one loves someone or something, he/she exalts it, he/she is close to it, and the love and affection is revealed in how the individual conducts him or herself toward the object of affection. For example: **When a man loves a woman**, he will express it to her by acts of kindness, giving, sharing, consideration, and by honoring her and her thoughts in the presence of her and others. His behavior will be an expression of someone that is in love with a particular woman. When her name comes up, you will have his attention. His thoughts will consider her needs and his plans are always with her consideration. Some will say, "A man does not consider the woman he loves all of the time and in everything." On the contrary, if he is a Christian man, yes he does! He will love her as Christ loves the church and considers the church/body of Christ in everything He does **(Ephesians 5:25-31).**

CHAPTER TEN

The Role of Closeness, Consideration, and Commitment in Partnership

One of the primary elements that defines the concept of love is addressed when discussing the concept of closeness. It appears that the closer two or more become, the more pronounced the elements that define the concept of love become. It also appears, as one draws closer to an individual, the more that person influences the individual's thoughts, behavior, and how he or she functions. Most will agree, one cannot be close to another and not influence how the individual functions. In other words, if one does not affect the thoughts, behavior, or decision-making process of a person, one does not have a close relationship with that person. Therefore, it is safe to say, when a person loves someone and does not consider that person in his or her decisions, that person has a misunderstanding of what love and closeness truly embodies. Closeness is a defining element in a relationship/partnership. How do we know this? This conclusion is clearly made when examining the concept of love that defines marriage between a man and a woman.

According to God, a married couple becomes so close that they function as one. The woman is the man's helper, one who is comparable to the man (complements the man), not subject to the man **(Genesis 2:18-25)**. This tells us that the goal God has for marital partnership exists in a setting that fosters the achievement of individual and partnership goals with **a combined mindset** that functions as one. **The question then** becomes, **how is it that two individuals with independent minds accomplish or develop the ability to function as one?** It is done with an active and conscious mind by both partners who are committed to God's will for them. Both partners embrace the will of God and work together to achieve individual and partnership goals. **This comes with an understanding that does not condone the perception that one partner controls the other or that one partner is better than the other.**

Ephesians 5:21, asks Christians to submit to one another out of reverence for Christ. This is because the redemption of God through Christ restores human interaction and relationships to God's original design for mankind. This is an act of submission that considers God's original intent for mankind to live in partnerships that acknowledge differences and strengths in love, liberty, and the truth of their equality in God. This submission is also done out of the respect that one has for God's will for mankind. The original social unit took place within the context of marriage; therefore, God's original design for marital relationships was about humility and love toward one another, which conforms to the authority of God, not the authority of mankind. God's design for marital partnership and human relations does not focus on a **big "I" or little "you."** God's design for marriage and human social interaction entails married couples and men and women coexisting in a social network that works together in closeness and in partnership to achieve God's goals for each individual and the social structure. A design that reflects Adam and Eve's lifestyle, prior to sin. This is a lifestyle that promotes submission, closeness, and consideration toward God and one another.

The partnerships that exist between husbands and wives and others are grounded in the understanding found in **Romans 2:11 and Acts 10:34-35,** which explains that there is no respect of person with God. Meaning, God does not value one of His people over another **Galatians 2:6**. This may be difficult for many to accept after being born into a world full of sin and iniquity that is geared toward racial, gender, and social status bias. God is captivated by those who honor Him in Holiness and not by one's race, gender or status. Additionally, each partner acknowledges that both the husband and the wife and other Christians are a part of one unit in the body of Christ. As members of the body of Christ, each partner is also captivated by each partner's ability to press toward Holiness in Christ and each partner's ability to humble themselves to one another in Christ. The humility of each partner in Christ is a stimulating element of closeness and helps to cultivate the understanding of how God would have them truly love one another. This understanding includes the knowledge of God's word found in **Romans 12:4** and **I Corinthians 12:12-31,** which expounds that "**all members**" of the body of Christ have an important role in God's plan for His people. This is an acknowledgment that recognizes individual differences and God given gifts. God is fair-minded and in His scriptures, He is encouraging His people to be fair-minded. He is looking for Christians like those found in Berea in **Acts 17: 10-12**. These individuals were willing and ready to receive Christ and His salvation according to the truth of God's word and God's actions in Christ, void of the traditions and doctrines of mankind.

God Has a Vision

God does not need the perceptions or visions of mankind to direct His people **(Jeremiah 23:16)**. He does not need permission from mankind to implement His plan for mankind. God has a plan/vision for His creation. God is not calling for the visions of men to direct His people. He is calling for His leadership and the body of Christ to submit to His perfect plan for them, the people of God, and others. Therefore, Christians need to be about studying to show themselves approved in understanding what God's plan is for His people and others and not focused on formulating or following traditions, doctrines, and visions scripted by mankind that God has allowed to operate in the land because of the rebellious disposition of many.

It is clear in God's word and in the history of His actions, God has allowed mankind to conduct themselves in ways that He is not pleased with. Mankind's persistence to run their own course and God's commitment to the free will of mankind, has caused God to remove His hand from the lives of many. As a result, God has allowed the operations of given behaviors, traditions, and doctrines that work against His plan for mankind **(Exodus 32:9; Acts 7:51)**. In **(Matthew 19:7-8),** Jesus demonstrated God's displeasure with mankind insisting on choosing their own way, when He spoke on God's perception of divorce.

In **Matthew 19: 7-8**, Jesus reported, divorce was not in God's plan for mankind. However, it appears that due to mankind's oppositional disposition against God's will for them to seek out and maintain appropriate marital partnerships, divorce was allowed **(Matthew 19:8)**. Meaning, many of God's people were refusing to consult Him when choosing a marital partner. Many were also resistant to His word and how mankind is to respect and love one another, as many do today. God's people were marring whoever they wanted to marry. Marriages were becoming more and more defined according to "religious" doctrine, cultural expectations, worldly philosophies, and/or personal principles and standards and not according to the loving partnership God designed for men and women. Also, God's people were becoming more and more committed to living marital lifestyles that did not honor Him. As a result of the abuse, neglect, and abominations that many were experiencing in these rogue/undesirable marriages, a merciful God allowed divorce. God's strong disapproval of divorce is seen in **Malachi 2:16**.

Therefore, if members of the body of Christ are all working to achieve what God has for them and mankind, it must be acknowledged that a Christian's role, and the love God has for a man and woman, extends beyond catering to the traditions, doctrines, and the selfish fleshly desires or comforts of others. Mankind is first asked to be committed and submit to obeying God's will for them and others in Christ. Christ's example never expected anyone to serve and cater to Him. Although he showed pleasure in the thoughtfulness of others toward His personal comfort, He was not committed to others catering to His personal comforts. We see this in **Luke 10:38-42,** when Jesus tried to convey to Martha that His word and appropriate Christian fellowship was more important than preparations done to address the physical needs of Him and others. Therefore, one must question the mentality of those who insist on being catered to. Upon acknowledging and submitting to the authority of God, the role God has for His partners is rooted in liberty, teamwork and a unified effort of love, commitment, submission, and consideration for the needs of one another in Christ.

God Has No Respect of Person

II Corinthians 3:17 reports, where the Spirit of God is, there is liberty/freedom. God said, His yoke is easy and His burden is light **(Matthew 11:30)**. Husbands and the wives are two free will minds that are committed to God and operate as one through the power of God's Holy Spirit. The couple also functions with the understanding that their ability to work together is best accomplished when each partner respects and considers the gifts and role the other has in God. This is a respect for one another's roles that extends beyond gender. God has no respect of person and His anointed calling for mankind in Christ is not dictated by one's gender alone. Let it be known, the liberty/freedom God has for His partners will not let Him tie them to anyone or anything that would try to muffle or limit their freedom to live within this liberty and the anointed calling God has for them, on a personal level and in partnership. Nor will God enslave His partners to those who are not committed to submitting to the will of God's liberty/freedom for them and others.

Therefore, God would have both partners in a Christian marital partnership be close to one another and acknowledge and accept His will for each of their lives and rejoice in the liberty and freedom offered to all through Christ. God is not oppressive or controlling and He does not condone an oppressive or controlling lifestyle for His people. In the uniqueness of closeness, both the husband and wife must consider and respect the freedom, gifts and role God has for each partner in the partnership and for each partner's personal walk in Christ! This is why in **Ephesians 5:21**, God ask partners to submit to one another out of respect of Christ.

Here, God is asking mankind to live unto Him, by recognizing and submitting to His original plan for mankind. God is asking mankind to respect, partner, and work close with one another with the consideration of God's plan for mankind. This cannot be done without the understanding of the freedom and liberty restored to them through the redemption of Christ with the power of the Holy Spirit under grace. God is asking mankind to accept the fact that Christ's redemption frees men and women from the curses and fallout of the original sin and offer them the opportunity to experience the respect, closeness, and partnership they once shared with God and each other prior to sin **(Romans 6:7-11)**.

Listen to the humble words of God in **Ephesians 5:21**. Out of respect for mankind's freewill, God is asking mankind to choose to return to His original plan for them. Even after giving His only begotten Son that mankind may have the privilege of being released from the curses of the original sin and draw close to Him and one another, God is asking men and women, not making them, to address Him and one another according to His original design for them. This is a design that is void of the curses of sin and celebrates the beauty of mankind within the context of liberty, consideration, humility, submission, closeness, love, and partnership. One cannot do this when operating in the flesh with partiality or according to doctrines and traditions that are scripted by men and not according to the history or precedence set by God.

A conscious understanding of God's will for the marital partnership works to help the couple submit to the word of God and the Holy Spirit. The Holy Spirit then empowers and strengthens the couple's ability to continually be mindful of each other. This Spiritual state of submission and mindfulness also help each partner draw close to one another and understand the importance of and the need for them to embrace their God-given status of oneness. This is done not only because they are committed to God but because they feel respected, considered and loved by the other partner. As a result, they can now fully experience their state of oneness that gives them the advantage spoken of in **Matthew 18:19-20,** where God revealed the power of two or more coming together touching and agreeing.

The Power of Consideration

When each partner understands the power of consideration and unity in God, the partners' strength in God and their ability to maintain a strong marriage through the will of God improves. The act of consideration is something that is entered into by each partner unto God and His will for them in spirit and in truth, and not as something good to do. Therefore, maintaining their attitude of consideration and spirit of closeness toward one another does not become a burden or a ritualistic act. The spiritual nature of this type of consideration and closeness operates within the workings of love and the genuineness of this type of consideration and closeness strengthens the partnership. As a result, each partner understands, accepts, and is empowered by the word of God and Holy Spirit to function as a considerate person toward each other and is close to one another, in spirit and in truth, unto God according to how God would have them.

This considerate and close disposition organically transforms each partner, as they operate in it, into functioning as a considerate being. Feelings of closeness and acts of consideration become a part of who they are; it becomes embedded in the operations of their being and rooted in each partner's cognitive and spiritual identity. This is an identity that will not break the marital vow or neglect the needs of the other partner. Nor will such a partner seek to oppress or control the other partner, out of respect for the gift of liberty and freedom given by God and perfected through Christ's redemption. Their godly nature of consideration and feelings of closeness will cause them to have consideration and compassion for their marital partner and other partners during times when their partner is working through personal, emotional or trying issues and/or are experiencing personal difficulties. These partners will not see these periods as a time to bail out of the partnership, may it be for business friendship or marriage.

The learning experience Christians gain from being in a partnership with God and through studying and following the selfless nature of Christ, as they are empowered by the Holy Spirit, will strengthen them and encourage them to be considerate and supportive of one another during difficult times. It will also encourage them to be faithful to the marriage or the partnership, not only because it is a good thing to do, but because they accept that their faithfulness to the marriage and other partnerships are not about them and their partner(s) alone. They acknowledge in spirit and in truth, their faithfulness to each other is also a reflection of their consideration and faithfulness to the word and will of God and their partnership with Him. So when their partner comes across difficult or the married couple is working through milestones in the marriage, each partner will brace and strengthen themselves in God according to His word, and Christ's examples of how to work through challenges.

Many Christian partners may use unorthodox thinking and language to communicate how they are feeling about difficult periods in their partnership such as: "If it was not for God, I would leave, divorce you or end the partnership." Christian partners should not be offended. These types of communications are okay, because this type of thinking, although a little rough sounding, indicates that their partner acknowledges and may understand that their actions in the partnership must consider God's desires for them and their partner. In spite of the Christian partner's current negative disposition and their current feelings of resentment, the complaining partner is voicing his or her willingness to submit to God's will for them to stay the course of the partnership. This is also a reflection of his or her resistance to answering the call of the flesh, and a reflection of a desire to resist putting his or her temporary feelings of discomfort above the partnership and God's desires for him/her.

This type of communication is also an indication to the partner/s that their partner has evolved to the point of knowing their commitment to the marriage/partnership is not just about them and their comfort level or the negative feelings they are experiencing in the moment. These are moments that the couple, business partners or friends will most likely laugh about in the future. This concept of marriage and partnership is difficult for the carnal mind or a selfish person to accept and is the primary reason Christians should not marry or partner outside of the body of Christ. However, it must be noted: **The considerate nature of a Christian is not**

that of one who condones backing or covering a partner with issues and/or difficulties that stem from a desire to be irresponsible, abusive, and unfaithful to the partnership or one who maintains a desire to continue in sin.

The Marital Partnership

The love that God has for men and women that lead to marital partnership binds them together in their hearts and in their sprits/souls. This is an act of God, not an act of man. They are one. The man and woman both have a relationship/partnership that is close and committed to the will of God first. A commitment that brings about rejoicing in each partner's spirit when he or she display genuine/authentic consideration and respect toward God and one another. Therefore, when a man loves a woman, or when a Christian man loves a woman, he is close to her, he is committed to her, and he will consider her in "all" his ways. This is the same for a Christian woman.

The love God has for Christian marital partnership is not a phase and occurs only once or twice in a person's life. The love God has for a man and a woman is Spiritual and transforming. Although sex is a wonderful part of a marital partnership, the love God has for Christian marital partnership is not a "hopping the bones" type of love (sexual). When one understands that a marital partnership is Christ-driven, one may appropriately conclude that Christian marriages must be founded in the principles and Spirit of God. The reason why many Christian marriages are failing may be because many Christians have a poor understanding of who they are in Christ and their partnership role with God. Many individuals may be nice noteworthy people, even Christians; however, their ability to function within a marital partnership may not be in place, because of their underdeveloped understanding of the meaning of salvation and their underdeveloped relationship with God.

In many cases, married couples are void of understanding of how God would have them to submit and partner with Him and each other in the union of marriage. Many fail to realize that marriage is about both partners and God. A marriage void of the acknowledgement of God is one that is void of what it means to be truly married. Most of the modern-day approaches or standards used by many to judge one's worthiness of marital partnership does not line up with God's plan for marital partnership. This is because this approach/standard focuses too much on a worldly perspective of marriage and one's ability to "hop the bones" of another (sexual abilities). In other words, many marital partnerships are entered into without the consideration of God and for worldly or fleshly reasons. They are not entered into because the partner has proven him or herself to truly be a Christian and is the person God would have the Christian marry. Many Christians follow the worldly approach and follow Christian approaches that are embedded in traditions of mankind and in doctrines of men. These approaches are causing marital conflict and moving Christian marital partnership further and further away from God's will for marital partnership, as observed in the History of His creations and judgments for men and women and His offer of restoration and liberty in Christ.

Consideration and Closeness Beyond the Marital Partnership

Commitment to consideration of others does not stop with marital partnership. Consideration of others, especially of those that are a part of the Christian body, is expected of all Christians and should be the norm. As a result, Christians are considerate of the unique differences that members of the body of Christ have. They are sensitive and considerate toward the various forms of suffering and ills that have happened to or befall various members. Although they do not allow themselves to get lost in another's pain and suffering, Christians are considerate and are expected to sympathize and seek to empathize with the pains and suffering of their brothers and sisters in Christ. This is why in **Romans 15:1-3**, Christians who are strong are asked to bear the infirmities of the weak. Christians do not seek to minimize or discredit the pain and suffering of another. God would have Christians help others bear their pain and suffering and not be indifferent to the pain and suffering of others. Note: A Christian's considerations and sympathies for one's self and another should not set aside or cancel out the word or truth of God. Christians do not console one's self or try to work others through pain and suffering void of God's truth. However, although Christians work through issues within the context of the Word of God and teachings of Christ, they do not blind themselves to the truth of another's experiences.

In other words, Christians do not tell those who have experienced a history of pain and/or suffering to, "get over it and move on." Christians, as partners in the body of Christ, seek to help their brothers and sisters who are suffering as a result of a history of abuse, neglect or injustice work through their issues in prayer and by embracing the application of the word of God. Christians are encouraged to help one another and others though outreach that embodies the power of the Holy Spirit helping them and their partner/s in Christ gain appropriate understanding of Christ and who they are in God.

Also, these Holy Spirit filled Christians are empowered with a form of outreach that can help mankind understand the love God has for them and demolish lies, stereotypes and strongholds that are hindering their partner and others in Christ from appropriately resolving issues and moving forward in Christ.

Christians should not be afraid to address issues because they are empowered with the Holy Spirit. The Holy Spirit is an extension of God and is empowered, with the understanding that informs Christians that they have the power in the name of Jesus, to enlighten, rebuke, educate, and help God's people transform and work through issues. The Holy Spirit is also empowered by God to help the people of God help others work through issues for the good of the individual, the body of Christ and any situation. The word of God, in **I Corinthians Chapter 12,** reports, individual Christians define the body of Christ. This is an indication that Christians should view themselves as a unit of oneness. Most will agree, **sane individuals will not try to damage or destroy parts of their own body**. Therefore, Christians should care for and draw close to one another; an act that requires consideration for each partner's needs and a willingness to pray for one another and help one another work through issues. This includes helping one another work through pain and suffering as they help each other answer their calling in the body of Christ.

When Christians work to achieve the closeness God has for the body of Christ, this closeness will work to diminish chaos and divisiveness within the body of Christ. God commanded His people to come out and be separated from unbelievers not from one another **(II Corinthians 6:17)**. God drew a line between those who love Him and those who chose to continue in sin. Christ came to help Christians draw this line and not to create divisiveness between those who are committed to being governed by the authority of God. God's line of divisions is not about separating His people according to their differences, life experiences, cultures or different forms of pain and suffering, but according to their commitment to Him. Therefore, Christians should draw close to one another, because of their commitment to God and because the strength of a Christian starts at home and is made even stronger through their contact and interactions with other members of the body of Christ.

It is united Christian partnerships, inside and outside of one's home and the house of God, that empower all Christians with the ability to embrace and maintain the Christian faith comfortably. Also, diminishing the commitment of the members of the body of Christ and their partnership role works against the body of Christ and is not the ministry God is calling for. Additionally, commitments to partnerships outside of the body of Christ will affect the wellbeing and the spirit of the Christian and the Spirit of God, which dwells with and within each committed Christian. Ultimately, it will affect the wellbeing of the body of Christ **(I Corinthians 3:17-17, Psalm 1, Proverbs 14:2)**. When the Christian interacts with an individual who is in conflict with God, the Spirit of God within them is alerted. The Spirit of God that lives within the Christian is in a constant effort to exalt God through His word and will resist coming into agreement with anyone or anything that opposes God **(John 14:26)**.

To exalt is to elevate or lift up. The word of God, in **Matthew 22:36-38 and Matthew 6:33,** states that we should lift God up above anything and everything. The Holy Spirit that lives within a devoted Christian will urge the Christian to do just that. It is the Christ-like relationship/partnership that an individual has with God and that person's ability to pay homage toward God that strengthens them. It is also this commitment to God that improves the Christian's ability to honor God, and it fosters the development of good partnership skills. The Christian who knows how to love and honor God for who and what He is, has become a Christian who knows how to love and respect the rights of others, whether it is for business, friendship or marriage.

Christ-driven Christians are in a constant state of learning, trying to grow in what is required to establish and maintain a true and meaningful partnership with God in Christ. This is because they have become aware of the fact, inspite of their love for Christ, living in a sinful world and being shaped in the iniquities of this world has embedded sinful and negative qualities within them that they must move away from. They learn and grow in their ability to forsake fleshly desires for the greater good and they also learn how to love and walk circumspectly, thoughtfully, and carefully with others. One's ability to grow in the things of God and honor God are the characteristics that will strengthen one's ability to successfully consider, honor, respect, and love those they partner with. **An Individual who does not have the training, discipline, insight, and knowledge that develops from having an appropriate partnership with God is not equipped with the skills needed to promote and maintain a lasting, appropriate, and successful Christian partnerships with others**.

A Further Examination of the Concept of Honor

It appears that it is a natural part of mankind's nature to want to reverence or exalt objects or persons perceived as positive and perceived as positive influences in their lives. This characteristic may be rooted in the theory that mankind was designed for worship. Some theologians believe that God's primary goal for man was to create a being that would worship Him within the uniqueness of personal choice and freedom.

Therefore, the concept of honor must be examined a bit further. The word of God clearly instructs us to learn of God **(Matthew 11:28-30)**. This is because God knows that with honor, comes commitment. This is to say, there is no honor without commitment. Therefore, many Christians and others may find it difficult to commit to God because they do not truly understand what it means to honor Him. Once again, there is no appropriate honor if there is no commitment. We see this when the word of God states, in **John 14:15**, "If you love (honor) me, you will keep (commit to) my commandments." So, if you love a woman, you will follow the commandments of God and marry (honor) her **(I Corinthians 7:9)**. In other words, if you are lifting something up, especially when you are attaching the concept of love to it, there should be an express commitment to display actions attached to this proclamation or statement of exaltation. **John 14:15** also conveys to us that the action taken will work on behalf of the object being exalted.

To Learn of God is to Know How to Honor God

God's request for mankind to learn of Him is extended to mankind as a principle of operation. God wants the Christian to understand what he or she is committing to prior to commitment. **God's request is His attempt to encourage all to develop a relationship/partnership with Him that is about asking questions and learning**. God wants mankind to develop and maintain a mode of inquisitiveness when it comes to Him and all things. He wants Christians to not allow circumstances to overwhelm them, due to a lack of knowledge. As a result, Christians should not follow anyone or anything blindly **(Roman 16: 18-20)**. Christians are encouraged to actively seek to learn how to work through issues in God with the understanding of what they are dealing with.

When God ask mankind to study and learn, He is trying to encourage the unfolding of the natural nature of mankind to be inquisitive. It is this organic inquisitive nature that help Christians grow in God and fosters a deeper union between God and the Christian. This is because when one ask questions and shares information with others, the thread that binds them together is strengthened and made clearer. This thread will define the path. In other words, the more one learns of another or of an organization, the better one will understand how he or she should deal with that person or organization.

God has the answer to all things. Mankind should look to God for the wisdom and understand of all things **(Colossians 2: 2-3)**. When mankind is not interested in looking to God for answers, mankind will most likely decide to look to other places for the answers of the nature of God, the origin and nature of mankind, and the existence and course of this universe. Looking to self and others for answers that one could never answer will drive mankind further and further away from reality and the truth of God and knowing who and what God is. Truth that is void of God will also help create men and women that have puffed up perceptions of self, their understanding of this universe, and how mankind should function in this world **(I Corinthians 4:6)**. This type of behavior also foster the development of a society that expands the devil's workshop.

Therefore, God's offer to have us learn of Him also reflects God's hope that we examine and learn of all persons or things before committing ourselves to them. God knows the nature of mankind and the detriment of overlooking mankind's need to understand the world and their existence in the world. When a person overlooks the reality/truth of others or any situation, one will make him/herself vulnerable to pitfalls. God is an intelligent being, and to partner with Him will bring about intelligent behavior in an individual. Note: God's perception of intelligence is more about one's ability to make sound decisions and not about puffed up dispositions or ways of behaving, which are scripted by traditions of mankind. There is no class or status structure in God. Therefore, one must understand: In order to honor someone or something, one must learn about it. One must learn about something, because to learn is to know and to know is an aspect of understanding. To gain knowledge and understanding requires an inquisitive and intelligent approach to collecting information.

Neither Christians nor non-Christians should establish relationships, partnerships or take any action based upon what they think or have heard alone. **God does not necessarily expect a person to accept that He is the almighty God of this universe just because a preacher said so**. God would have all seek to know that He is God. He encourages us to learn of Him through an intensive evaluation process that entails personal observation (assembling one's self with the people of God who bear Godly fruit), a personal search of the God's word, and by investigating the object in question (Him) through the history of who God is, the creation of what He has made, and a personal, one-on-one encounter with Him in prayer **(Matthew 11:29-30; Jeremiah 33:2-3; II Timothy 2:15; Hebrews 10:25; Romans 1:20; Matthew 6:6)**.

This intelligent approach is important because God does not want us to make the mistake of giving honor or commitment to an object or person without having a sound understanding of who or what the object or person is. God is all about individuals making informed and insightful decisions. It is God's desire, according to **Proverbs 4:7**, that "In all your getting, get understanding," meaning that men and women should seek to learn as much as possible about all things, prior to deciding to endorse or reject it. This is because God knows that **when one is committed to giving honor to a person or an entity, the honor will be given to all of what the person or entity is, and not to a portion of the person or subject in question**.

Consciously or not, when an individual gives recognition or honor to an entity, that individual is honoring everything about a given subject or person. This is because an object, subject or person is a byproduct of all the characteristics that

305

define it. **Therefore, one cannot give recognition to a portion of the subject in question without giving recognition to the entire characteristic and makeup of what defines it. Therefore, when honor is given to a thing, object, or person, it is given to the whole thing, object, or person.** One either embraces the object of affection or not.

You are either with me or not, said the Lord in **Matthew 12:30.** This Scripture suggests that one cannot honor parts, portions, or segments of God. Once one is committed to God, God expects total commitment. He invites you to learn of Him and make a choice. In **Joshua 24:15,** He said, "Choose this day who you will serve." God is asking individuals to make an absolute choice. God went further to say in **Revelation 3:15-16** "... lukewarm and I will spew you out." Here we learn, **partnership is about choosing to commit to all of who or what that person is**. If one is not willing to commit their all, one is not an appropriate candidate for Christian partnership, whether it's for business, friendship or marriage.

Deviant Sexual Behavior

Therefore, when a person decides to partner with a person in business, friendship or marriage, remember that the individual is partnering with all of what that business, friend or husband/wife represents. Therefore, if a woman is considering marrying a handsome man who is, rich, a good businessperson, good provider, but has freaky ungodly tendencies in the bedroom; one cannot forget that the person's bedroom behavior is very much a defining part of his character. Meaning, the Christian woman or man cannot embrace bedroom characteristics that are in conflict with God's word and be what God is calling for in Christ (this will be discussed further in future writings). A Christian cannot partner in marriage trying to block out this ungodly characteristic about that person and think it will not affect the partnership, the salvation of the partners and each partner's partnership with God. Also, remember it is the totality of what an individual's character is that defines the function and the course of the person and partnership.

To partner in marriage with a person who has freaky ungodly behavior in the bedroom makes a statement. This act of partnership states that you are acknowledging before God that you support all of who this person is. Although you may not have come to the point of admitting to this, subconsciously you are telling God and the person you are partnering with, I honor and support and I am willing to commit to the act of engaging in freaky, ungodly behavior in the bedroom. You are also telling God, in spite of the fact that I am rejecting your will for me not to partner myself with a person who is engaging in abominable behaviors in the bedroom, I want you God, to honor and bless my marital partnership. I want you God, to bless the abominable. Now, how does that sound? God's word does not change. He will not bless that which He has defined as an abomination, because the abominable behavior(s) take place within the confines of a marriage.

It must be made clear to the Christian who wants to continue in the body of Christ and is contemplating entering into such an unacceptable marital union, is asking God to give them all the rights and privileges of Christians who have chosen to try to live Holy in all their ways. Now, the word of God instructs us to follow His commandments and "be Holy as I am Holy" **(I Peter 1:16)**. The question then becomes, "Do you really think God is going to condone such a marital partnership?" No, I don't think so! A partnership that causes a person to be at odds with God's desire for them to live Holy, is not acceptable to God, nor will He condone such a partnership. God is watching and listening, so pray before speaking as you read this.

Now, there is a demonic myth in the Christian community that states: Whatever a married couple does in the bedroom (sexually) is not defiled, is of no concern, and is condoned or is blessed by God. This myth is not biblically supported and caters to those with itching ears and to those who are more focused on participating in sexual behaviors, which are designed to establish and maintain strongholds on the flesh. **These strongholds work against nature for which God made one's sexual organs and work against the natural affections between a man and a woman.**

This myth also is the gateway that leads to the workings of **deviant sexual behavior** in the lives of God's people. The perpetuation of this myth may be embedded in a deficit of the knowledge and understanding many Christian have of what is deviant or lascivious sexual behavior. Also, they may have a lack of knowledge and understanding of God's perception of deviant sexual behavior and why this perception persists. This myth is maintained in the lives of many individuals who have chosen to participate in or have been exposed to deviant sexual behaviors prior to choosing to come to Christ, but do not have the understanding and wherewithal to seek deliverance from the demonic strongholds and evil spirits that attach to or follow those who engage in deviant and/or lascivious sexual behavior.

Through the workings of sin and the detrimental fallout that could occur from engaging in or continuing to engage in deviant behaviors, Christians are failing in their efforts to be what God is calling for. Christians need to seek the truth of God in all things. This includes, seeking the truth of how God would have a husband and wife truly love and make love to one another. Myths such as this work to seduce men and women of God into walking away from the truth of God and living substandard lifestyles in Christ. **Many who follow such myths about bedroom behavior end up spending too much of their intimate time focusing on sexual acts, the amount of sexual activity and thrill-seeking in the bedroom and not on cherishing one another throughout the relationship and making love**. For the sake of time, this myth and many like it will be addressed in future writings.

However, many Christian men and women do not concern themselves with the truth of how God feels about their sexual behavior or many of them enter into marital partnerships, such as this, and try to make the partnership acceptable to God, after the fact. They do so by trying to negotiate, rebuke, and/or argue their partner into changing or compromising his or her freaky ungodly bedroom behavior to suit what is more acceptable to them and/or God. By focusing on positive and acceptable behaviors or attributes, many Christians overlook the fact that "their" chosen partner has ungodly characteristics that will jeopardize the partnership and the Christian's ability to please God. **Compounded with this fact, their marital partner's bedroom behavior is not a reflection of sexiness and is nothing new, but just a perpetuation of age old deviant sexual behavior, sin!**

An Alignment Can Define Your Profile

An alignment and partnership to something is not always spelled out. Sometimes honoring and committing to or giving a form of support could cause others to interpret this as an alignment or partnership. Remember, everything a Christian does should first and foremost be about honoring God and strengthening their relationship and partnership with God. The Christian's partnership with God through Jesus Christ should be a Christian's primary concern and serves as a driving force behind their decision-making. It will also serve as the primary characteristic of the **Christian's profile**, and what a Christian honors or endorse will add to that profile.

Christians seek to please God in all the entities and the partners they support as they work to strengthen the body of Christ. A Christian's goal should be to become more and more like the example that Christ gave us. Therefore, it should be acknowledged within the Christian lifestyle that one can jeopardize their partnership with God and their ability to become more like Christ, in a Spiritual and overt manor as previously discussed. However, it is important to note, damage to one's partnership with God is not always overt and obvious. One can also destroy or hinder a partnership with God and other Christians and hamper a Christian walk in subtle, worldly acceptable ways, such **as allowing your profile to be ambiguous or conflicting in Christ**.

These subtle ways of neglecting one's duty in God can be seen best when observing who and what one chooses to honor or commit to. Once the understanding is accomplished, honor is about acknowledging all of what a subject is and the act of honor forms a type of commitment, which could possibly lead to an interpretation of a type of partnership, the Christian

310

must become acutely aware of who or what they express homage to for business, friendship or marriage.

For example, when one publicly reports that they like a given artist, this person has given reverence or honor to the reported artist. In most cases, this act of honoring the artist brings about a type of emotional connection and a form of commitment to the artist. This can be concluded because the person is committed enough to publicly state their appreciation for the artist. For one to come to the point of openly acknowledging an artist or anything, most will agree, one must first develop some type of appreciation for the artist or thing in question, for whatever reason. Note: One's reasoning as to why one appreciates the artist is not relevant because one cannot always explain their reasoning to the observer. The Christian need only to understand, their public expressions of support for anything can serve as an endorsement of the totality of what the individual, entity or organization is.

One's appreciation for the artist may or may not be well defined. However, a connection and a type of commitment that has led to the individual publicly giving credit to the artist is acknowledged. Others see you and what you represent (Christ) as one who like or appreciates the artist. A form of honor has been established. This association creates a type of connection or partnership that is open for public interpretation and the Christian's appreciation for the artist characteristics are added to that Christian's profile.

As a result of the Christian's desire to publicly show appreciation for a given artist, an unassuming/modest maybe even insignificant connection between the Christian and a figure has been made. This public endorsement will, most likely, create some level of the appearance of association between the Christian and the artist. It may also be viewed as or associated with some type of profile about the Christian or about Christians and God in general. This public endorsement has established a type of connection and no matter how minor this connection is to the artist, this connection may cause many, Christians or unbelievers, to position or align themselves with the artist. This alignment may persist even when the Christian discovers that the artist is promoting concepts and issues that oppose many of your Christian beliefs. This is because people do not normally publicly acknowledge admiring or liking anything without having some type of positive feelings toward it.

These positive feelings can hinder one's ability to stand firmly against the artist and/or openly denounce the artist on other issues. Now, remember in **Thessalonians 5:22,** God asks his people to shun the very appearance of evil/sin, and **Ephesians 5:7 & II Timothy 5:22,** God asks us not to participate in the sins of others. When one places his or her seal of approval on something, whether it is by omission or commission, the individual may be unknowingly participating in the promotion of or the perpetuation of whatever the individual or organization they are endorsing engages in. **Note: Endorsement is a form of participation.**

When an individual endorses an artist who is engaging in sinful behavior, rather than oppose the artist on issues in conflict with the principles of God, **the Christian may hold his or her peace or walk away. Believe it or not, these are acts of defiance in God. This is because the Word of God reports that Jesus said,** "If you do not acknowledge Me before men (what Jesus represents), I will not acknowledge you before my Father in Heaven" (**Matthew 10:32, Luke 12:8**). Some Christians may also try to rationalize or try to justify the unacceptable behavior(s) and/or the philosophies of those they support. We see this when Christian women stand by their husbands after being abused and/or betrayed by them and chose to hide and/or defend the wrong or sin of their husband's behavior.

No one is asking the wife to put her business in the streets or her husband on blast. However, when necessary, acknowledging the truth of the husband's behavior can serve as a testimony against the husband's sinful behavior and servers as a godly attempt to bring shame to those who engage in such behavior **(I Timothy 5:20; II Thessalonians 3:14; Proverbs 17:10). Sin likes to hide in dark places and grow like mold when covered up**. This is one of the reasons why God promises, all things done in the dark shall come to light **(Luke 8:17)**. We also see this type of commitment in Christian parents who defend their children even when the child is clearly behaving badly. We may also see this when one embraces the music of a given artist and supports the promotion of the artist's, musician or politician even after discovering the artist, musician or politician is a person who promotes and/or engages in ungodly and/or dehumanizing activities.

When there is a conflict between the object of one's affection and one's beliefs, one will most likely experience some level of anxiety. This anxiety can cause stagnation and cloudiness in one's decision making. It can also affect one's ability to make appropriate decisions in Christ. This is because once an emotional connection, for whatever reason, is established between two or more, this emotional attachment and sense of commitment has the potential to affect or cloud one's judgment. Clouded judgment can hinder the ability to make appropriate decisions in Christ, an act that can be costly to the individual and others as they try to maneuver this life journey.

CHAPTER ELEVEN

Summary – Revisiting the Principles

Christian partnerships are established between two or more people who honor God. As God, members of Christian partnerships should have no respect of person **(Acts 10:43, Romans 2:11).** Meaning, Christians do not fixate or focus on one's status or express partiality when addressing others except toward those who are committed to the authority of God through Christ **(Galatians 6:10)**. The partiality Christians have toward one another is the byproduct of a natural affection and closeness that emerges when individuals identify, as all Christians should, as members of the same group/body. Christ-driven Christians learn through their partnership with God and God's relationship/partnership with Christ and the Holy Spirit, all members of the body of Christ are a unit of one. They also understand that all members of the body of Christ are valued by God and have a role in the ministry of Christ and each member's role is assigned by God and not mankind **(I Corinthians 7:17; I Corinthians 12:12-31)**. This type of understanding is what keeps a devoted Christian humble and on his/her knees praying for understanding and guidance.

Fervent prayer will help these Christians quickly learn; characteristics such as gender, race, status and visual or physical appearances are of little concern to God when addressing the body of Christ and others. As a result, when accomplishing goals, Christ-driven individuals focus on the word of God and their partners calling in Christ to dictate the role each partner will play in the task at hand and the relationship that will be established between the two.

Despite social norms; Christian partners seek to honor one another for the love of God they see within each other, as God honors all who honor Him **(I Samuel 2:30)**. God confirmed this when He chose and honored Abraham, Isaac, Moses, Job, Debora, Mary, and all the historical men and women of God for their love and honor for Him. Therefore, following God's example and with no disrespect for those who are not committed to God's authority, the conclusion can be made that a Christian should first and foremost honor those who honor, respect and love God **(Romans 12:10)**.

In **Romans Chapter 12 & Ephesians 4:32,** God is trying to help Christians understand that members of the body of Christ should share a special love, consideration and respect toward each other, as God has a special love for all who love Him and respect His authority **(I Samuel 2:30)**. As a result, His people do not develop relationships with those who do not respect God and their membership role in the body of Christ. One of the primary goals for a Christian is being committed to acknowledging and accepting that all Christian are valuable and that they are valued by God as individuals and as members of the body of Christ. Also, there should be a clear understanding in the body of Christ, there are no partnerships found in God between a Christian and those who do not respect the fact that "God" is the authority; Jesus is the way, and God has a calling for all mankind.

Therefore, Christians accept and understand that all mankind is to be loved and respected. However, they must also accept and try to understand and acknowledged that God has a special love for Christians. This special love is a result of God's acknowledgement of the Christian's love of God and willingness to follow their calling in Christ. The Christian's acknowledgement of each other is an acknowledgement that appreciates the belief that there is no respect of person in Christ. Meaning, Christians accept and acknowledge that there are no big "I's" and little "you's" in Christ and the ministry of Christ is not about one's personal ministry or biological family bloodline. God's ministry in Christ and the love God has for the body of Christ is not a family (blood relatives) affair, only! This is said, because it appears that many churches are primarily all about acknowledging the ministries of family members and sharing love and kindness with respect of person. They appear to overlook or minimize the ministries of others who have been called by God to partner with Him to do great things in Christ. The leadership of these ministries also appear to limit their expressions of love to those who support them personally and/or others who mirror them. The leadership of such ministries needs to address this issue, because this is not acceptable to God and works against the nature of true Christian partnership in the body of Christ.

The Body of Christ is, simply Christians working to acknowledge, respect, and help one another through Christian partnership fulfill the will of God for them and others. This is accomplished as they put forth their best efforts to live Christ-driven lifestyles and answer the anointed call of God in Christ on a personal and team level. This acknowledgement and understanding speaks to Christian leadership first, because leadership has been given the responsibility under the authority of God to be first-line examples of service and commitment to the desires of God for mankind. It is in leadership, if nowhere else, in the body of Christ, others should be able to see what it means to be appropriate partners with God and others. Leadership is not about an untouchable kingdom of special beings on earth. Leaders in the ministry of Christ are the first-line workers in the body of Christ, not Kings and Queens or Lords and Ladies.

Like Christ, Moses, and Paul, leaders of today are [should be] servants who answer to the command of God for themselves and others. In other words, God is the head of His people, the King of Kings and Lord of Lords. Therefore, leaders are at the command of God and leadership should conduct themselves according to God's commands. These are commands that reflect God's history and His creations and are filled with the mentoring of His Holy Spirit, in accordance with His word. God's leadership is [should not be] not self-willed. Their role is to follow through with what God has envisioned for leadership and others. Leadership, as others, should be seeking God for a better understanding of what God has envisioned ("past tense") for them and His people. Leadership was not appointed by God to formulate personal visions/goals for God's Church or His people. God has a vision for His Church and His people as seen in His word and commandments. When God's people address leadership, leadership should address God. Leadership should also encourage the people of God and all mankind to personally pray and enquire of God, concerning God, life issues, and all things. **(I Corinthian 11:1)**.

Note: Many problems in the churches of today may be due primarily to too many members of leadership applying personal and worldly principles and perceptions when governing God's people. A Godly leader is one who will always seek to answer the command of God for them and others according to God's word and the creations He has made, as seen in His word. Also, God's leaders will always work with others and encourage others to seek answers from God that can be justified according to the word of God and the calling of God in all things. This is because the final say in all things is found in the word and command of God and not in mankind, leadership or not. The word of God is the embodiment of God, is God, and one cannot follow God without His word. Paul described his ministry as one that does not abuse its authority and renders him a servant for the gospel of Christ **(I Corinthians 9:18-19)**. Here, Paul is reporting that he is a slave to the word of God, which Jesus said He did not come to abolish.

Paul did not report that he is a servant of Christ, according to what "he" envisions for God's people. Nor did Paul proclaim, he is a servant of Christ according to how "he" thought the people of God should be led in "his" day and time. Paul did not discredit, minimize or rationalize the truth of God's unchanging word to accommodate the ways, times or traditions of mankind. Matter of fact, Paul confronted Peter for focusing on the traditions of mankind and/or prioritizing the traditions of mankind over what God has for His people in Christ, according to His word **(Galatians 2:11-14)**.

Paul presented his position in Christ as it was. He was a man in leadership, who answered to God according to the word of God and the teachings of Christ and not a leader who answered to himself, mankind or the ways of the times. This is because Paul knew God's word stands and does not change. The word of God does not evolve, change or tailor to the ways of mankind, because the thought patterns, ways and evolutions of mankind are the byproduct of mankind being born in sin and shaped in iniquity. Mankind's thoughts and ways are not like God's ways and God is not calling for leadership that would change His word or the intent and meaning of His perfect and Holy word **(Isaiah 55: 8-11)**. As a result, we learn there is no perfection or redemption in the ways of mankind. Therefore, **mankind cannot become fixated on carnal minded thinking and behavioral patterns, which are the byproduct of an evolution of imperfect beings who have been tainted by sin and must stay focused on the perfect and redeeming word of God**. This is a word that is in place to guide mankind and to encourage them to press toward staying the course that God designed for their humanity, their wellbeing, and their redemption in Christ. God will reveal and give more insight and understanding of His unfolding word, but the fundamental truths and principles of His word will never change **(Colossians 1:23-28)**.

Oh Leadership, where is your humility? Leadership must learn to discipline themselves to stand down to God's authority as Jesus did, the Capitan of their ship in Christ. Leadership and all Christians must learn to bend the knee to God, according to His word, which is embraced by the teaching of Christ. It is required in stewardship that one be found faithful and committed (**I Corinthians 4: 1-2**). Leaders in Christ should be faithful and committed to being truth seekers, accessible and being the troops that are willing to die on the front line, like John, Paul, and Stephen standing up for the things of God, if necessary (**I Corinthians 4: 9-13: II Corinthians 6:4-10 and II Corinthians 11:23-33)**.

Therefore, leaders and others in the body of Christ must dedicate themselves to developing an appropriate understanding of who

God is, how God operates, and how God would like to have His people operate within His Word and how He would have them develop partnerships. Within this understanding, leadership must acknowledge and accept that there is nothing a leader in the body of Christ can do, say or accomplish that will diminish or change the anointed word of God or the anointed calling or role of others in the Body of Christ **(I Corinthians 12)**. One's leadership role does not give him/her the authority to redefine the word of God, nor the calling of another.

All mankind must accept that God's plan for mankind does not revolve around the will of mankind, but the will of God. They must understand that it is not within their authority to appoint the calling of fellow partners or to attempt to change the word of God or minimize, overlook or diminish the calling of another in the body of Christ. Such actions will put those who do so at odds with God. This is because the word of God does not change and the calling and appointments of those in the ministries of God are assigned by God **(I Corinthians 12:11-18; Galatians 2:5-6)**. The role of leadership in Christ is to strengthen others in Christ and to help others in their ability to embrace their personal calling in the body of Christ. It is not the role of leadership to assign a calling to anyone. Leaders in Christ are, as Christ's example, about watching and praying in the Holy Spirit for God's direction and help in all situations **(John 12:49-50)**. The example of this expectation is seen when God sent Samuel to anoint David, King **(I Samuel Chapter 16)**.

Recognizing who is the Authority (God), all leaders must accept that God has appointed them to the role of leadership, according to His will for them and others with impartiality and with the explanation that they (leadership) will submit to His authority and His word. Many leaders must begin to understand, their position in Christ is contingent on their willingness to submit to God's authority – a submission that is reflected in their lifestyle. This is a lifestyle that shows respect and impartial treatment toward others in the Lord as they seek to maintain an appropriate partnership with God and others in Christ.

With this understanding, leaders must accept that their unwillingness to maintain an appropriate relationship and partnership with God and others and put forth their best efforts to stay committed to God's plan for them personally, as Jesus, can cause them to lose their leadership position in the sight of God, as Saul and Eli. This demotion is in place no matter how others may perceive them or honor them. Leaders who fail to discipline themselves to put forth their best effort to submit to the authority of God and to be an appropriate partner with God and do not partner themselves with other Christians unto the glory of God, as all Christians should do, miss the mark **(Jeremiah Chapter 23)**.

Due to the fact of many leaders' unwillingness to partner themselves appropriately in Christ and follow God's plan for them and others, they have run a race that disqualifies them in the sight of God as leaders and as members in the body of Christ **(I Samuel 15:18-28; I Samuel 16:1; I Corinthians 9:24-27)**. The topic of leadership is addressed because one of the primary reasons many Christians are failing to understand their role in Christ and how to fulfill their role in Christian partnership, is because of poor leadership. This is a leadership, by too many leaders, who refuse, for whatever reason, to seek and adhere to the truth of God, as found in His word and is evident in His history and the creations He has made.

Many Christians have a poor understanding of the meaning of living for God through submission to God and appropriate partnerships in God, primarily because of Christian leadership that does not exemplify the characteristic of Christ, does not submit to the authority of God, and is undisciplined, self-willed and burdensome to the people of God. This leadership, in many cases, is weak in Spiritual strength, arrogant, selfish, stubborn, and rebellious to the authority of God. It is also frequently biased, showing partiality toward members of the body of Christ, and others, and has a poor understanding of who and what God is. Many of these leaders are focused on keeping the people of God's eyes on them and not on God. Too many Christian leaders are focused on running the house and ministry of God according to the traditions and doctrines of mankind and their personal viewpoints. They are not committed to studying and/or following the word of God, praying, and seeking the guidance of God regarding how they should address Him and His people beyond these personal viewpoints. Worship in too many churches has become more about song and entertainment than encouraging the people to learn of God and to worship God in spirit, with the understanding of the truth of who and what God is. As a result, many are not being properly taught what it means to truly be a Christian and how to truly love and worship God.

Also, many Christian leaders have an underdeveloped understanding of the meaning of salvation and their partnership role in their salvation. In too many cases, Christian leadership is not committed to maintaining an appropriate relationship and partnership with God and others, nor are they committed to functioning and operating in God appropriately. Additionally, in too many cases, the house of God has become a dictatorship that is laced with traditions, commanded by doctrines and rules that have been scripted by the selfish nature of men and not the word and authority of God, as seen in His word, His creations, His history, and the love and liberty offered by the grace of Christ. These are issues in many churches and are most likely the primary reasons why God addressed the churches in **Revelation**, when He repeatedly stated that He has a problem with some of the churches.

God is concerned with all forms of discrimination and inappropriate partnerships, especially within the body of Christ. God's word and His judgments concerning the characteristics and nature of mankind are in place for the definition and livelihood of His will for mankind. They are designed to address the spirit, truth and heart of an individual and not the physical appearance or status of a person **(John 4:23-24; I Samuel 16:7)**. God has little concern for the fleshly qualities of mankind because they are temporary. God's focus is on the spirit of an individual, which is eternal **(II Corinthians 4:18)**. If you are having problems accepting this truth, resist the devil and receive the word of God! God's judgments do not discriminate, but offer wisdom, knowledge, understanding and correction as to God's will for mankind in Spirit and in His Truth. Also, God's judgments address all operations in and out of the body of Christ/church, and He opposes those operations that divides His people and work contrary to His word, His history, His creations, and His will for mankind. Many Christians are faithful and love the Lord, but because of corrupted leadership, those that are self-willed, divisive, burdensome, greedy, arrogant, and who are peddling the word of God for their own benefit, these Christians are led down the wrong path and are failing to fulfill their partnership role in Christ **(II Corinthian 2:17)**.

Many faithful Christians are failing to properly partner with God and others and live an appropriate lifestyle in Christ, because they are too focused on leadership that resemble that of the Pharisees and Sadducees, which governed during the times of Prophet Paul. The primary reason for Paul's resistance against God's will for His people in Christ, was established in his training and commitment to God under the governing of a leadership which was self-willed, selfish, and greedy. Paul truly loved God, but it appears that his commitment to the established governing leadership and unwillingness to seek the truth of God concerning Christ for himself, placed him in an oppositional position against God and made Paul a murderer of God's people. Yes, this is very serious, people.

Paul's failure to seek and acknowledge God's will for him and the people of God prior to the damage and disaster he heaped on Christians, is a reminder to Christians and others that they should not follow leadership or anyone blindly. The leaders of the body of Christ and the leaders of this world should only be followed, as they operate in the eternal unchanging word of God, according to the teachings of Christ. Paul confirms this when he commanded the people of God to follow him as he followed Christ **(I Corinthians 11:1)**.

It is the appropriate understanding of leadership that helps the members of the body of Christ develop appropriate partnerships and operate appropriately in God's most guarded partnerships between mankind, marriage. To operate or partner outside of the yoke of God in marriage will force the Christian to eventually do one or more of the following: (1) Compromise or reject many principles of God; and (2) Reject the definition of an appropriate partnership between them, God and others.

To reject a partnership founded in marriage on the grounds of incompatibility is not an acceptable reason for divorce in the sight of God. Now what! A Christian is married to a person who does not share his or her belief system and God does not allow the Christian to divorce on those grounds alone. God's principles for marital partnership direct Christians to not marry a person whose belief system is contrary to God's word in Christ **II Corinthians 6:14-17**.

Therefore, a partnership operating outside of the will of God will cause chaos in the life of the Christian partner. (3) The Christian partner will attempt to remain in the partnership, through compromise with the unbelieving partner. Successful compromise with an unbelieving partner will most likely require the Christian to minimize or ignore many of their Christian values. Christians do not compromise in God. Note: Christians may compromise on value differences unrelated to the principles of God, due to culture, ethnicity or race, but they do not differ in their Christian principles. This is because the principles of Christ are rooted in the unchanging word of God and in a truth that is good for the uplifting of a nation.

God's value system is not culturally based or bias, but faith based. Therefore, God's values supersede the concept of culture, ethnicity, gender, and race and when an individual follow the statutes of God, all these elements become secondary. This does not mean they are not relevant or important, but they are not a Christian's primary focus and will not be a defining factor in their relationship with God, the Word of God, and the members of the body of Christ or others. This is because what God has designed, judged, or commanded is for the livelihood and unity of all mankind and through the power of the Holy Spirit, will root out and rule out any and all factors that may hinder His design for mankind or cause division in the body of Christ. This is made clear in the History of God's commands as seen in His actions **(Numbers 9: 13-14; Romans 2: 24-29; Book of Ruth)**.

Compromise between an unbeliever and a Christian is difficult, to say the least. Christians who try to maintain a partnership with an unbeliever through compromise, will most likely begin to minimize or rationalize (creating reasons for) why his or her partner's ungodly characteristic(s) and/or values should be tolerated or accepted to commune peacefully with them. The believing partner may also try to manipulate or pray the other partner into accepting God's way of life. This second approach of dealing with an unequally yoked relationship/partnership is also not acceptable to God and is a reproach to another's free will. This approach will cause the Christian partner to be at odds with God. To be at odds with God will hinder the Christian partner's ability to accept God's truths and be what God is calling for. It will also cripple his or her walk with God because it will serve as a stumbling block in the life of the Christian. The compromise needed in an unequally yoked partnership will create stagnation in the life of the Christian that will hamper their spiritual and general growth in Christ. This stagnation will also hinder God's ability to unfold His full/complete plan in their life and hinder, limit or stop the blessings He has for that Christian.

Compromise with an individual or entity not governed by God will also force the Christian to deal with and/or possibly submit to characteristics and factors about their partner that contradict the will of God, in order to come into agreement with the individual or entity. Therefore, one will have to be subject to the totality of who or what the individual or entity is. One may not be aware that he or she is embracing the total package of a subject when endorsing it through partnership. However, once again, a person or object does not exist or operate as a fragment. The individual may present in fragments, but it is the totality of what a person is that defines them and dictates how the person or entity will function over all. Consequently, an individual who interacts and develops bonds with presented fragments of an individual develops a connection with and develops a type of relationship or partnership with the whole of who that person is. This is because once again, the person or object in question does not exist as a fragment, it may only present in fragments.

The relationship or partnership the individual has with the unknown fragments of an individual may be vague and/or malformed. This is because their connection is not established with the full knowledge and understanding of who or what the individual is. However, it is a relationship and/or may be an un-consenting partnership just the same. You may not have agreed to subject or bind yourself to the unacceptable characteristic of an individual, but you have by association subjected and possibly committed yourself to those unannounced fragments. This is because just as a person does not exist in fragments, the individual does not surrender him or herself in fragments. A person may present in fragments but is bringing all of his or her baggage. This is baggage that will be dealt with eventually.

When it comes to partnerships, it appears that our society would like to eliminate the concept of applying the principle of considering as many variables as possible before making a commitment. Many of us would like to stay focused on the positive element of a subject. Such an approach is faulty and not logical and is the gateway that leads to bad decision-making. **Poor decision-making is a hallmark characteristic of a poor candidate for partnership**. Therefore, when communicating with someone who suggests ignoring various key factors when making decisions, keeping your distance from that person is advised.

The following example sheds light on the pitfalls associated with honoring objects and persons without considering their total package: Most would agree that a man with characteristics of being law-abiding, hardworking, and a good provider for his family should be acknowledged and recognized for doing so. However, if the man in question is also an **adulterer** or one who emotionally and/or physically abuses his wife, should he be honored? Can this man be honored for his positive qualities without giving some credence/credit to his negative qualities as well?

Once an object or person is given honor or positive acknowledgement and negative facts about the individual present themselves, one cannot demand that the public focus on the positive characteristics of this man alone. A woman cannot demand that her parents ignore the fact that the man who reports he loves their daughter is the same man who abuses her or neglects the financial needs of their grandchildren. Nor can a man expect his parents to honor a woman who is disrespectful toward their son and one who creates conflict within the family structure, just because he loves many of her characteristics.

From an emotional standpoint, it is also difficult for a person who is emotionally attached to reject the person or object in question upon discovering unacceptable facts about them. This inappropriate emotional attachment can be best seen when individuals chose to involve themselves sexually with an individual he or she knows little about. The effects of emotional attachments are also reasons why the **Word of God** discusses the importance of knowing the characteristics of those in leadership positions in **I Timothy Chapter 3**.

Now once again, **no matter how hard one tries to highlight "positive qualities," the totality of who or what a person is will make a statement to their partner and others**. Also, the agency presenting the individual with honor cannot control the interpreter's view on why such a man or woman should be honored. The individual is presented in a positive light and nothing can stop others from embracing positively all of who or what that individual is, the positive and the negative. A Christian's endorsement of such a person, knowingly or unknowingly, is an endorsement of the negative characteristic as well. As a result, a Christian is participating in the perpetuation of those negative characteristic in a family structure, the body of Christ, and in the society.

So, when an adulterer or physically and/or emotionally abusive person is seen in a positive light, some may conclude that it is okay to be an adulteress and an abuser of one's partner in marriage, as long as the individual is a good provider. Thereby, setting in motion an evolutionary process that supports and perpetuates the subliminal message that it is okay to be sexually immoral and abusive, divisive or disrespectful as long as one is a good provider, good businessman, good friend, student, coach, politician etc... This is a message that becomes stronger and more acceptable as the message of honoring individuals with such characteristics is perpetuated in a family structure, society or within the body of Christ. As a result, marriage and social lifestyles evolve to become disconnected from God's truths, making room for selfish rationalizations to justify sinful behavior.

Therefore, what was once unacceptable or a questionable characteristic is now the norm. This normality is a byproduct of an evolutionary process that attempts to neglect the need to consider the totality of what an entity is. Society and too many members of the body of Christ then become comfortable with turning a blind eye to the negative or sinful characteristic of an individual, organization or object and ultimately turning the blind eye to the consequence of the subject in question's negative, unacceptable or sinful behaviors or positions. This is why God put forth unchangeable truths. God's truths work against the workings of sin and the evolutionary process of mankind's experiences on earth that are subject to sin. God's truths work against sin's ability to distort and destroy the humanity of mankind.

Some may say, this is a world of sin and everyone has problems. As a result, it is okay to align one's self with those who support many of your views and values, Christian or not. This may be the case for many, but mind you, the negative and/or sinful factors about the individual will eventually present themselves. When having to deal with these opposing elements, Christians must acknowledge, in the process of supporting their partner, that they cannot position themselves against the principles of God. Meaning, the compromises the Christian partner makes with the opposing element should not be in conflict with their relationship with God according to the principles of Christ. Also, these compromises should not leave room for others to assume the Christian endorses their partner's questionable or sinful values. Remember, your representation of Christ should have priority in your life and your actions or endorsements should be mindful of God and others. The word of God reports, we should do nothing that may cause others to falter or become a stumbling block in the life of another **(Romans 14:13-23; I Corinthians 8:9-10)**.

Now, let us fully convert this type of thinking about honor to the concept of partnership. When we do, we quickly learn that partnership is a form of honor. This is because through partnership, we learn when one partners with someone, the individual is honoring that person. Partnerships make a statement that says: I identify with this person, group, or icon so much so that I want to develop a relationship with it in a way that others will know or respect how I feel about it. One's feelings of connection can be expressed through contracts, verbally or actions. This expression of connection can be well developed, vague or malformed. However connected, it affects one's behavior and forces one to formulate a position that shows a form of respect or honor for the object or person in question. In other words, in some respect, like it or not, your partner's characteristic become a reflection of you.

Therefore, before formulating a position that an object or person is worthy of your attention, learn of the subject in question. This is because honor is the first phase of partnership. There is no true partnership without respect and honor and what you honor will affect your decision-making and define many of your choices. For example: If one honors a particular type of beauty or body type, he or she has defined/limited his or her options in a mate. A definition such as this is carnally based and limits God's ability to give you a marital partner that will empower your walk in Christ. Remember, although God is concerned about the desires of your heart, His primary concern is about your ability to get saved, stay saved, live Holy, and prosper in Christ and be ready for Jesus' return. If one honors money and the things that money can buy, his or her goals for business partnerships may cause him to focus more on profits than on business ethics and the social contributions the company makes to society.

Christians must begin to understand that they should not establish partnerships based on segments, portions, or parts of anything or anyone. When Christians partner with groups, organizations or individuals that have qualities that are in conflict with God, the Christian is sending a message to God and to the public that he or she may, in some way, also identify with these qualities. An act that could be characterized as the appearance of sin. This appearance can cripple the growth and development of the Christian and others. This is why in **I Thessalonians 5:22,** God asked His people to abstain/shun the very appearance of sin. **Ephesians 5:7 & II Timothy 5:22** also ask us to keep ourselves pure and not to share in other people's sin. **God is not calling for Christians who do not make it clear that they are not in conflict with the word of God.** The reason why many partnerships fail, lie in the partners' belief that a constructive and productive relationship can be built and maintained by focusing on the positive parts of who the partner is without considering the totality of who or what the partner is.

Although many may choose to partner with entities without considering the totality of who or what the subject is, this is not acceptable in Christ. Most people normally choose to partner with others because they believe the individual or groups they are choosing to partner with have values and/or beliefs that they can abide by or tolerate. Now, Christians do not tolerate functioning in sin, nor do they partner themselves with others who view sinful behavior as an option. This is because **Christians understand that Satan's success is found in the workings of sin. This is because Satan will use sinful acts to gain strongholds in the lives of all individuals and in the lives of their partners, including Christians**.

Strongholds are spiritually based and express themselves through demonically motivated thought patterns and behaviors. If not resisted and allowed to grow/linger, they will fester, causing a malfunction in one's ability to be what God has commanded mentally, physically, and spiritually. They will also cause mankind to consider and hold on to deviant sexual thought patterns and operate in behaviors that they have been exposed to that work against God's design for mankind. These sinful behaviors and thought patterns can become habitual in the minds and lives of individuals. Strongholds are like slime that is almost impossible to wash off. These behaviors and thought patterns are destructive to the individual and to the people around them. They are also most crippling when the individual seeks to define who he/she is, develop healthy relationships and/or try to understand the meaning of what an appropriate partnership in Christ is. Strongholds can express themselves through unresolved emotional and psychological issues and/or deviant sexual behaviors, fetishes, obsessions, and moral conflicts.

People with psychological strongholds may experience dysfunctional and negative thinking, sinful or conflicting thoughts and feelings that hinder their ability to live at peace with themselves, God, and others. **Christians must begin to understand the depth and the breath of what it means to be a Christian, to be in the middle of spiritual warfare, to be a partner, and to be in an inappropriate partnership, if they intend to live Christ-driven lifestyles**.

Proverbs 4:5-7 informs us that having an understanding about anything is very important. Understanding who you are and what you should stand for or engage in as a Christian is very important. God would not have us ignorant of who we are, nor would He have us ignorant about how we should evaluate any situation when making decisions. It is one's ability to assess the total situation that sharpens one's ability to be a good decision-maker and improves one's willingness to question the Godly nature of all situations and individuals. The ability to examine the total picture before drawing a conclusion is a quality that God is calling for in these days and a quality that will empower any partnership.

God presents Himself as a total package in **Matthew 12:30 & Luke 11:23** where He stated, "You are either with Me (God) or Against Me." In other words, take all of Me or nothing at all. It is all of who God is that makes Him the merciful and just God that He is. Therefore, do not deceive yourself that acknowledging God and His Son Jesus is enough to give you an inside connection with God. You must learn of God. It is what the Christian learns of God through prayer and study that helps the Christian understand how he or she must commune with God. As noted, partnerships with God require a transformation and a personal adjustment. Christians who partner with God are empowered with the understanding of what it means to be humble and to submit. They learn what it means to listen and how to position themselves in Christ. Strong willed dispositions are defined differently in God. The strong-willed disposition favored by God is found in one's willingness to be strongly fixed on the things of God, not a will that is strongly focused on personal perceptions, emotions, and comforts.

Christians may not always agree with what is being said, but they will listen to gain an understanding of the situation. This does not mean a Christian will allow others to dump ungodly and distorted concepts on them. Not at all! One does not submit or listen to or engage in conversations that distort the truth of God and the truth of their salvation. However, a Christian does not make decisions without listening to the basics of what is being said and looking into the truth of the matter from a worldly perspective and from how the perspective aligns with the word of God. Christians are truth seekers. They know, it is the truth of a matter that furthers their ability to make appropriate choices in Christ.

Considering the total package of a subject or situation in question is one qualifying factor associated with Christian partnership. One's ability to listen, respect God's ordinates and creations, show mercy, show hospitality, gentleness, and strength in God are all characteristics of someone who has a true relationship with God. These are also characteristics of those who should be considered for partnership. Those who have a relationship with God also understand the meaning of discipline, self-sacrifice, and they will produce productive fruit of the flesh, according to the will of God. The fruit of the Holy Spirit will be seen in their lives and their lifestyle will make a difference in the lives of others. Discipline is not just a concept, but it is a reality for those in Christ. In other words, a relationship with God teaches the Christian how to view and consider others and how to deal with the pains and joys of life. These individuals learn to move beyond their comfort zone to accomplish the things of God and to love others. These individuals think before they act and are more than willing to extend themselves to answer the call of God and to assist others when it is appropriate in Christ. A candidate for Christian partnership will embody these basic characteristics and it can be said, God will not offer an individual up for partnership who has not shown development, growth and a willingness to learn in all of these areas.

Although a person may display many Christ-like characteristics and this person may present well as a candidate for Christian partnership, an investigation into the character of that candidate in Christ is still needed. This investigation process shows God that we take nothing for granted when it comes to our salvation and God's consent about how we should conduct our lives. It is like seeking consent from a parent on an issue that a child feels the parent agrees with. However, out of respect for or to honor the parent, a conscientious and astute child will examine the candidate with eyes that have been trained by the parent. These are eyes that ask the question: What will my parents think about this or that? In the case of a Christian, these are eyes that have been trained in Christ (eyes that have been trained through their experiences and exposure to the word and Spirit of God) to ask the question: What will God have to say about this or that?

In other words, a Christian should confirm with God through His word, His Spirit, wisdom of other Christian partners, and prayer that a candidate under consideration for partnership meets God's approval and is the one whom God would have him or her partner with. In most cases, this examination process requires prayers, collaboration, and time. In some cases, there are supernatural connections between two Christian parties that can lead to partnership. Either way, all Christian partnerships should be confirmed through the word of God and the Holy Spirit.

The confirmation process for partnership requires impulse control. Impulse control is something many, including Christians, have not displayed a mastery of. Most impulse control issues start in childhood with a child's inability to learn boundaries. The fact that many parents do not consider the importance of working their children through issues in a way that teaches them boundaries and self-control, may explain much of our society's impulse control issues. Therefore, parents should seek to help their children learn to be patient and insightful. Childhood is a time for learning, not a time to allow one's child to be selfish and display behaviors that are unacceptable in Christ.

Many will say that one's behavior does not necessarily define the heart of a person. Yes, only God knows the heart of a person, but a man's life history is evident and is a reflection of what is in one's heart. Paul tried to relay this in **I Timothy Chapters 3 & 4** when he addressed the behavioral expectations of church officials and members. The word of God in **James 1:14-15** states, **sin is first conceived in the heart of mankind. Therefore, if sin is evident in the behavior of a person, based upon this Scripture, it is safe to conclude that the individual has sin in his or her heart**. If concluding that the heart of an individual behaving badly is sinful, is too much for some to accept, one can at least conclude that an individual who is behaving badly, behavior is in conflict with the word of God and not a reflection of someone that seeks to honor God.

Therefore, it is safe to conclude about a person behaving in conflict with God who makes the statement: **"God knows my heart,"** God knows such a person's heart contains sinful content! Better yet, God knows this person's heart is in need of a cleansing. In other words, such a person has issues! An individual's most current lifestyle can never be overlooked. And, an individual who is behaving in ways contrary to his or her heartfelt beliefs is confused, a condition that adds to the tragedy of his or her sinful behavior. This is not a person who is ready for Christian partnership. This is a person who needs repentance and an understanding of what it truly means to love one's self; others; to love and honor God; and the meaning of being a Christian. It is also a person that a Christian should not try to fix, because only God knows and can fix the heart of a man or woman. This is a **Red Flag** and unless commanded by God, one should consider leaving those types of people alone.

Again, the partners who God presents to you should be confirmed through the word of God and Spirit of God. Just believing God will work all things out is not enough for a dutiful Christian. Yes, God will work all things out for the good of those that love Him, but Christians who love God and is faithful to His word, will put forth his or her due diligence to do what God requires of them according to His word **(John 14:15-31)**. This display of faithfulness and diligence by the Christian, strengthens God's favor toward them and opens the door for God to effectively work on behalf of the Christian.

This is because the Christian who is faithfully operating within His word and within the understanding of who He is (to the best of his/her ability), as defined by His precedence, is operating in a state of Holiness. They are operating hand and hand with God, and their actions should be a reflection of and an expression of the partnership that exist between them and God.

Holiness is a state that unties the hand of mankind with God and allows God to address and bless mankind according to the fullness of what He has for His people. You see, when one is operating outside of a state of Holiness (outside of the word of God), God's ability to work on his/her behalf is limited. This is because God cannot effectively fulfill His desires and blessings for mankind outside of His word and the nature of who and what He is. God is Holy. Being Holy requires one to work and operate within the word and will of God. God is the Word and the Word of God is who He is **(John 1:1).** He will not operate outside of His word. He is Holy, because He operates within His word and He is most effective when He is free to be whom and what He is. He is a being that is defined by His Word according to His established precedence. Accordingly, living for God and following the commands of God is not about how one feels or one's social or cultural traditions, but about the word of God, which is an expression of who and what God is. God's word also defines His ability to operate effectively in this universe and with others. Therefore, Christians are expected to watch as well as pray (be active, not passive) in the things of God. Meaning, Christians are committed to doing what they know to do in God, to the best of their ability, according to His word, that they may abide in God's word and the Holiness of God may abide in them **(Luke 21:36).**

 Being active in God will not get in the way of God. An active Christian conducts himself or herself as Jesus did when He was on earth. Jesus was actively involved in God's will for Him and mankind by following through with what He knew God expected of Him and as seen in God's word. Jesus actively operated within a state of Holiness. This was a state that commanded the favor of God and allowed God to effectively move on Jesus' behalf. Christians can and should ask God for confirmation and wait on God for His revelations. At the same time, Christians should be following through with what he or she knows is right in the Lord according to His word and the precedence's He has made. They should be waiting on God and operating within Holiness **(James 4:17)**. This is a mouthful and this is the life of a Christian who has a partnership with God. God teaches the Christian responsibility and diligence and instills in them necessary boundaries in Christ that empower them to be productive partners in Christ and appropriate Christians in any partnership or society.

Christ's redemption was designed by God to realign mankind with the ability to walk and live within the established will of God, Holiness. Christ's redemption does not change God's will for mankind. **Jesus said, I came to FULFILL THE LAW (Matthew 5:17-18)**. Christ's life was an affirmation (declaration) to mankind that, although God's grace is in place to help whoever will come and is willing to live an affirmed life in Christ to do so, God has never and will never tolerate sin in any form. Also, that mankind must accept **ALL** of who God is. **(Matthew 12:30)**. Christ came not only to redeem mankind from sin; He also came as an example for mankind to follow. He came to show us that **we can live according to God's will with the help of the Holy Spirit through grace**. Christians should seek to walk according to all that God has commanded, to the best of their abilities, and to think it is okay not to do so is a **"form of godliness."**

Do not be deceived Christians! A form of godliness is seen in one who has Christian characteristics but refuses to accept the fullness of what God is, what He expects of mankind, and refuses to submit to the true meaning of Christ's redemption. Christians must seek to accept and walk in the fullness of what God has for mankind. Upon learning what the expectations of God are, one must seek to conform, to the best of one's ability, to all of what God requires of mankind. At this point, one may conclude, the ability to maintain one's salvation is impossible. Such a conclusion would be a mistake. **The definition of following the commands and principles of God is found in the act of pressing toward the mark of perfection in God's will, not in being perfect (Philippians 3:12-14).**

It is the pressing toward God's expectation of us that defines the state of one's commitment to God and one's state of Holiness. God's word attempts to convey the nature of such a press in **Mark 12: 41-44** when discussing the poor woman's offering. Paul also tried to convey this when he discussed the concept of long suffering and warring to maintain one's faith and desire to do the right thing in **Romans 7:21-25; Philippians 3:14**. However, just as the Cyrene (Simon), in **Matthew 27:31-32,** helped Jesus in His time of pressing toward the mark God had designed for Him, God will also send help to His believers as they press toward their mark of perfection in Christ Jesus. One's salvation is perfected in God according to his or her best efforts in God's word through the grace offered by Christ and the moving of His Holy Spirit.

This is a spiritual and behavioral process, not just a heartfelt notion. Our pressing toward God's mark of perfection may start in the heart, but it is defined by one's persistent and consistent patterns of behavior and dispositions that are in line with the Spirit of God, according to His established commands, principles and precedencies. This is why the word of God informs us in **James 2:14-17**, faith without works is dead. The question then becomes: Are you doing your best? Are you doing your best to move away from sinful activity and thought patterns and making every effort to discipline yourself to be more committed to the things of God? All Christians should take a look in the mirror and ask, is that man or woman in the mirror putting forth his or her best efforts in Christ? They should also seek to recognize and accept that their salvation is a vow that embodies a contract and a partnership between them and God. As a result of this understanding, they are expected to try to understand and perform their roles in their salvation/contract/partnership to the best of their ability.

Knowing that perfection in God is all about an individual's determination to live according to God's will in Sprit and truth, other relevant questions for Christians are: (1) Do you want to be in the Spirit and will of God? (2) Are you trying to do the will of God? (3) Do you do what you know is right in God? You may not know all there is to know about loving God and living for God, but are you doing what you know to do in God? Do not focus on what you see others, who say they love God, fail to do in God. The focus is on you because remember, this is a personal walk with God that each of us are held accountable for, and God does not hearken (listen) to the blame game; and (4) Do you search the word of God and pray in the Spirit of God to inquire more and more about the righteousness of God? In other words, do you want to grow in the will of God or are you happy with just knowing enough about God to make yourself come across as "Christ like", which is a form of godliness. Do you just want to look like a Christian or do you want to be a Christian? This is the question, because being a Christian is what Christian partnership is all about! Focused, Christian partnerships are not about the world and its' definition of partnership. No! No! No!

The world's concept of partnership may be based upon having a number of things in common. The definition of Christian partnership, on the other hand, is much more profound. This partnership is based upon the totality of what two or more members seeking partnership are made of. The concept of Christian partnership comes from a holistic perspective. These partnerships are formed from well-developed perspectives of whom or what each partner is and are byproducts of logical and integrative thinking that incorporates the principles of God. The people of God should pray and commune with God in the Holy Spirit when choosing to partner with anyone or any entity.

Christian partnership foundations should not be established or created in emotions and most of the time they are not established easily or quickly. Christians do not just walk into partnerships with others because it may be a good thing to do. They are established because it is what God would have them do. Christian partnerships are defined and built by the Christian qualities of the partners involved and each partner's ordered steps in God. Christian partnerships are those that involve people whose personal and private lives are well established in living a Christ-driven lifestyle. **A qualified Christian, who is appropriate for Christian partnerships and relationships, live a lifestyle in Christ that may have questions about the ways of God, but are not defiant or indifferent toward the things of God**. Therefore, a Christian who is seeking partnerships is seeking to connect with those who fit these qualifications.

God seeks to partner His people with people who have a mentality to press forward in God. It is this ability to press toward the mark in Christ that builds the character needed to be a God given partner. A God- given partner has evolved (over time) in God to become a person who will submit to the will of God, even when they are not comfortable with what God is asking of them. God has empowered this person with the capabilities needed to press toward the mark of maintaining a constructive God filled relationship with Him and others. Babes in Christ should not be fixated on partnering with anyone. This is because a babe's goal in Christ should be primarily about growing in Christ. True partnership is about establishing growth and gaining maturity in Christ. Note: A babe in Christ is not about an adult's biological or chronological age. A babe in Christ addresses one's spiritual and psychological state in Christ.

Therefore, knowing how God perceives partnerships, one may begin to understand that both private and public behavior is important to God. This understanding will help all acknowledge that one's ability to be a qualified Christian partner is a private and public matter. This revelation holds true even in the bedroom. God expressed His feelings of one's need to let the world know publicly that he or she is a man or woman of God when Jesus stated, "If you acknowledge me before men, I will acknowledge you before my Father" **(Matthew 10:32 & Luke 12:8)**. Acknowledgement is a verbal and behavioral process. God also addresses one's private life when He addressed His people in **Matthew 6:6**. Here, God reports, He sees in secret and will reward/address openly. This is also seen when God addressed sexual behavior in **Leviticus Chapter 18**.

Matthew 5:14-16 reports, Christians are the light of the world. As Christ's life on earth was an example for us to follow, so are our lives examples for others to see Christ's exemplified qualities in us. Therefore, ask yourself, do others describe your character and behavior as one in line with Christian principles? Will those who are close to you describe you as being a Christian or will they say you are "A kind of Christian"? Do you have Christian characteristics, but the history of your lifestyle is not a reflection of one who is committed to living by the principles of God daily? In other words, are you a little shady (shallow) in the Christian lifestyle department?

A person with Christian characteristics, but who is not Christ-driven is one who goes to church most of the time and believes in God; however, drinks excessively or becomes fall down drunk, parties like a rock star and fornicates on Friday and Saturday nights. It may also be a person who does not believe in sex before marriage but is a liar and backstabber. Such a person may also be one who cries Jesus in the church house but looks down on others as soon as they walk out the church doors, if not before. As noted, a Christian's perfection in God is found in a continual and diligent effort to do God's will and to share the love of Christ. Anything less is a form of godliness.

So if we are not trying to be better Christians and show this, we are not what God is calling for and we are not prepared for Christian partnerships. In fact, you need to be alone with God allowing Him to help you work through issues that hinder your desire to press forward in Christ, because the concept of partnership starts with you and God through the grace of Christ with the power of the Holy Spirit. The Christian who is seeking partnership cannot afford to and will not overlook un-repented sinful behaviors and characteristics present or in the past that are displayed by themselves, or those who are candidates for partnership. Christians understand that such behaviors and characteristics are a **red flag** that suggest a person is not prepared for partnership in Christ.

By now, one can conclude that an appropriate Christian partner has Christ-like qualities that are defined by God. As Christ,

Christians accept and follow the commands of God. Christ-like qualities also empower Christians with the ability to receive and accept the fact that appropriate Christian partners must be founded in God. **A Christian should not say, "Who should I choose to be my partner?" in anything.** However, he or she should look to God for the appropriate partner in every situation. **Your wife or husband should be God's choice for you. Your business is God's business and your friends should fellowship with God first.** When a person allows him or herself to be duped into believing that they can choose better partners for themselves than God, the person is operating according to a form of godliness. This disposition is not according to God's will for mankind. This person is also opening the door for Satan and others (many who are well-meaning people) to disrupt his or her Christian walk.

A Christian's life serves as a witness that a form of godliness does not meet with God's approval. Jesus' walk met with God's approval because He did **"ALL"** that God commanded of Him, even when He did not want to **(John 15: 10, Luke 22:42-44, Philippians 2:8)**. Jesus struggled when drinking the bitter cup of suffering and accepting death on the cross **(Matthew 26:39-42)**. However, Jesus was faithful to God and committed to the will of God; a will that Jesus knew was for His good and for the good of all mankind. God's will for mankind will work to the good and edification of all mankind. Jesus has faith in God and Christians, who say our faith is in God, should also trust in His will for us. Just as Jesus, our trust in God should show itself in the form of submission to God's word and will. Do not be confused, God is not asking a Christian to be a person who submits to everyone or everything that says it is of God. God's word informs us to try the spirit (of them that approach you) by the Spirit (Spirit of God through His word) **(I John 4:1-5)**. God's Spirit will speak to His people through the context of His unchanging word, judgments, and commandments, the history of His works and creations, and the power of the Holy Spirit that operates within and around the lives of Christians.

Christians should be led by the Spirit of God. The Spirit of God is full of God's commands, judgments and expectations. These commands, judgments, and expectations can be found and confirmed in His word. Note: Don't forget, in **Malachi 3:6** God informs us that He changes not. Therefore, the word of God does not change. If God's word does not change and the definition of God is defined by His word, as reported by **John 1:1-5**, **what God expects or requests of mankind through His Spirit will not make His word void**. This is important because when a Christian is approached by anyone or faced with any situation, Christians must know that it is their duty to consult God's unchanging word concerning the matter. It is also the call of the Christian to pray in the Spirit of God for God's direction on any given matter.

God will direct the Christian through His word and His Spirit. God's Spirit will reveal to you the true nature of any force that asks a Christian to act on God's behalf. God's Spirit will also confirm God's revelation on the matter according to God's word. If a Christian does not get a clear revelation from God that is confirmed in God's word, according to the history of His actions and His creations, the Christian should not accept the revelation or act. This is a history of God's word that extends beyond one noted scripture in the Bible. A wise man once stated, one should not make a religion out of a single scripture, but study to gain understanding of the word of God through the totality of the expression of God's word and actions. The truth of what God is trying to convey to mankind permeates and is found throughout the Bible. Remember, the duty of the Christian who is searching for answers from God is to study, watch, and pray, then wait for God's revelation on the matter **(II Timothy 2:15; Mark 13:33)**. This should be a recurring theme in the life of all Christians, and all Christian partners are in place to help each other acknowledge and adhere to this approach in all problem-solving situations.

However, the problem with many Christians is many of them appear to display more faith in the perceptions of others and their personal viewpoints than in God's desires. Additionally, many do not like to pray before making decisions. The concept of waiting on an answer from God before deciding is out of the question for many Christians. Sad to say, praying to God, consulting God's word, and waiting for a revelation from God on a matter is not a reality in the lives of many Christians. "Whoa! No! I can't do all that," or "it doesn't take all that!" is the average Christian's response to studying the word of God, praying and waiting on God. These individuals appear to know the path of Calvary better than Christ, who did all that and suffered through it all.

As noted earlier, discipline and impulse control issues appear to be a major problem for many Christians. Many Christians appear not to have the ability, for whatever reason, to wait on God. This lack of self-control and impatient disposition binds and limits the ability of many Christians to function in God as dutiful and wise individuals. Most businessmen will agree, timing is important when deciding to invest in a product. Christians must understand that timing is also important to God. However, God's timing is not dictated by immediate gratification or mankind's limited perception of possible outcomes. God's timing is in place to perfect the outcome of a situation on multiple levels. God's timing will work to the advantage of all Christians and others associated with the situation. His timing will also work to the advantage, growth, and discipline of all parties involved and beyond. This is for the believer as well as the unbeliever.

God's timing is not all about you, nor is it all about what you think He should do for you or what He should do to address others. Knowing you are not the only priority with God when He addresses your life issues is not always easy to accept. However, understanding that God's priorities are not like ours when He addresses issues, will help Christians learn how to trust in God for His perfect resolution to a problem **(Isaiah 55: 8 & 11)**. The history of who God is, through His word, tells us His approach to problem solving will always extend beyond personal needs, desires, and issues of the individual petitioning Him. So, whatever the situation or concern wait, pray, and wait some more on God. He knows just what to do and God will fix and perfect any situation for you and your Christian partner(s), (to make complete) according to His perfect will, whether it is for business, friendship or marriage. Amen!

P. S. Until we commune again: May we all worship God in Spirit and in Truth. This is a truth that is defined within the word of God according to His creations and the history of His actions.

Remember: Do not forget the Spirit of God tempers the hearts' of mankind and the heart of a person will direct one's path. Therefore, nothing can separate a person from the love of God (stop you from obeying God) or hinder one's ability to operate in God, when he/she commit, submit, and press forward in God according to His word, His Creations, and the History of His actions under grace, within the power of the Holy Spirit **(Romans 8:35-39)**. Amen!

Don't forget to share your experience reading this book with others.

REFERENCES

Ammerman, Robert T. & Hersen Michel (1993). Handbook of Behavior Therapy With Children and Adults: Developmental and Longitudinal Perspective (ed.). Needham Heights, MA.: Longwood Professional Book.

Barton, L.G. (1997). Quick flip questions for critical thinking: Improve thinking skills at any age with the flip of a page! Edupress, Inc., Lab Safety Supply Inc.

Cavendar, N.M., & Kahane, H. (2010). Logic and contemporary rhetoric: the use of reason in everyday life, 11 ed. Wadsworth Cengage Learning.

Curtis, Rebecca C. & Stricker, George (1991). How People Change: Inside and Outside Therapy (ed.). New York, NY: Plenum Press.

Ennis, R.H. (2011). The nature of critical thinking: An outline of critical thinking dispositions and abilities. Retrieved from http://faculty.education.illinois.edu/rhennis/documents/TheN atureofCriticalThinking 51711 00.pdf

Fiscalini, John & Grey, Alan L. (1993). Narcissism and The Interpersonal Self. New York, NY: Columbia University Press.

Heron, William G. (1999) Narcissism and the Relational World. Lanham, New York Oxford: University Press America.

Inzlicht, Michael, Tullett, Alexa M. & Good, Marie (2011). The Need to believe: a neuroscience account of religion as a motivated process. Religion, Brain & Behavior, Vol. 1, Issue 3, pgs. 192-212.

Langs, Robert (1993). Empowered Psychotherapy: Teaching Self-Processing – A New Approach to the Human Psyche and Its Reintegration. London SW7 4QY: Karnac Books.

Mackay, L.K., Stock, A.T., Ma, J.Z., et al (2012). Long-lived epithelial immunity by tissue-resident memory T (TRM) cells in the absence of persisting local antigen presentation. Proc National Academy of Science, USA 109:7037-42.

Paul, R. & Elder, L. (2013). The critical mind is a questioning mind.
Retrieved from: http://www.criticalthinking.org/pages/the-critical-mind-is-a-questioning-mind/48

Schenkel, J.M., Fraser, K.A., Beura, L.K., et al (2014). T cell memory. Resident memory CD8 T cells trigger protective innate and adaptive immune responses. Science 346:98-101.

Suinn, Richard M. (1990). Anxiety Management Training: A Behavior Therapy. New York, NY: Plenum Press.

The Holy Bible (1994). The Holy Bible: The New King James. Nashville, TN.: Thomas Nelson Publishers

Tishman, S. & Andrade, A. (1999). Thinking dispositions: a review of current theories, practices, and issues.
Retrieved from:

http://learnweb.harvard.edu/alps/thinking/docs/dispositions.htm

Watanabe, R., Gehad, A., Yang, C., et al (2015). Human skin is protected by four functionally and phenotypically discrete populations of resident and recirculating memory T cells. Science Translational Medicine 7:279ra39.

Made in the USA
Columbia, SC
23 November 2020